Bridges People Built

To Gisele

Happy reading

♡ Tina

Bridges People Built

CHRISTINA SCHILLING

Bridges People Built
Christina Schilling

Copyright © 2016 by Christina Schilling
All Rights Reserved

Book and Cover Design by Karoline Butler

ISBN-10: 1530353734
ISBN-13: 978-1530353736
Library of Congress Control Number: 2016904561
CreateSpace Independent Publishing Platform
North Charleston, South Carolina

Dedication

This book is dedicated to my family and to those in the human family who are facing changes or made changes in their lives.

Index

Introduction ix

Chapter 1. Walking On A Troubled Surface
A Bridge For Simon - 1939 1

Chapter 2. War Becoming Reality
The Loss of Bridges - 1939 to 1941 25

Chapter 3. Destruction, Death And Violence
A Land Without Bridges - 1942 to 1945 53

Chapter 4. Hardship And Survival
Rebuilding Bridges - 1945 to 1950 83

Chapter 5. Hope For The Better
A Bridge for Michael - 1951 to 1955 113

Chapter 6. Love Built And Trust Destroyed
A Bridge for Rose. Simon's Disappointment - 1955 to 1961 137

Chapter 7. Simon And Martine
A Bridge With Letters - 1961 to 1963 179

Chapter 8. Love, Forgiveness, Death And New Beginnings
Bridges That Continue – 1964 231

Introduction

This book tells a story of people who were facing war, discrimination, persecution and hostility. Large numbers of them fled a country and had to start over. Others stayed and battled incredible hardship. Human losses were heartbreaking, and those who witnessed the destruction were haunted by memories that were disturbing and traumatizing. Of those who survived, many sought to create a new life in another country.

In many ways the story about people facing and surviving the horrors or war and destruction is as valid in the twenty-first century as it was a century earlier. It is still happening right now, as this book is being written.

However this novel will take the reader back more than 70 years. It tells the story of people from Germany who lived through World War II. Large numbers of people who faced persecution and death managed to flee the country before war broke out. They lost their homes and lost contact with friends and loved ones for the sake of survival. For the population of the country death, destruction and deprivation were constant companions for several years. Once the war was over a lot of survivors decided to start over. Millions left a country that had been torn apart by war and hardship. They became immigrants who went overseas, and they made a decision that was not easy. They faced profound changes, cultural differences, and they had to master a new language, but they became builders of a better future for themselves and for their families. They also contributed in the shaping of the countries where they had made their new homes. In the process they built invisible bridges that spanned the continents. This story concentrates on immigrants who arrived in Toronto. It depicts the harrowing war and post war period of Germany and a new start in Canada. The book is not a biography, but a mosaic of lives of persons I have been privileged to know and whom I crossed paths with. They had their own stories to tell. My parents and neighbors told me about the tumultuous times they went through. I'm also deeply indebted to my brother, Harry Liedtke. His vivid written accounts of war and post war times, as well stories of his own experiences coming to Canada by boat like many other immigrants like him, have greatly assisted me with my research and writing. I was fortunate not to have witnessed the terrors of war directly, but I lived in a country that still showed the results and scars of bombings and destruction. Also I still witnessed the post war years, the associated difficulties, and later the economic growth.

    The story that is about to unfold here will remind many readers of their own journeys of starting over, making changes, and leaving a country. Regardless from which country they came, they will discover a lot of common experiences. The deeply traumatizing effects of war and the disregard for human dignity in war-torn nations is as painful and present now as in the past. May the book not only be a look at the ugliness of war, but also be a call for peace and tolerance as well as a reminder of the goodness that can be found in people.

One

Walking On A Troubled Surface

A Bridge For Simon - 1939

It was still early in the morning, yet the sun found its way through the slits of the shutters casting a bright stripe of light onto the wall. Michael observed the dancing light patterns on the curtains and listened to the sounds around. It was not time yet to get up, and he did not have to hurry, as the summer school holidays had just begun. Still, he wanted to get up early. He had plans to help his father build a lean-to tool shed in the yard for the shovels and garden tools. His dad did not have much time, but he had told him what to do. They had sat down together, and his father had drawn a plan. Michael had watched. He loved drawing plans for projects, and even though he was just going on ten, he was skillful and competent. He had helped his father with the frame, holding materials, and nailing. This would be fun today! The roof shingles had to be nailed onto the roof, and his two friends would help him. It was a bit like building a big birdhouse.

He yawned and tried to see the clock, but it was still too dark in the room. It would be so easy, if he had a wristwatch with lit up numbers like his friend Peter! He was proud of it and never missed a chance to brag about it. Oh well, maybe some day I'll get a watch like this, Michael thought. After all such a watch would be expensive! He had to wonder how Peter's parents managed. Nobody was rich in this neighborhood, and Peter lived in a house, which was occupied by three families. He and his parent lived in this small, stuffy, three room flat under the roof. Everything was always spotless and tidy there, but the place was like an oven on hot summer days and resembled an icebox in winter. Michael had to think that he actually should not even complain. A watch was not such a big deal. He lived in a nice place, a lot nicer than where Peter was living. His parents had moved here from a city in the middle of Germany just over two years ago. His dad had found work as a bookkeeper at one of the larger breweries in the city, and he was pleased with the job. The move had been a good change for the family. They had a ground floor flat with four rooms, there was a small patio they enjoyed in summer, and a garden too, which was shared with two other parties that lived in the house; except the other two parties were not even interested in gardening. So the garden was really the domain of the Laumann's, and they did not mind it. The landlord lived in another town, and he would just make his appearance once or twice a year to see that the house was not falling apart. Poor Peter had a landlord who lived in the same house. Worse of all, Mr. Kerner was an ill-tempered man who did not even allow a kid to play ball in front of the house.

The annoyingly shrill sound of the alarm clock made Michael jump. Time to get ready! There was never much time in the morning. He hurried to the washroom and turned on the water tap. His hair defied the efforts of water and comb. Back in his room he grabbed his shorts and quickly stuffed them under the mattress of his bed. His mother should not see what happened to them yesterday evening! He and his two friends Peter and Simon had run into a bit of a problem the evening before. They had climbed a barbed wire fence of a farmstead near the open fields. The cherry trees looked too tempting! Michael was not careful enough, and he had split his shorts right at the back seam. After stuffing themselves with the luscious fruit he and his friends made their way home. Probably it had been too much of a good thing, as Michael's stomach and guts had rebelled throughout the night. His mom wondered whether he was getting sick, and he vaguely mumbled something about an upset stomach. He shouldn't have said it! Next his mom gave him a cup of chamomile tea, which tasted awful! He grimaced: no, it was not the greatest idea! And now he would have to snitch a needle and some thread from his mother's sewing box to mend the shorts. He put on a pair of old pants and went into the living room. His parents were sitting down for breakfast. His dad was never a big talker in the morning. His mother gave her son a surprised look. "Long pants today? It is going to be warm. Are you still feeling sick?" Michael looked for warning signs on his mom's face. "No, mom, I'm much better now. Peter, Simon, and I are going to work on the lean-to shed today, and these pants are old and good for working." The answer seemed to satisfy his mother. He finished his bowl of porridge and went to the kitchen sink to wash the dishes. During the school holidays he would help his mom. She was always getting stuck with the dishes. His father had left for work, and his mother had gone out for groceries, when the door bell rung. His two friends, Simon and Peter arrived. Both eyed Michael curiously. Simon was concerned: "Hey, did you get into trouble because of your shorts?" Michael grinned. "No, they are buried under the mattress of my bed. But I have to fix them now. Mom just went for groceries!" The boys exchanged sheepish glances, before Peter laughed: "Well, we just talked that we did not get into trouble with our parents. But did we ever get into other troubles instead! Ha-ha! Revolution in the stomach! Too many cherries! Not enough toilet paper!" They laughed at their toilet humor. The trio, Michael, Peter, and Simon were in the same school. They were hardly like peas from the same pod. There was Michael, a lanky boy who would be ten years old on the first day of the New Year. He always joked about his birthday. It was too soon after Christmas, and he got his presents already. He had straight medium blond hair, a face full of freckles, and pebble-grey and observant eyes. He was the observer in this group, critical and outspoken. Peter was a year older than Michael, but he was a short, wiry boy whose blond sun-bleached hair was cut to a brush cut, and his blue eyes seemed to reflect the color of the light summer sky. He was forever in motion, always quick to do things, and always excited about new ideas. He was the doer of the three. Simon stuck out in every way. He was the youngest of the group, not even eight years old. He was a tall boy and looked older than his age. As a result of this nobody in school called him "little guy" or "pipsqueak". Also he was smarter than the rest. His face was framed by wavy brown hair, and his gentle, dark hazel eyes seemed to reflect his personality. He was the thinker of the three friends, quiet and friendly with everybody. His high academic performance left the teachers somewhat helpless. As he was too gifted to stay in the lower grades, he had been placed in the same grade as Michael and Peter. The three friends were entirely different from each other, and yet they had banded together after Michael and his parents had moved into the small suburb of the city. Michael and Peter were neighbors; Simon lived at the other end of the suburb.

Michael deftly mended his shorts and joined his friends. They went outside and attacked the pile of materials. Simon critically looked at the structure. "We may run low on shingles. Are there any more?" He wrinkled his forehead. Peter waved away his concern. "You know, let's just get at it." Simon's father was an architect, and the boy seemed to have a keen interest in anything that was a building and absorbed knowledge like a sponge. He had looked at the plan and told Michael's dad that there would be a support beam missing for the roof. Martin scratched his head: this kid was even right! Michael looked around and got a ladder, nails, and three hammers, and Peter could hardly wait to start with the work. Soon the sound of hammering could be heard across the yard. The three were busy, and in the early afternoon they were finishing their work. Peter stepped down from the ladder. "Hey Simon, genius kid! You were right again! There are two rows of shingles missing. Time for a swim in the pond."

They walked out of the subdivision to the edge of the forest. The pond was their favorite place to cool down in summer. It was a carefree afternoon with all the glory of summer wrapped into one day. Michael's mother had prepared a big bowl of pudding with berries from the garden for the hungry threesome, and they cheerfully demolished it. They finished by taking turns licking the bowl clean and wound up with traces of pudding all over their faces. Michael's mom shook her head as she observed their antics: "What are you doing? You guys are making a huge mess of yourselves! Do you want me to call you the 'Three Little Pigs'?" They just laughed, licked their fingers and wiped their messy faces. Later Michael's friends made their way home, and his father came home to admire the handiwork of the boys. He was duly impressed with the teamwork of the three boys. It would not take him much time to finish the project. Summer was a time, which they enjoyed, a wonderful array of sunny days. School seemed far away. Nevertheless there were headlines in the newspaper and newscasts on the radio that threw somber shadows into the sunny days. The specter of unrest and turmoil, of political muscle flexing, and hostility moved more and more into the foreground of daily living. It felt uncomfortable even to a young boy like Michael.

The noises of passing vehicles and the busy sounds of the day were ebbing away in the stillness of the late evening. The mind of the young boy however had not settled down after a day of disturbing news. It had started with going back to school. Normally school was not something that Michael disliked, but his friend Simon had been standing around in a corner of the schoolyard looking like a lost soul. His face had been somber. Simon was usually not acting this way, and Michael stood beside him, wondering whether it was school that was getting to him after the long summer holidays. Simon shrugged away the fact that school would be trouble. If anything, school was way too easy for him. The teachers had given him study materials for yet a grade higher, and that after he had already jumped two grades. It was something different that was troubling him. His mother was a well-known artist in the city. Ruth Hoffer's sculptures and oil paintings were beautiful, expressive works that had attracted a lot of attention. She worked from home, but recently she had arranged for an exhibit in an art gallery in the city. The display had been very successful till the previous day, when two official looking individuals walked in and requested that all her pieces were to be removed instantly. This not being enough the two visitors returned within a few hours and took any work with them that she had not managed to remove. It was gone, her work, her art. She was told that it would be destroyed. Michael was stunned. He could not understand what was happening. Simon's eyes were filled with sadness. The art of his mother had been condemned as "degenerate". Simon's father was deeply concerned. Ruth Hoffer was an artist whose art did not fit the current norm of the country, and she was Jewish. The family had talked before about possibly leaving Germany. The warning signs had long been there, and now Simon's family found themselves as a target of hate and discrimination. Simon feared for his mother. Michael felt that school was a light load. The heavier load was the prospect of seeing his friend move far away. At the same time he realized that his load was light in comparison to the difficulties, the anguish, and the uncertainty his friend and his family were facing.

The evening at home was not any more uplifting than his day at school. He shared what Simon had told him at school and noticed the somber face of his father and the anxious expression in the face of his mother. They were deeply concerned. Lately the topics of their conversations had been repeatedly worrisome, even for a young boy like Michael. The word "war" was reoccurring on a daily basis in their conversations. It was like a shadow of a predator that was hovering over the sunniest day. Other people in the neighborhood seemed to have the same concern. The prospect of war was like a menacing cloud over everybody. The last war was still all too fresh in the memories of many people, including Michael's parents. It had wreaked havoc in the country just a little more than twenty years ago. Even though there had been no official news on the radio or in the paper that there actually was a war in progress at this point, disconcerting news items were plentiful. Michael's father read the evening paper after coming home from work. He was a silent man, but his furrowed forehead was a clear signal, that not everything was well in the news. He put down the paper in exasperation and mumbled something about troop movements. Michael's mother quietly nodded, but her eyes were wide with unspoken anxiety. It was difficult for Michael to fall asleep, but he finally did.

School was finished and the schoolwork was done. Michael decided to leave for a while to catch up with his friend Peter who lived on the same street. He whistled a shrill signal, and his friend came down the stairs. Michael hoped that they would go to the public sport field and play ball but Peter had other ideas. He invited him upstairs. His father was a machinist, working the evening shift at the clothing factory nearby, and his mother had gone out to see a neighbor. Peter turned on the radio, and the boys sat down to surf the radio waves. Peter loved listening to any station, especially if it was from another country. He had an intense curiosity about other countries, loved maps, and found it intriguing to decipher foreign words. A foreign language station caught the attention of the boys. Michael was not too thrilled, as he grumbled, "You and your foreign radio stations buddy! I don't understand a word of that garble! What is the point?" Peter put a finger to his mouth: "Even if you just get a smidgen of what is broadcasted, you still get a little bit closer to the facts of what is really going on. The German stations all broadcast the same stuff, so it's a one-sided picture." Michael nodded: "Sure, I see what you want. What station are you trying to get?" Peter fumbled impatiently with the dial and mumbled: "You know, this is really strange! I'm trying to get into the Polish station of Gleiwitz, but it does not work. And usually that is clear and easy to find." He continued searching for another station. The reception of an English station was somewhat fuzzy, but the boys listened, as they both had recently started to learn the English language at school, and they found it interesting to try out their new language skills. Michael nudged his friend. "Just listen to that, will you? No wonder that Gleiwitz is off the air! There has been an attack on the station, and the Germans say that it's Polish saboteurs that are broadcasting hostile anti-German messages. One person has been killed." Peter shook his head and replied: "Hey, but it sounds like the English don't believe the story. They claim that the Germans set this up." The news speaker continued, and his clear and crisp enunciation made it easier for the boys to follow the message. Michael turned very quiet. He was the thinker, whereas Peter was the talker. "What's your take on that, Michael?" Michael's face was serious, as he thought aloud: "If that is a set-up by the Germans, it means that they will take this event as a reason to march into Poland. It makes it sound that Poland has been an aggressor to Germany..." Peter looked at his friend. "Yes, and the next thing will be war. That does not sound like a nice end to summer!" Michael stretched and looked at the old wall clock that seemed to tick warningly. "We can listen to the news some more, but not tonight. I'd better go home, or the war will start right at my place. My dad can get really mad if I come home too late. So, see you tomorrow. I'm afraid the news won't get any better over night." Michael patted his buddy on the shoulder and took his shoes off. He did not want to make the slightest bit of noise when he went down the two flights of stairs. The landlord, Mr. Kerner, lived on the first floor. It was not enough that he was an awkward, grumpy man. He was also a forever-curious individual, who made it his business to watch over all the comings and goings in the house. Besides that he was also a big wheel in the local Nazi party and looked with disdain and suspicion at anybody who was not a diligent party member. His short stature and small clipped moustache had garnered him the nickname "Little Adolf", alluding to his similarity to Adolf Hitler. Michael and Peter had an intense dislike for the man, which was also shared by many residents in the neighborhood. Contrary to him his wife was a kind-hearted, gentle woman who was well liked by her neighbors, and their little daughter Rose was a sweet, happy girl. The neighbors also noted, that she was expecting again. Some people shook their heads: here was a family that was divided by ideology and political muscle flexing! How could she stand it? It was not the happiest situation, which was obvious to anybody who saw the patient, but repressed expression in the face of this woman. Not everybody was a party member. Even a lot of the card carrying members were less than lukewarm in their involvement and had signed their name on the list in order to avoid harassment by the zealous leader figures that were throwing their weight around. Michael was satisfied to notice that there was no sign of "Little Adolf" taking note of his quick departure. He avoided the click of the garden gate by vaulting over the fence and went home. His father noticed that he was at the door. "This is kind of late for a young lad like you." He sighed: "But it is of no use to give you lecture number 1001. Get into bed, but be quiet. Your mother is tired and has gone to sleep already. What important stuff did you guys have to yap about again?" Michael looked at the quiet, probing eyes of his father. He could fib and tell stories to his mother, but his dad seemed to look through him, if he tried to fabricate a story. "Dad, you better sit down. We listened to the radio, and we did not do much talking at all. There is this one station in Gleiwitz, Poland. Usually it's clear like a bell, but it went dead today. So we fiddled till we caught an English station, and I'm afraid we got some news, which are not in the paper, at least not yet." Michael's father nodded. "There is trouble brewing in the east. Hitler would love to take over Poland." Michael agreed: "So, this is what we heard on the English radio station. The story on the news said that Polish saboteurs took over the radio station and broadcasted anti-German propaganda. One Polish man was killed. But the English aren't buying it. They claim that it is a set up by Germany to justify action against the Polish aggressors." Michael's father whistled through his teeth. "I never knew that you two were getting into news this way; smart fellows! Well, we'll read the German version in the morning paper. In the meantime we'd better get some sleep. There is just one snag: after this piece of news I may not sleep that well. You know what this will mean, of course, son?" Michael looked at his father. Even though he was just a young boy, he had witnessed so many conversations between his parents and their friends. Being an only child he had always been included in their conversations, and somehow he had grown up faster than many of his peers. He had seen a time that was tumultuous and unsettled. Everybody who listened to the radio or read the paper could see a country that looked like it was heading for trouble, despite big promises and boisterous speeches that were broadcast. The country had become a dictatorship that was strengthening. But the leadership held the population in a stranglehold. Michael's alert eyes seemed so much older than those of a young boy as he answered: "Yes, dad, it's as plain as day for anybody. Peter knows it too. This will mean war."

Michael heard his father lock the front door, and he noticed that there was still light shining through a slit beneath the door of the room next door. Obviously his dad found it hard to settle down for the night. He wondered what he would be thinking about.

There were so many thoughts that were swirling through his mind. Would his father have to go to war? But then he was not a young man. It was the young who had to join the army. He thought of the students of his school that were graduating. Of course, they had to join. And there was the specter of a war itself. He had heard stories about World War I from his parents. His dad had been drafted into the army at the end of the war, barely sixteen years old, and he had suffered a bad head injury. The big scar was still visible, a constant reminder, that wars were not war games. His father had been lucky. He had seen several of his friends die in the trenches. Michael also knew a neighbor who had lost a leg in the war, and another one who was blind from poisonous gas. He had heard his mother recount stories of danger and deprivation. She had grown up in a large city, had ducked into door openings to avoid shots that were fired, and starvation during the war had been the norm. In the meantime the cruel techniques of war had become so much more developed. There were still armies marching and tanks moving, but in the meantime attacks through the air were a reality, and these war techniques were different from the previous war. That had been a war that had lasted four long years. How long would this war last?

Michael tossed and turned. No, he could not even imagine what a war would be like. There were not just armies marching and tanks lumbering through the country. He had witnessed conversations where stories were recounted in whispered tones. He had been too young to understand it all, but he had seen faces that showed expressions of anguish, sorrow, and distress. Nobody could predict how it would all go on. He saw that the light had been turned off next door. Dad had gone to sleep, and finally he fell asleep too.

He woke up from quiet steps and the sound of rushing water from the bathroom. One of his parents must have woken up earlier than usual. Normally it was the annoyingly shrill ringing of the alarm clock that woke up the family. Michael walked out of his small room and saw his dad come out of the washroom. He looked tired, and his face looked somber. "Dad?" Michael eyed his father, and he gave his son a tired nod. "Yes, good morning! Let us hope that it is a good morning." His tone was guarded and had a pessimistic undertone. Michael was curious: "Did you tell mom?" He knew that the news of the previous evening were deeply disturbing to his dad and were heavy on his mind. "No son, not yet. I did not want to ruin her sleep, and waking up mom with news like that…hmm…that's not good either. But I have to share it with her after breakfast. She has to know." He sighed and turned to get dressed. Michael's mom was busy fixing lunch for her husband and after that joined the two at the breakfast table. During work days breakfast was never a leisurely meal, and everybody was quick to rise from the table and to bring the dishes into the kitchen. Mr. Laumann cleared his throat. "Louise, there was something in the news yesterday night that did not sound good." His wife looked up quietly, but the anxiety in her eyes was obvious. "What is it now? As long as I can think, there has never been much good in the news." Michael's father quickly relayed the events that Michael had described to him the evening before to his wife. Louise shook her head. "There is nothing that you or I can do about it. We have to wait and see. Let's hope that nothing comes of that Gleiwitz story. In the meantime life has to go on here. You always say this, Martin." She tried to sound reassuring and calm, but it was not convincing, not even to her.

Michael and his father turned to leave, the one for work, the other one for a day at school. Mrs. Laumann stayed back to do the daily chores around the home. It was a peaceful morning here in the outskirts of the city, and it turned into one of those sun-filled late summer days. Looking out of the window into the small garden with its fruit trees, garden beds, and berry bushes was like looking into a world that was beautiful, whole and undisturbed. Louise thought back to the remarks of her husband this morning. Even though the world here seemed to be in order, she knew that nothing could be taken for granted. Quietly she did her work around the house, before she took her shopping basket and

Walking On A Troubled Surface

walked to the grocery store, which was a distance away from the settlement where the family was living. The grocery store was in the center of the suburb. The area was still very rural; only the busy road and the rails of the tram and the railroad line showed that the city was not very far away. On her way Louise Laumann met Peter's mother who was also on her way to the store, and the women walked together companionably. Peter's mom was less talkative this day than usual, but after some time she opened up. "You know, Peter told me some wild stories this morning. He and your boy spent the evening listening to the radio. I was out, as I was meeting with my neighbor to do some sewing. These two seem to find it entertaining to listen to foreign stations. They are just curious, and they seem to like trying out their English knowledge. But what my boy told me sounded pretty crazy. It was something about a takeover of a Polish radio station. And the English news agency seems to claim that this is fabricated by the Germans." She looked at her neighbor with wide-eyed concern. "Did you hear anything about that?" Louise nodded. "Yes, we talked about that this morning too. My husband is very concerned. Of course he is worried that this action could be followed by a war. She sighed and shrugged her shoulders. "I don't know what to make of it. I guess we'll have to wait and see. It is probably going to be all over the news. But then the newspapers may tell us a story that's glossed over and not true."

The two women entered the store. The storeowner eyed the two and shouted a loud "Heil Hitler!" as a greeting. Neither Louise nor her neighbor liked this greeting. Louise looked straight at the man and smiled at him. "Good morning, Mr. Braun. It is a beautiful morning, isn't it?" The man looked back at her, and there was a condescending note of self-righteousness in his voice. "You may not have lived in our town for very long, but this should not stop you from using the proper German greeting." He clearly alluded to the fact that everybody was exhorted to utter the "Heil Hitler" phrase as a greeting in loyalty to the government. Louise gave him a mild but steady look. "But Mr. Braun, I do believe that it will always be in good taste to wish a person a good morning. Wishing somebody well can hardly be marked as impolite, wouldn't you agree?" For a moment there was the trace of a smile on the man's face. "Have it your way, I'll have it my way, Mrs. Laumann. Just don't get yourself into trouble."

The two women selected their groceries. They avoided further talk in the store. Some other customers entered, and there was a lively exchange of news. The two women heard the storeowner talk about the event in Poland. He sounded outraged as he recounted the story, that Polish rebels had taken over a radio station and shouted anti-German propaganda messages. Another customer agreed loudly. "It's about time that the government steps in. They should send the troops! This has to be stopped. Germany should get the army into this area."

The women paid for their purchases and quietly left the store. Louise was the first one to speak after they were out of earshot. "This is exactly what my husband is concerned about, a possible invasion in Poland." Her neighbor sounded less concerned. "Why worry? Poland is far away from us." Louise could not share this opinion. "Other countries will not quietly look on if there should be an invasion. It will have terrible consequences for Germany, even though Poland seems far away on the map."
In deep thought the two women walked home, and to both the previously sunny morning seemed to be obscured by an invisible, ominous cloud.

Michael met his friend Peter at the street corner, as both were heading to the same school. They had to walk to the next tram stop, as the grammar school was in the city. Peter was curious and wondered whether Michael had upset his parents by arriving home late after they had listened to radio stations. Michael dispelled his friend's concerns: "No worries! Dad let me off easy, and my mom was asleep. But I told my dad about the stuff we heard." Peter wanted to know more. "And? What did your old man have to say about that?" Michael grimaced. "Oh, it was worrying him, of course. I could tell, as he did not go to sleep for quite a while after I had come home. The light was on for a long time, and this morning he looked like he had not slept a wink. He also told the story to my mom, and she looked like this did not exactly make her day."

They had reached the tram stop, and a streetcar arrived with screeching breaks. They stepped into the tram and quickly found a handhold in the jolting and rumbling vehicle. As always it was crowded with passengers heading to work and students heading to school. They looked out for their school friends. One of them, Simon Hoffer, was close by. They moved closer together to chat about school and the day. Simon was quiet this morning, and he looked preoccupied. Peter gave him a friendly nudge. "Hey, talking with you today is like digging for treasures. What's up?" Simon's facial expression became even more pained. He looked at his two friends and replied: "I guess I won't be around here much longer. It's no good. You remember what I told you about my mother and what happened to her art exhibit!" Peter stared at him, realizing the seriousness of his friend's situation. Michael nodded. His face mirrored the somber expression of his friend Simon. He knew what he was talking about. Simon's dad was German. His mother was a gifted artist. Her art had been labeled as "degenerate", and she was Jewish. As a result Simon and his little sister Sarah were considered "Half-Jews". The noose around the Jewish population had been tightening more and more. His parents had talked about Hitler's approach to create an Aryan state and to eliminate anything non-Aryan from the country. He heard stories about boycotts of Jewish businesses and attacks on them. This had happened several years back, when he had been too small to understand the sinister plans that were brewing. But he had listened to enough stories that left his young mind horrified. He had also seen that their caring, competent family doctor, Dr. Rosenbaum, had closed his office without any notice. The neighbors found it upsetting. The office space was empty, and people talked that he and his family left the country virtually overnight. The boys got out at the station close to their school and walked the short distance. Michael spoke into the silence. "So, what are you going to do?"

Simon's head was bowed, and he sounded scared: "My dad told me that we are definitely leaving. It has to be soon. My uncle Jacob, the brother of my mom, has made all the arrangements. He lives in Toronto in Canada. Normally we would take a train and make it to Italy, but we may not be able to get out of the country this way. We heard that some people went by truck like stowaways. But we don't know anybody. And we are supposed to catch a freighter in Genoa. The ship is bound for Montreal, and from there we have to travel by train to Toronto." He was close to tears, but bravely he tried to smile. A sudden thought shot through Michael's mind and catapulted his thoughts into overdrive. He had to think of the Menzinger's, farmers they knew well. The farmer's wife Marie was a friend of his mother. Leo, the bachelor brother of Mr. Menzinger, lived at the farm too, and he was a truck driver. He had heard him yarn about driving all over the place, and he was mostly driving loads of mixed cargo to Italy. Harbor cities like Genoa had been mentioned in his stories. He had to speak to the man. Maybe he could help. It was a bold idea, but he had to try. He decided to mention his thoughts to his friend: "Simon, I have an idea. We know a farmer, and his brother is a trucker..." He shared his idea with his friend. Simon looked like in deep thought. "Thanks, but I need to know soon. This is going to be hard. I'll miss you guys. We have been friends, and I hate losing my friends." Michael tried to sound reassuring. "I'll know more tomorrow, Simon!"

The three boys entered the school building and went to their classroom. Michael sat beside Simon during Math. Normally Math was an easy subject for Michael, but today he found it difficult to concentrate on numbers, fractions, and decimals. The events of the evening before had been disturbing as had been the reaction of his parents. The conversation with his friend before school was disconcerting as well. He had to think what he could do, and he

Walking On A Troubled Surface

made plans for the afternoon. He had to find an excuse to go to Menzinger's farm. Should he share his plans with his parents? He was not so sure. His mother would probably get worried, and he did not want to upset her. His dad was different. But his father was not home at the time when he came back from school. Should he just go to the farmstead, talk to the Menzinger's and Leo and tell his parents later?

"Laumann, come forward, and convert these decimals into fractions." The teacher's voice cut through all his planning. He sighed, and walked to the blackboard, took the chalk, and started writing. He was nervous, pressed too hard, and the chalk made a screeching sound on the blackboard. There was snickering from the class, but he managed to get the calculation done. The math teacher eyed him and shook his head. "You can do better than that! Maybe it is time for you to concentrate a bit more. You have that look on your face like you were sleeping with your eyes open! Sit down." Michael slunk to his desk and tried to stay focused. School seemed to be endless today. During recess he accosted Simon. "So, I'll see what these people will have to say later today right after school. Do you want to call me, or should I call you?" Simon shook his head vehemently. "Whatever you do, don't call. Don't use the phone. "When he saw Michael's questioning glance he continued, "I know from my parents, that the government is watching everything, mail and phone calls too." Michael nodded. "Understood. But how are you leaving? You have a house, furniture, and all those things. That sounds difficult!" Simon looked straight at his friend. "You know, there are decisions that are really hard. My parents said that staying alive is more important than a house and furniture." Michael thoughtfully looked back. "Life is the most important part. The rest...forget it! But I would really want to stay friends, no matter how far you are away." He had to think of the city his friend had mentioned. "You talked about Toronto; that sounds interesting! I never knew that you had relatives in Canada. And Canada sounds like an adventure, like a big country and lots of wilderness. You know, some day I may want to leave here too and move away." Wistfully he looked at his friend. Simon nodded thoughtfully: "Yes, but first we have to make it there! I'll stay in touch. There are letters. Big promise!" He hoped to stay in touch, but would the letters even make it out of the country, if there would be a war? They went back to their classes.

After school was over, Michael went home. His mother was out. She had left a hastily scribbled note. "Went out to get some material for a dress." Michael grinned. Good! That was a process that could take time. He took a pencil and added his own note to the message of his mother. "Going quickly to Menzinger's. No homework today. Getting two rabbits." He was satisfied. That was easy! He did not even have to tell a lie. It was the perfect truth: there was no homework, and he and his parents had talked about getting rabbits that would inhabit the rabbit hutches his dad had recently built in the backyard. As far as Simon was concerned, that was a topic he did not mention. He went to the drawer of his small desk where he had stashed away his allowance, pocketed some of the money, got on his bike, and pedaled off. The farm was not far away from the suburban area where Michael lived. The houses of the neighborhood were close to open fields, and forests. Michael's mother had made the acquaintance of Mrs. Menzinger at the market right after they moved here. They had a small farm, sold produce at the local market, and Mrs. Menzinger took in sewing and mending; she was doing house cleaning as well. They had become friends with the family. Their son Hans was a bit younger than Michael, and there was Resi, the little sister of Hans. Besides them Mr. Menzinger's bachelor brother Leo lived at the farm as well, unless of course he was driving cargo loads across the country and abroad. He was the vagabond of the family, always on the road and rarely home. Menzinger's farm was located on small country roads that lead to the "autobahn", the new highway that connected larger cities. Nevertheless it was quiet, as the noise of cars or trucks was just a distant hum, and the closest neighbors were far away. The old half-timbered house, which had been in the same family for generations, was hidden behind a dense beech hedge. To his relief Michael noticed that Leo's large truck was parked on the side; he was home, and he could talk to him. Michael leaned his bike against the gate and entered the yard with its fruit trees, berry bushes and tidy garden beds. A large dog came bounding out of the doghouse under the stairs of the house, barking furiously. Michael patted the shaggy head. He went up the steps to the kitchen door and knocked. Mrs. Menzinger opened the door. She was busy with a basket full of mending and offered him a cheerful greeting. "Come in! Nice to see you, Michael! I guess you wanted to talk to my husband about those rabbits." Michael nodded eagerly. She leaned out of the window and called for her husband, and Mr. Menzinger came in. He greeted Michael, and Michael felt hands that were rough from the relentless everyday work of a farmer. He was a man with a face on which wind and weather had left their marks, and the stubbles of his beard showed that the end of the week was near. He had to get decent and shave for Sunday. Despite all of the hard work and daily toil he was a man who was content and happy, and a pair of observant, cheerful eyes scrutinized Michael. "So you want to start a farm, huh?" Michael laughed. "Not quite, but I wanted to ask whether I could buy two rabbits from you." The farmer chuckled. "I'll give you a male and a female, and come next spring you'll have a farm!" Michael wondered quietly whether his parents would object to having a few rabbits populating the hutches. He had mentioned that he wanted to get only two. He grinned. "I'll take them, Mr. Menzinger. And if things get out of hands, I'll have to find a way to get rid of them." The farmer laughed. "That should not be a problem! Just harden your heart, young man. You can always put them into the frying pan." When he saw Michael's pained facial expression, he gave him a friendly pat on the shoulder.

"Don't get upset with me. I'm a farmer, just seeing the practical side of things; I can help you out to get them ready for Sunday dinner. And you can also sell the critters at the market." Michael sounded relieved. "That sounds good to me." He made a pause, and the farmer observed the boy. "You look like you have something else on your mind. What is it? Is your bike broken again?" Michael was surprised how observant this man was. "No, my bike is not the problem, but I have a friend at school. His mother is Jewish, she is an artist, and her art was condemned. The family is worried. They have to leave." Mr. Menzinger nodded. "Oh, it is a terrible thing! I can't even understand how things like that can happen! It's this Hitler and his inner circle! They are like poison to peoples' minds! I have heard so much. Let us hope that your friend and his family will be able to leave the country like so many others." Michael told the story that his friend Simon had relayed to him at school and the need to find a ride to Genoa. He wondered whether Leo would be driving there soon. A smile crinkled Mr. Menzinger's face. "Well, you have guts and ideas, Michael!" He got up from his chair and shouted upstairs: "Hey, Leo, you better come down and listen to this!" Heavy steps came down the creaking stairs, and Josef Menzinger's brother Leo, a hulking and rough looking young man, lumbered into the kitchen. Despite his intimidating appearance he had kind eyes, observant and cheerful like those of his older brother. Quizzically he looked at the boy. He knew Michael, and he listened to the story about Michael's friend and his family. He snorted with a short laugh, and a sly expression was spreading over his face as he looked at the boy. "It's funny that you should ask. I have done that a few times over the last two years. My cargo hold has a hidden area, and so I have taken people down to Genoa on my trips. Yes, mostly they were Jewish." He chuckled: "They all wanted out, of course! A bit risky, maybe, but what the hell! It's the right thing to do! Damn Nazi government! My way to kick them in the ass!" Michael looked surprised. He always thought that Leo looked tough, but he never guessed that he was a daredevil. He described to Michael that his friends were not in for a comfortable trip. It would be a bit drafty in the cargo hold, and it could be a bumpy and very cramped ride too. He explained that he did not want much money for it. Some beer money would be nice or a contribution to gas would be appreciated. Usually he stayed at a place called "La Paloma", a small albergho or guesthouse near the Genoa harbor, when he was in the city. They could stay there till they got on the boat. It was a cheap place, which was populated by sailors. Not the cleanest place, he warned; a few spiders and cockroaches could be part of the company, but the people were good and very kind. He concluded his description. "Leaving in two days from here at night. Probably my last trip out of the country. They may close the borders with the war coming, and next I may have to serve in the army. Tell them to be here, and I'll take them." He nodded to Michael with a reassuring grin and went outside to do some work. Mr. Menzinger chuckled: "Well, we seem to get one problem solved. Now let's go outside, and you can pick up your rabbits. I have a cage that you can strap onto your bike carrier." They went out to the rabbit hutches that were beside the small barn that housed two goats and included a pigpen and the chicken coop. Michael looked at the small balls of fur that were hopping around in the hutch. "Oh, they are so cute," Michael exclaimed. "Just don't get too attached to them", warned the farmer. "Here, these two are ready to go, and they look healthy to me. Just give me two bucks for them; that will be good." Michael got a two-mark bill from his pocket and thrust it into the farmer's hand. He strapped the cage with its furry occupants on his bike carrier and pedaled home. It was satisfying that he could let his friend know that he and his family would have transportation, and he felt relief. At home he quickly put the two animals into their hutches and went into the house. His mother was not home yet, for which he was grateful. Later his parents arrived home almost at the same time, his father from work, his mother from her errands. There was not much of a conversation going on. Michael's father picked up the evening paper. As usual, he was brooding over politics. He sounded agitated and upset. "It is just what I predicted. Germany will march into Poland. And I tell you, this will lead to war." Michael tried to listen away. It was always about war, war, and more war. The anxious face of his mother did not make things any better. He realized that he could not take off and spend every evening with his friend. That would not go over too well with his parents either. Instead he tried to divert their attention. "Oh, by the way, I did go to the Menzinger's today, and I got two rabbits." His mother did not sound too thrilled: "If you think that I'll be the one to feed these animals and clean out the rabbit hutches, you are mistaken." Michael tried to calm her down. "No, no, that's my job, Mom." Michael's father looked up from his newspaper and grinned. "So, here comes the new business owner, Michael Laumann, proud owner of 'Laumann's Rabbit Farm'. You can always sell them, if it is getting too crowded out there. And I won't mind something tasty for dinner from the production." His comment sounded almost a bit like what Mr. Menzinger had said earlier! Michael was pleased with the end of the day. It looked like his plan would be working for his project at home, and it looked also like there would be help for his friend and family.

Michael spotted Simon in the tram on his way to school. He gave him a big smile and a thumbs-up signal. They did not talk during the ride in the tram, but Michael immediately gave the positive news to his friend after they started walking to school. Simon sounded relieved. Of course he knew the Menzinger's farm, as he had gone there with Michael on a few occasions. He sounded somewhat relieved: "This is almost too good to be true. We will be at the farmer's place the day after tomorrow late when it is getting dark!" Michael promised his friend to pass the message on to the farmer or to Leo. This time he needed to get more creative to find an excuse for his visit to the farm. He pushed aside his concerns: something would come to him! He found it hard to concentrate on his schoolwork. Too much had been happening. On the one hand it felt like a burden was being lifted from his shoulders, as his friend would hopefully be able to leave the country safely. On the other hand he felt profound sadness. Simon, Peter, and he had been buddies for two years. They had played together, gotten into mischief together, now they were in grammar school together, and all of this was coming to an end. This was not like a death, but still it was a loss. It hurt.

He came home after school and silently sat down to eat his lunch. He did not feel like eating much and left a large share of his meal for his dad. His mother was in the basement laundry room of the house. Cautiously he ventured downstairs. His mom was bent over the steaming washtub and was scrubbing towels and linen sheets. She looked up. "What is up today? Do you have homework?" His mother sounded relieved, when he mentioned that he only had a project to finish for next week. She started rinsing the bulky load in the large tin tub and seemed to disappear in wisps of steam, as she mentioned: "I don't need help here, but it would help me if you could run an errand for me. We need bread from the bakery, and we are out of eggs. Mrs. Menzinger would be able to sell us a dozen, I hope." Michael found it hard to control his enthusiasm. Here was his chance! No stories were necessary; everything went better than expected. He nodded in agreement, got his bike and pedaled off. A big grin was spreading over his face. Sometimes life seemed to be less complicated than expected! After having bought the eggs at the farm and having discussed the details about his friend Simon and his planned trip, he felt a sense of relief and satisfaction. Leo gave him a bone-crushing handshake, like one man to the other. "Don't worry about anything. It is a bit uncomfortable for them, but they will be fine! And tell your friend not to be scared when he sees me. I look tough, but I don't bite!" The farmer shook his head: he had never thought that Michael would come up with the suggestion of people smuggling! He was curious. "What do your parents know about all of this?" Michael grinned an uneasy grin. "Nothing, but I swear to God that I did not lie! I just told them yesterday that I wanted to get the rabbits. And today it was my mom who sent me to buy the eggs. So, I did not tell them a lie. I just did not tell them everything I was doing." The farmer nodded. "You've got the nerve that not many would have. But in time you probably should come clean with your parents, my friend." Michael agreed. In time could be a while away! He jumped on his bike and passed by the bakery to buy the bread, after which he went home.

    The next morning at school was a painful experience for the three friends. Simon was still there. He only mentioned to Michael and Peter that it was his last day. Nobody else in the classroom had been informed about his departure. The three boys sat at the edge of the sports area, each of them in deep thoughts. Simon heaved a sigh. He was close to tears. "Don't get me started", said Michael, "this is hard." Peter blew his nose. "We just hope that your trip will go well." Simon looked at his friends. He did not look like the precocious youngster he was. Knowing about the precarious time ahead his face was that of a vulnerable, scared little boy. Bravely he tried to manage a crooked smile, but his eyes were filled with sadness. "You will hear from me. I'll never forget you. You'll get a letter, but once there is a war, you'll probably never get it." Underneath his sadness was determination. "You'll get that letter, even if it takes till the war is over! Trust me, I don't give up." They watched Simon walk away to the tram stop, the tall boy who was younger and yet seemed so much older than his classmates. Peter's voice was very quiet. "If we could only look into the future! Will we ever see him again?" Michael shook his head: "I don't know. Time will tell. I wish him the best. But we'll miss the genius kid! This is sad." He had stopped himself from crying when they said their good-byes, but now the tears were coming. Both of them sat together on a wall by the football field. They were silent and in deep thought on their way home. Now it was just the two of them, and they felt a painful gap.

Two

War Becoming Reality

The Loss of Bridges - 1939 to 1941

Michael had been busy in the backyard of the house. He had his chores to do, and he spent some time gathering dandelion greens for the rabbits that were the new addition to the yard. He was pleased with the new acquisition. They were growing fast, and the lively animals immediately started nibbling at the offerings, while Michael cleaned out the hutches and filled the water bowls. He heard his mother calling him to come in. It was evening. Probably his father had come home from work, and it would be time for supper. He entered the house and found his parents sitting at the table. The radio was turned on, and he caught the words "aggression", "enemies", and "battle". It hardly sounded like good news. The expression on the faces of his parents only confirmed this feeling. His father turned the volume of the radio lower. "We have been listening for a while already. So the news is out. Germany is at war. England and France have declared war on the country." Michael bit his lip. "Well, we have been talking about that possibility for a while." He had to think back to the evening when he had heard about the attack on the Polish radio station. His father continued. "So the Germans marched into Poland, and the other nations are not taking that lying down." He sat slumped over in his chair. Michael's mother looked preoccupied, as she reported her observations: "The signs are everywhere. Today I wanted to go to the store for groceries, and they handed out ration cards there." She described that they had to sign up at one grocery store to receive the cards and the groceries. It involved filling out forms and papers, the typical control measures of government. There was a certain allowance for meat, bread, a quantity of potatoes, and other items. Only people who were doing heavy physical work would receive more. It sounded like belt tightening, and for Michael's parents it felt like a replay from the time of World War I. This rationing happened very sudden. Michael's father voiced his opinion that all of these measures had been planned well in advance, so they could be put into place very fast. Louise looked at Michael with a smile. "You know, as I think of it, this idea of you keeping rabbits is not even so bad. Next spring we'll get a few chickens. Eggs are rationed too. And Marie Menzinger will have to deliver the eggs to a collecting station." Michael's father raised his hands. "Oh, please! Does that mean that I have to become a builder and design a chicken house next?" His wife patted him on his shoulder. "No, Martin, don't get upset! Our neighbor has a small garden with fruit trees out in the fields five minutes from us, and there is an old, empty chicken coop. I have asked them already. They are not using it." Mr. Laumann grumbled, but it sounded like a good-natured grumble. "Fine, if you want. I guess it will help. But let's not get a zoo." They all laughed. It was a laugh that lightened the mood after the uneasy news of this evening. Even though there was the news that a war had broken out, it was almost a sense of relief. There had been uncomfortable feelings before and a sense of foreboding. Everybody had been thinking about the possibility of a war, but nobody had known the time. The time was now. Michael would always remember the date. It was September 1, 1939.

Life went on as usual. Michael was getting used to the fact that the papers reported about war action. It was like a dark thread woven into the days of the year. He also got used to his father's daily commentary, which always circled around war and fighting. But he never became indifferent to it. At times he had to compare it to a fire that was burning and spreading. In the meantime more nations seemed to be involved. He had to think: his parents had talked about the war of 1914 to 1918. It was called the First World War. What was happening now sounded even more alarming. This war had all the makings to become a world war as well, as it was growing fast. He noted that young men of the neighborhood were drafted into the army. They left, and the mood of the population showed a variety of reactions. There was exuberant optimism. Rousing speeches praised the "Führer" and the superiority of the country that would win any war. Flags were raised, the band played marches, and some individuals saw the war just as a minor annoyance that would be over as fast as it had begun. Others were more cautious. The adults had seen the previous war, and they were guarded. A lot of the adults hoped for prosperity and had no appetite for wars. They knew that wars inflicted wounds and came with the cost of lives. His parents were very private people. They never freely shared their opinions with the neighbors and kept for themselves. But Michael knew their opinion. Both, his dad and his mom, were feeling helpless about seeing their lives in danger. They were deeply upset about the leader of the country who had constructed a reign of oppression, disregard for human dignity, and despise for anything that did not fit into the mold of being "true German".

Once again the mood at home was down and negative. Michael's chores were done, and he went to see Peter. The boys met outside Peter's house and slunk up the stairs. His friend seemed a bit more secretive today. Both parents were out, and the boy went to the radio and turned on the dials. Triumphantly he held up two earphones. "You heard the newest, didn't you? Now it's illegal to listen to foreign radio stations." He handed one of the earphones

to Michael. "If my mom or dad find out what we are doing, we are going to get it. They are afraid that we are going to get into a heap of trouble. But I'm going to play it safe."
He grabbed a thick blanket from his bed. Both boys sat under this noise-muffling shroud and listened intently. Finally they had found Radio Luxemburg and Radio Moscow, both of them stations with German language programs. They were kept up to date with news about the war. Michael clapped his friend on the shoulder and grinned: "Man, you are a real whiz! This is exciting! Let's not get caught."

Michael was waiting for another opportunity to go to Menzinger's farm. It came soon enough. His father had a few knives that needed sharpening, and Josef Menzinger was a jack-of-all-trades who would be able to help. Michael put the knives into the saddlebags of his bike and headed to the farm. The family was busy with the potato harvest, and Michael started to help collecting the dug up potatoes and put them into burlap sacks. Their young son Hans was working beside Michael, and he was happy that the work was done faster with both of them working together. Michael noted that Leo's truck was gone. But Mr. Menzinger could probably tell him how things had been going with the journey to Genoa. After a while Mr. Menzinger ambled over to Michael. "I guess you have something to get fixed or to buy?" Michael nodded and handed him the knives. The farmer looked at them. "That should not take too long. Just carry on. I'll be back in a while." He disappeared into his workshop and got busy with the sharpening job. They were almost finished collecting the potatoes from the ground and putting them into the sacks, when the Mr. Menzinger returned. "There you are! Your dad can pay me the next time he comes by. Oh, and there is something I wanted to tell you! Everything went smooth like butter with your friend and his family. They came here when it was pitch dark, and we went into the house for a while. You know, your friend Simon was really brave, but the little girl, Sarah, was crying and carrying on. That was exactly what they were worried about." Michael expectantly looked at the farmer. He knew that resourceful Mr. Menzinger had his ways of finding a solution to any problem, and he was curious. "So, what did you do? Did she finally stop bawling?" Josef Menzinger's face broke into a broad grin. "It was not exactly something that momma would approve of under normal circumstances. But no matter what, it worked! I made her drink half a bottle of beer, and she was out like a light after that! I also gave them two bottles of beer along for the journey. As I said, that's not exactly appropriate for the care and feeding of a five year old, but it did the trick! So, they huddled into the cargo hold, and away they went. Leo is somewhere driving cargo to northern Germany now. He won't be doing it for long. He has been drafted. Lucky they went when they did. The borders are closed now! He told me that they had a good drive, and they had to stay at this fleabag hotel for two days till they left by boat. They should be on the other continent by now. With the windy weather they probably got a bit seasick, but that's harmless. Let's hope and pray that they will be safe!" He looked like he was trying to see something far away in the distance. "We may never know. With the war there will be no letters and no news. We did everything we could, and no matter what: living is about the courage to trust and carry on. May God help them!"

Michael had to think about Mr. Menzinger's words. He would remember them on many occasions after this day.

Fall turned into winter, and an early spring had arrived. Mrs. Laumann had walked to the farm and came back with a cardboard box in which a few baby chicks were chirping and scratching. Michael observed the new addition to the household with interest. He knew that there were government regulations. They would have to deliver the eggs to a collection station if they were keeping a large flock of birds. Mrs. Laumann had no intentions of doing that. "I'm not raising a bunch of chickens for the government! We are only entitled to keep two chickens per person, so that's six for our own use." Michael looked at her. "So how is that with the mathematics, mom? I see ten." His father commented: "Well, let's hope that there are a few roosters in the flock. That should solve two problems. We are going to have a few good Sunday dinners, and the rest of the crew will give us some eggs." Life at the edge of the city seemed to go on in its regular fashion, but Michael noticed that quite a few of the younger men in the neighborhood were absent. They were involved with war action. Michael's father was over forty, and due to his prior head wound from the previous war he was not required to join the army, at least not for now. Their life seemed to be peaceful. If only his dad would not get so worked up about the war! Michael looked out of the kitchen window. His father had gone to the mailbox, and he watched his dad standing outside in front of the house in a lively conversation with several neighbors. He did not like the angry expression on his dad's face, and he nudged his mother who was washing dishes in the sink. "Mom, I think that Dad is angry about something. He is talking with a bunch of neighbors."

His mother looked up and hurried to the door. The expression on her face showed worry mixed with fierce determination. She had to step in and stop his rant. Louise knew her husband; if he got angry it would be about politics. Quickly she went to the front door and called him: "Martin! Come in quick! Telephone for you!" Michael took note. His mother was right. She knew that it had become dangerous to discuss politics and speak freely. Some time ago a neighbor had a huge argument about war, Hitler, the party, and its leadership with one of the big wheels of the local party. Not long after that a police car arrived at the man's residence. The man was arrested. He simply disappeared from the neighborhood, and nobody knew where he was. Some neighbors said that he had gone to jail for uttering threats to the government. Others had voiced the opinion that he had been taken to an institution that was called "KZ", a concentration camp where everybody wound up who did not fit into the concept of the state. It was like a way of warehousing the "undesirables", and many of them would never return. Mr. Laumann came hurrying up the steps. "I'm coming already! Who is on the phone?" Mrs. Laumann calmly looked at her husband. "Nobody!" He stared back at her, visibly irritated and bewildered. Calmly she looked at him: "Martin, nobody called. But I saw what was going on outside. Actually Michael saw you and told me. I tell you, political discussions and altercations with the neighbors will land you in a place where you don't want to be. And we don't want you there either! So, please…" Mr. Laumann became calmer. He heaved a sigh. "You are right, Louise. I should know better. I'll be careful." Louise stared at him and emphasized every word. "Just- don't- do- it! - I mean, stop talking politics with the neighbors!" She went back to her work, and her husband went to the back yard and took out his frustrations on a pile of firewood that needed splitting.

Another summer was coming to an end. It was a brooding, overcast day, and school had started again after the summer holidays. Michael sat down at the kitchen table. His facial expression seemed to reflect the mood of this day, and his mother gave him a questioning glance. Somehow he seemed out of sorts and sad. He was in his own world and quietly thinking. Maybe he had problems at school. She asked him, but he waved away her concerns. School was fine, and he was happy to start with the next grade. For the longest time she had not seen his one friend Simon. Several months ago she had asked Michael about him and the family. She had not seen Simon's parents, Ruth and Paul Hoffer, at any meeting in school, but Michael just mumbled something vague to the effect that they were probably busy. She also observed that now it was only Peter and Michael who were buddies. Strange! The three always had done things together. This time she decided to get to the bottom of things, and she asked whether he had a falling out with Simon. Michael realized that he had to finally "come clean" as Mr. Menzinger had put it. He had to tell his parents what had transpired exactly one year ago. It was today to the day that he had seen his friend the last time. It made him sad. He leaned back and gave his mother a questioning glance. "Can I wait talking about it till dad is back in the house? Otherwise I have to tell a long story twice." His mother understood. "Sure, good idea!"

Martin came in. It was close to suppertime. Michael eyed his parents cautiously. "Mom asked me why I was looking sad today. Today one year ago was the last day I saw my friend Simon." The parents looked surprised. Michael's father cleared his throat. "Simon…yes, I remember. I always liked him; such a nice boy, and his parents are nice people! But I was not even sure that you were still friends." Questioningly he looked at his son. Michael shifted uneasily on his chair. "I better tell you the entire story. Simon is in Canada. The family had to leave. It was getting too dangerous here. His mother is Jewish." And first haltingly, then faster he told his parents the story of the family having to leave, about him asking Leo Menzinger to take them by truck to Italy, the trip in the cargo hold of the truck, and their plans to make a journey by ship out of Italy. He finished by adding. "One year ago Mr. Menzinger told me that I had to come clean and tell you about all of that. It is done now." There was uncertainty in his eyes. "I just hope that he and his family will be safe. With the war there is no way to send mail overseas, and we don't get any either." The clock ticked into the silence of the room. Michael waited. He had done what had been necessary; he had told his story. Now he was prepared that his parents would scold him severely or ground him. But nothing of that transpired. His father gave him a rib-crushing bear hug. "I know that it is difficult to not know. But I am proud of you, son!" His mother smiled through tears. "Thank you for helping to get them out of the country, and thank God for people like Leo. I believe that it happened in time. The borders were closed after the declaration of war. They would have never gotten out as passengers on a train." Silently they sat down to eat their supper.

Life was still peaceful in their area despite the fact that the war had been going on for two years. Michael had observed large squadrons of twin engine Heinkel bombers taking off to the North. He knew from listening to the radio stations that they would take part in the conquest of France, but nobody was too concerned that their area here would be in danger. The hilly region of southern Germany did not have too many large cities that would be likely targets, and the valleys were often shrouded in fog, which made direct aims at the area even more difficult. Sunny fall days had given way to clouds and drizzle at the end of November of 1941. They were all sound asleep when the wail of sirens sounded through the quiet night warning the population of an imminent attack. Immediately after the short thunder of anti-aircraft cannon boomed. The Laumann family went down into the cellar to seek protection, but Martin and Michael looked outside first. In the night sky they saw clusters of multicolored magnesium marker flares that were slowly floating down on parachutes. Scouting aircraft had planted these markers to stake out the areas that were to be attacked. It was unlikely that the houses here would be the targets, but nevertheless they hurried downstairs. The sound of bombers followed the scout aircraft and unloaded their deadly cargo onto an industrial area that was about a mile away. The bigger danger was a hail of thousands of shrapnel from anti-aircraft grenades that rained down on the area with a high-pitched whine. They could hear the pinging sound of the shrapnel as it ricocheted from the roof and from the cement sidewalks. After a while the sirens sounded again as a signal that the danger was over. After this interrupted night they looked around to survey the house for damages. There was nothing of note, but they heard that a garment factory close by had been destroyed, and two night shift workers were killed there. Peter had walked around and collected some interesting specimens of grenade fragments, and at school they were traded between the classmates. It had been one unnerving night where war made its appearance in the area, but after that a treacherous sense of false security prevailed. For now no further attacks were happening in this area.

The seasons ebbed and flowed. The Laumann family sat at the breakfast table. Michael grabbed another slice of bread and spread it thickly with mother's homemade plum jam. It was not that sweet as there was no sugar available, but the plums made up for it. It did not matter, as long as there was something to eat, as he seemed to be permanently hungry these days. He had grown two inches taller than his father, in many ways like a young edition of him, except that he was the communicator in the family. Mr. Laumann was his usual silent self. He shortly asked his son about the day at school ahead. Michael gulped down his cup of roasted barley coffee. It was the daily breakfast drink, as real coffee was only available on the black market at exorbitant prices. For him it did not matter. His parents missed the real early morning brew of fragrant coffee. He responded to his father's question. "Oh, it's nothing big today, dad. Except there will be an assembly in the hall later. It's about some announcement for a meeting. So I'll be home a bit later." His father's face showed signs that this

War Becoming Reality

would be the end of a quiet breakfast. "This is what I hate! They constantly come up with these assemblies. It is just another form of manipulation from the Nazi party, and this is happening in the schools too! Last year they made you sign up for the youth group." Martin Laumann lost his composure, and his fist hit the table that the coffee cups clattered. "Nobody can tell me to become a party member, damn it!" He was visibly upset. "Why do we have to have an argument about politics even at the breakfast table now? Can't we at least keep some peace here? I dislike this so much." Mother's voice rose, and there was a painful, pleading note in it. Michael looked back at his parents. "Just don't get so worked up dad. So I was signed up for the youth group! But I avoid those meetings like the cat the cold water." He took his dishes out into the kitchen and washed them. Next he grabbed his satchel. He waved to his parents and shot out of the door. He whistled the shrill signal for Peter as he approached his house. Peter caught up with him, and they broke into a swift trot to reach the tram stop. "Stupid assemblies," Peter huffed. He was not pleased. "If they want to sign me up for another group, I won't do it. And this youth group is crap too! I hate it!" He was in a fighting mood. "Ha! I got a yellow ticket because I missed two meetings." Michael chuckled as he commented: "Guess what, I got a red ticket. I missed three meetings! I can just hear the leader going on like 'Lack of effort towards your fatherland, young man, and lack of respect'. What a bombastic idiot!" He mimicked the preaching tone of the youth group leader. Both burst out into laughter. Michael shrugged his shoulders. "Oh, well, so I'll go to the next meeting to keep the old fart happy. After that it's back to the same old tricks: blue ticket, yellow ticket, red ticket, after which they'll see me again. Let's run! Here is the tram!" They flashed their student tickets and stepped into the vehicle. They did not see any fellow students. The tram was full. Something was unusual. Michael squinted, when he saw several people wearing a badge on their clothes. What was that? He recognized a yellow six- pointed star-the Jewish star. So this was the newest regulation: all Jews had to wear the Star of David! He quietly told his friend about his observation. Peter thoughtfully looked at the persons. "This is just not right", he murmured under his breath. "Is the government crazy or are we nuts?"

The tram came to a jolting halt. An old woman who wore the star badge almost lost her foothold, and the boys stopped her fall. She gave them a shy, grateful look. "You better hold on, madam. Don't fall!" A fat man laughed contemptuously: "How can they fall? They are thinking that they are the chosen race!" Hot words stung on Michael's lips. This fatso did not even have the decency to offer his seat to an older lady! He should just keep his mouth shut! Michael gave the fat man a grin. "The only chosen people in this popcorn popper are people like you who have a seat under their butt." The passengers nearby laughed. One man got the message and offered his seat to the woman. The fat man's face contorted with rage. "That is youth today! No respect, no decency…" Peter stared at him contemptuously: "And certainly no seats in the tram", Peter finished the sentence of the complaining man. How could anyone have respect for a person like him! The tram stopped and they walked to the school building.

They joined the large crowd of students milling around the door, waiting for the bell. The head teacher stepped out and shot an energetic glance at the crowd. "Line up", he barked. He raised his hand. "There will be an important assembly at noon in the hall. Everybody must be present." The bell started to ring, and the boys filed into their classrooms. Michael's thoughts went back to the people in the tram who had worn the Jewish star badge. He had to think of Simon. He missed his desk neighbor, but he had the feeling that he was safe. He willed himself to belief it, even though he had not heard from him. There was no mail coming in from overseas. It was war. He wondered how he would be doing with the new language. He would have to learn it fast. Michael's English was growing in leaps and bounds, as he was listening to all the forbidden English radio stations. It served two purposes: on the one hand he was always up to date with the news, on the other hand he was learning a language so much faster. With the knowledge of the news had come disturbing facts: there were reports of attacks, bombs, grenades, and warplanes. He had seen the one night with sirens and shrapnel raining from the sky. There could be more. He had to think about yesterday's news. Gosh, it had been scary! The voice of the teacher cut through his thoughts. "Laumann, please carry on and translate the next passage!" Peter's finger was unobtrusively poised on the page that needed to be translated, and Michael surfaced with his thoughts back to reality like a diver who was coming out of an eerie cave. His eyes swiftly went across the page, and he cleared his throat. Thank God, this was an easy story about the maiden Pocahontas! He had devoured the entire book already earlier, and his translation came out smoothly and clearly. "Well done, Laumann!" The teacher was pleased. He added: "By the way, I need to talk to you after class." Michael felt uneasy. He was uncomfortably aware of his lack of attention today. Maybe that was why the teacher wanted to have a word with him. After the bell went, he cautiously stepped up to the teacher's desk. "Yes sir?" The teacher's eyes rested on him: "Well Laumann, let's have the good news first. You are doing better than anybody else in English. As a matter of fact, you are way too far advanced as to stay in this grade. You should go to the material of the higher grades. Next, tell me, where do you pick up all the words and especially the idioms?" Michael was guarded. Of course he could not tell his teacher that he was listening to forbidden radio stations on a daily basis! Instead he had to confabulate and improvise: "Oh, my uncle had a stack of English books. He doesn't want them anymore, so he gave them to me; these are books about England and America. They are interesting to read." Hope to God, that the teacher would never find out that he had no uncle! The teacher's eyes looked at him thoughtfully. He nodded, but Michael sensed that the man was not entirely convinced. "Very good; this probably explains why you have so many unusual terms in your English." Michael sounded nonchalant: "Yes, of course." The teacher looked at him again.

"Here is the bad news: your attention during class is absolutely the worst I have seen. Smarten up, even if the material is too boring for you. So, up at least one grade for now in English, and otherwise you'd better get going or you'll miss the next class." Michael felt relieved: "Yes, sir, and thank you very much!" He went on to the science class, and at noon the crowd of students milled around on their way to the assembly. The younger grades were dismissed after some brief announcement, however Michael's grade and the higher grades all had to stay. The principal stepped up to the lectern. "Gentlemen, two of our most outstanding local party leaders are giving a presentation next Tuesday at four in the afternoon at the Beethoven Hall in town. It is obligatory for all students grade eight and higher to be present. Attendance will be taken." Peter nudged Michael. "What is that again? More party shit?" Michael silenced his friend: "Shhh". Carefully he glanced around. His lips barely moved as he mumbled under his breath, "This does not sound right. We will have to go there, but we'll go together. I think I have an idea..." The principal's voice droned on. He mentioned enrolment in the SS group and extolled the virtues of becoming a member of an elite to serve the fatherland. Michael tried to listen away from the ramblings about a glorious victory and building of the greatest empire of the world. What a lot of predictable platitudes! He had heard these phrases so many times before, and he had an overdose already. His eyes looked attentive, but in reality his mind was already leap-frogging ahead to the meeting of next Tuesday. No doubt that he would have to show up there, but he had no intentions of staying longer than necessary. And signing up for the young SS group...no, this was something to avoid! He would figure out a way around it. He got home late due to the assembly and expected a frown from his mother, but she was not in the flat. She had left a note. The residents of the house had to take turns using the basement laundry, and despite the fact that this was not her turn on this day to do the washing, she was downstairs. This was strange enough, as everything in the household went on like clock work with an almost predictable

War Becoming Reality

regularity: laundry on Tuesday, ironing on Thursday, house cleaning on Saturday. This was certainly not the routine today. Michael went to the stove. An enameled soup pot was on the small wood burner. He was hungry, and the stew smelled delicious. He helped himself to a generous portion. There was not much bread left. It would have to last, and the small margarine cube would have to last too. He could have eaten a horse today, and he lifted the lid to scan the contents. No, he could not have more, as there would have to be enough for his father when he came home. Curiosity drove him downstairs, where his mom was toiling over a load of steaming wash. "Why do you have to wash today? This is not your usual day," he wondered. His mother wiped the steam and sweat off her face. "It has to be. We are getting company. I had a postcard in the mail from your aunt Alma. She and cousin Hilda are going to one of those women party meetings in our area here, and they'll stop by on their way home." Michael studied the expression on his mother's face. Aunt Alma was a difficult person, and it was obvious that his mother was guarded about the news. "I wonder what dad will say." Michael looked at her with a lopsided grin. His mother shrugged her shoulders: "Look, let's face it; he won't be thrilled either. It is rather short notice too. They'll arrive on Saturday and will take the train home on Sunday." Michael groaned. "Aw, darn it! Another weekend shot to hell!" She shook her head. "Michael! Let's just leave it. There is not much that we can do. But I believe that it should be possible to be pleasant and polite for one day. We still can go for a walk on Sunday afternoon. At least that should be relaxing." She added: "But we have to get some supplies. With the rationing getting worse we don't have enough. Could you make your way to the farm and ask whether they would trade our tobacco coupons for some milk and bacon or ham?"

Michael was only too willing to jump onto his bike. He pedaled through the neighborhood with its tidy front yards and the three story houses. Everything had looked so pretty till recently, but now the houses looked like drab monsters. They had been painted in ochre, dark brown or dark green camouflage colors. It was a regulation to make the structures less visible "just in case of an enemy attack". He arrived at Menzinger's farm where the family just sat down for their late afternoon meal. Mr. Menzinger pulled up a chair for Michael and invited him: "Here, sit down! You look like you may have a hole in your stomach. The way you are growing we'll have to saw a hole into the ceiling next." He put a plate on the table for him. Gratefully Michael sat down and munched on a huge slice of bread and a generous piece of bacon, which Mr. Menzinger had sawed off from a slab of smoked meat. They had done some butchering, but it was all done "black", of course. Michael mentioned the tobacco coupons his mother wanted to trade, and the farmer had a cheerful smile on his face. "Oh yes, any time! It's good of you to keep me in pipe tobacco." He went to the storage cellar and cut a piece of ham for Michael and added a ham bone too. Mother would be happy! He also filled an empty wine bottle with milk. Michael sank all those treasures into his saddlebags. He prepared to leave. "Just make sure that nobody sees the loot! This is "black ham", Mr. Menzinger cautioned him. At home he put the traded groceries on the kitchen table. His father was home and was engrossed in the evening paper. Michael sat down opposite of him. It was difficult to tell whether dad had a good day or not. Mr. Laumann put the paper aside. "How was school?" Michael mentioned the meeting next week where he would have to show up, and his father's face looked like a big thundercloud was approaching. He sounded angry: "More manipulation, of course. Always the same rubbish!" Michael remembered how upset he had seen his father before. He told him, that there was a plan to enlist students in the SS. Mr. Laumann clenched his fists. Michael stopped his father's next outburst: "Listen dad, please! I know what is going on. I'm not a dumb kid, and I don't plan to get dragged into this. Trust me! I'll figure something out. Please, don't tell mom. I know, that she would just be worried sick." His father sighed. "Son, I know that you are not stupid. Just realize that I am upset with a system that

War Becoming Reality

is built on false promises and hatred. It will drive this country to destruction. Thousands of innocent people have lost their homes, God knows how many have lost their lives, and I know from reliable work colleagues that there are plans to exterminate the Jewish race and also others that are inconvenient in the political scheme." There was profound distress in his eyes, as he pointed to a small passage in the newspaper. "Here is more; I just read it! People who are considered "inferior" or not worth to continue living will be removed. This is a disgrace and an insult to anything that is right and just! It makes me feel ashamed to be a citizen of this country." He interrupted himself and looked at Michael. "You just got home. Where have you been?" Michael replied: "Dad, I was at Menzinger's farm." A sudden realization hit Michael like a thunderbolt. He had to think of the Menzinger's little girl. The sweet-tempered five year old with her almond shaped, slanted eyes was not a child that would grow up to be a normal adult. Mrs. Menzinger had said on several occasions that she was slow and "not right" for her age. His parents had mentioned something about a problem she was born with. The doctor had mentioned his suspicion to the parents that she had signs of an abnormality. Michael had looked around in an encyclopedia at home. He loved this book, as it provided him with an endless source of information to satisfy his curiosity about anything, and he had found a term called "mongolism". Resi was simply born different. Michael had to think about all of that after listening to his dad. It occurred to him, that the Menzinger's life would be shattered, if officials found out that Resi was not fitting the "norm" of the government once she had reached school age. Mr. Laumann observed the troubled expression in his son's face. "You look upset, Michael. What's going on?" Michael heaved a deep breath. "Dad, this is scary! You just said something about people that are considered "inferior". What about the Menzinger's little girl? Resi is not right! Her mother has said that before. What will happen when she has to go to school?" Michael's father looked at his son, and his face seemed chiseled in stone. He breathed heavily like he was laboring under a load that was too much to shoulder. "Michael, you thought of something that had not crossed my mind yet. O my God! I have to go and see Josef Menzinger. They have to get her away from here soon, before she enters school and the authorities catch up on the fact that she is not developing normally. I'll go there on the weekend. He has to know." They sat in silence. Mrs. Laumann came into the room. She saw the tense expression on her husband's face. He explained to her what he had just read and explained: "It is about Menzinger's Resi. They have to hide her. They have relatives in the country far out. If they don't do it, they'll lose their child." Her eyes were filled with horror. "Dear God, so it is true! There are innocent people being killed." He nodded. "Yes, Louise, it may be millions of them, and it is all kept hidden. What is worse is the fact that we haven't seen the end of it yet. It is war, and we can only hope and pray that we will survive." Michael had to think; of course they had not seen it all. He and Peter had listened to the forbidden stations. More and more parts of Europe had become embroiled in war action. Like a consuming blaze the war had spread to other countries. Japan was involved; terrible fighting was going on in Russia; the United States were part of it. He heard that rationing would be getting worse. He had heard of bomb strikes. Everybody in the neighborhood had received notices that a bomb shelter had to be excavated, and whoever worked on it would receive permission to use it in the case of a bomb attack. He and his dad were assigned to work on this project several hours in the late evenings, and all the neighbors did their share too. The wall clock in the living room was ticking ominously into the silence of this evening. Time was ticking ominously as well.

Saturdays had a way to make Michael feel uneasy. He woke up to the swishing sound of the wet floor rag and the scrub brush that signaled the Saturday housecleaning ritual. Every Saturday was the same. He hated house cleaning! Sometimes he wondered how his mother could stand it. His father had already left for work, and he quickly downed a cup of barley coffee. The hot, bitter brew had qualities that could wake up a corpse! Next he rushed out of the door. Saturday's cleaning frenzy was no fun any time, but today it felt even more uncomfortable. His aunt and cousin were scheduled to arrive at the railroad station, and he would have to hurry up after school, as they had to be picked up.

School on Saturdays seemed to crawl along at a snail's pace. Longingly he looked outside. It was a wonderful fall day, but he would not be able to spend much time outside. He had to stick around with the relatives, and he told Peter about their impending visit that put their outdoor plans on hold. It was the last class of the day, and it did not help that the class clown Thomas lit a cigarette, puffed away in the classroom and disappeared into a storage closet when the teacher arrived. Thirty boys observed the closet with interest. There was chuckling and mumbling. The teacher, a somewhat humorless middle-aged man, entered the room and bellowed his customary "Heil Hitler." Thirty unenthusiastic voices mumbled a reply. He eyed the restless crowd with suspicion, as he had smelled the tobacco smoke despite the air from the windows that had been hastily opened before his arrival. He remarked: "If you think, that I don't smell the cigarette smoke, you are mistaken!" To drive home his displeasure he barked: "Detention after this period for the entire class." The teacher's facial expression froze, when he saw a wisp of smoke coming from the storage closet. He strode to the closet to open the door, and Thomas nonchalantly walked out with a goofy grin and sauntered to his desk. He had done it again and provided some entertainment. The boys shook with laughter! A knock at the door stopped any comment the teacher wanted to make. The school secretary walked in apologetically. "Very sorry for disturbing, but there is a phone call for you Dr. Schmid." Amidst all the chuckles and talking the bell went. Michael was not pleased. Now they had a detention. He would be home late! This day was a mess already! Shortly after the bell signal the caretaker of the school appeared. He was eager to close up the rooms for the weekend and saw the students in their desks. "What's up with you fellows? Get out and move it! I haven't got time on my hands to wait for a bunch of slowpokes like you." The boys gleefully hurried to follow the caretaker's order, and Michael heaved a sigh of relief. No detention for the class! They all got off easy today. Somehow he would survive the visit of aunt Alma too!

He arrived home and found a flurry of activity. Dad was standing by the shed splitting kindling for the stove. A few scattered feathers lay by the chopping block. That meant chicken dinner on Sunday, Michael observed. Visitors called for a special effort in the kitchen. Too bad that the visitor was aunt Alma! Michael knew from previous experiences that the mood would tense up with her arrival, only to relax again after she had left. They walked to the train station in silence, and the dark, menacing shape of the locomotive appearing in the distance was like a fitting picture. The squealing brakes and the rattling wheels overpowered any other sound. Doors opened and travellers exited. Some were farmers returning from the city market with empty crates and baskets, others were visitors. Aunt Alma was approaching from the distance followed by her daughter Hilda. Louise was determined to make the best of the short-notice visit and gave her sister a cordial hug. Alma's face showed a satisfied smile of a person who was pleased to harvest the respect of her relatives, but it lacked any cordial note. Cousin Hilda nodded stiffly and pulled her thin-lipped mouth into a forced smile. With the cruel realism of a thirteen year old Michael observed his cousin. It was hard to find anything likeable about this seventeen-year-old girl: she was unsmiling, unattractive, unsociable, and her colorless eyebrows and pale eyes just matched the unpleasant overall picture. Dutifully he carried one of the suitcases. His aunt was rambling on about the party meeting. His dad listened politely. He was clearly not interested in a fight about politics. She was dropping subtle hints, mentioning how every person would be needed in supporting the party, alluding to the fact that he had not become a party member, but Martin just nodded absentmindedly. Michael observed that she took a break, but he knew that she was just waiting for another opportunity. Louise and her sister went into the kitchen, and Michael overheard how aunt Alma was carrying on, bragging about how her husband had become a block leader and their son had been chosen to join the SS. It sounded like a display of fanatic pride, and he admired his mother, how she put up with this verbal avalanche that was annoying enough for him to listen to through the closed door. He noticed that the two came into the dining room, and his mother cheerfully called out for everybody to come to dinner. He had to think that his mother was trying to keep things peaceful and pleasant, and he also observed the expression of haughty self-righteousness in the face of his aunt. His father said a simple prayer, as they would usually do before dinner, and he noticed the expression of disdain on the face of aunt Alma and a sneer on cousin Hilda's face. Obviously staunch believers in Hitler like these two could not relate to saying grace. His aunt's eyes went over to him. "So, what is Michael doing these days?" He was cautious with his reply. No matter what anybody said to belligerous aunt Alma, she always turned it around and used the answer as ammunition. She was always right, and the rest of the world was forever wrong. He looked up from his plate. "Oh, I've got lots to do. There is school, homework, and my chores. I'm also helping with the excavation of the neighborhood bomb shelter. And I have half a dozen rabbits now, so I can sell a few and make extra money." Obviously she was not impressed. "You should see your cousins! Look at Hilda! She is the leader of her youth group, and her brother Albert is in the SS. You should do something like that." Michael leaned back in his chair, his face a study in boredom. "Oh yeah? Well, that is nice." His unenthusiastic tone and his facial expression were in direct opposition to his reply. His father observed the conversation, and his mouth twitched with quiet amusement. Immediately aunt Alma caught on. "I don't think that there is anything funny about Michael's indifferent and phlegmatic attitude, Martin. But a good example has to start with the parents, of course." Michael felt that he was running out of patience with his relatives. The old cat! She was really showing her claws! Defiantly he looked back at her. "There is nothing wrong with my parents. But it seems that some people here are thinking that life consists only of party meetings." He rose from the table. "If you could excuse me now. I've got a meeting with my school books called homework." He pushed back his chair, took out the dishes and retreated to his room, leaving the adults in tense silence. The adults stayed behind, and the evening dragged on with a polite exchange of news and trivialities, and later he heard the murmuring voices of his parents. They slept in the living room, leaving their bedroom to the visitors. Mother's voice sounded strained and discouraged, his father's reassuring and patient. "There is nothing you can do, Louise. She is a poisonous fanatic, and her daughter is just a brainwashed, colorless nobody. Poor girl!" He continued: "Well, I like peace in the family too, but I draw the line once they trespass on the rules of normal courtesy." It was good to know that his dad was standing his ground. Sunday morning would usually mean that they would go to church together after breakfast, but Michael's mother and father stayed behind. They had company, and they wanted to be available for them. Michael was glad to escape, and as he prepared to leave he almost collided with his cousin in the hallway. When she heard that he was going to church, she looked at him incredulously. "You must be joking! We are not going there. Who needs it?" He did not feel like arguing with this girl, waved and left. Peter was joining him out on the street. They walked to church and sat together with some of their friends. A powerful choral filled the old sanctuary and seemed to resound off the high arches of the building. It was Thanksgiving Sunday, and it occurred to Michael that there was a lot to be thankful for. So far there had been no bombs and no destruction in their immediate area. Daily life had become restricted, but in other areas of Europe things were much worse. They had food to eat every day, but the "daily bread" mentioned in

War Becoming Reality

the Lord's Prayer had been reduced to small rations, and it was a tasteless product consisting of some grain, bran, and potatoes. He had to think about the part of the prayer "...and deliver us from evil". What was happening in this time was evil. How could God allow this to happen? But God did not make wars. It was people who made wars. How long could it last? When would this be over? The hour in church became like a quiet retreat and a peaceful haven. He forgot about the awkward presence of the relatives at home, the apprehension about war, and the deprivations that had crept into daily life. Sunlight filtered through the old stained glass windows, and the silvery organ sound that was filling the church building followed him on his way back home.

The streets were quiet and Sunday-like, but the sense of peace and calm did not seem to prevail at his home. As he opened the door he heard a conversation in the living room that seemed to have escalated into an altercation. His father's voice was calm, but firm. "You will not tell me that supporting hatred and injustice is right, Alma." She was in a fighting mood. "Keeping the German race pure and Aryan and eliminating anything undesirable is justifiable and necessary. There have been other worthless populations exterminated in the past." Michael had his hand on the door handle. Uh- oh! It sounded like trouble in there! For a moment he wondered, whether he should simply go out into the yard or go to his room but he changed his mind. Why should he be banished from the living room because of an obnoxious relative? Resolutely he walked in and sat down on the couch. His father nodded to him briefly, and his aunt went on with her rant: "There is enough life around that is not worth living. It is a burden to society and the entire country, and it has to be eliminated." Michael had never heard overt statements like that, and he was stunned. This was incredible and pure evil! It was about killing people, something that filled him with horror. His father replied evenly: "This sounds highly questionable to me, Alma. Who are you to judge?" She became even more agitated, and there was a fanatical glow in her eyes. "I have every right to judge. I am in full support of Hitler and his ideas, whereas you…" her colorless lips curled into a contemptuous smile. Martin Laumann was prepared for confrontation. "Yes, so what about me? Carry on! You have my full attention!" She accused him of neglecting his duties, of not being a loyal citizen and exclaimed at the end: "And not enough with that, you are sending your son to church on Sunday instead of getting him involved in a healthy activity that prepares him to be loyal and of service to this country." There was brief silence, before Michael decided to speak up: "Actually, I went, because I wanted to go there. I'm not being sent like a parcel in the mail!" His preciously silent cousin decided to add her opinion: "And what do you learn there anyways? Stupid waste of time!" Cousin Hilda wanted to add some more vitriolic comments, but Michael grinned at her. "Interesting that you should ask. After hearing your conversation before, it is all the stuff that is missing with you. What happened to 'loving your neighbor', for instance? Oh, but you must have skipped over that! And there is the small detail of the fifth commandment that must have been lost in your wonderful meetings. It says 'thou shall not kill'. What happened to your brain, Hilda? Did you lose it in one of your meetings too?" She stared at him, unable to come up with an answer. A shade of doubt was visible on her face. She seemed to think about what he had said. Michael's aunt stared at her nephew and was speechless. Icy silence filled the room. Michael was grateful that it would only be a few more hours till these two would leave. Louise looked at her sister's face, which was cold and closed. They were preparing lunch, and Louise tried to be conciliatory. "I feel sorry that we seem to be getting into arguments about politics. We don't see each other often, and it's such a waste of time getting stuck in differences." Her sister's facial expression seemed to be a barrier to any further communication, and her answer reflected her cold attitude: "There cannot be any point in getting along, as long as you are showing an attitude of irresponsibility and disloyalty to the country. I don't need family like that! The party is my chosen family now." Louise stared at her in disbelief. "Then why did you come and see us at all, if you feel this way?" Alma shrugged her shoulders indifferently. "I wonder about this myself. But then I couldn't have made the trip home in one day." Louise soberly looked back at her sister. "I see. It was advantageous! Well, lunch is ready. We can sit down, and after that the train will leave. I guess that makes it convenient enough." She added: "Nevertheless I want to tell you, that you are my sister and welcome here. You should know that. But the rest is really up to you." Alma's face was sullen. She had nothing to say, and the meal was consumed in silence. After that they packed their luggage. The rumble of the small wagon that carried the luggage accompanied the walk to the train station. The hiss and rattle of the arriving train was punctuating a feeling of relief in Michael. There were no hugs, just a short good-bye, and they got into the train without looking back. Hilda was the only one who had mumbled a barely audible "thank you". Michael saw that his mother had tears in her eyes. His dad patted her on her shoulder. "It is the war that is getting worse, Louise. It seems to even creep into families. But we will get through this too."

He looked at the clear, sunny fall sky and suggested that they should all go for a walk together. They would go into the forest and collect pinecones and small twigs to start the fire in the stove, and they pulled the empty, rattling wagon behind them. Michael felt happy with his father's suggestion. He did not feel like staying at home. Somehow he still had the image of his aunt in his mind, the way she was sitting in the living room, criticizing and arguing. Any other place would be much more relaxing than sitting in the living room right now! They walked, passed Menzinger's farm, and went over the bridge across the highway. Underneath fleets of military vehicles were speeding by. It was a sign of troop movement, and the steady drone of the motors followed them as they walked into the forest. They got busy collecting windfall branches and pinecones. The wagon was getting full, a bulky but lightweight load, and they started to walk back as the evening sun filtered through the green-golden trees. As they passed the Menzinger's place, the farmer was standing by the gate. He had seen them and invited them to come in to rest a bit and have a glass of cider. They were happy to accept and sat down on the bench by the house. Hans, their son, and Michael were climbing into the apple tree to pick apples. It felt like being on top of the world in the evening sunshine. Martin Laumann had brought the newspaper article that he had found upsetting and alarming, which had dealt with the government's plans to eliminate life that was "not worth living", and he showed it to his friends. They had not heard about it, and shock was in their faces. They were looking at the information, and the farmer shook his head in dismay: "We cannot keep Resi here. Once she is old enough to go to school, it will be obvious to everybody that she is not normal like the other children." His wife immediately understood the implications. She had been quietly working in the kitchen, her hands busy as always, but she stopped, looking up aghast. "They are going to kill her, my baby." The two men talked together. There was time, but Martin Laumann urged his friend to act as soon as possible. Josef Menzinger agreed. His sister's family lived on one of the many remote farmsteads in the Black Forest. They carved out a living like most of their ancestors had done it: small farming, woodworking, and charcoal making. It was a solitary existence, but it was the safest place for a person who had to be hidden away like Resi. He planned to take her there. There was no public transport, no bus, and the railroad station was far away in the next town. Martin Laumann wondered, how he would get there. Josef shrugged his shoulders. He had to do it alone. His brother Leo was in the army and could not help. He had a sturdy bike, and Resi would have to sit in the small trailer. It would take them almost two days to get there, but it had to be done. He looked at his little daughter, who was playing with her doll. "Resi, tomorrow we go to auntie Veronica. Do you come along?" The trusting eyes looked back at him. "I come. Can I take my doll?" He was close to tears, but he smiled at his little girl: "Yes, but you will be going for a long time." The realization that she would be gone for a long time hurt him more than it disturbed his little daughter. "A long time," she echoed, nodded, and kept on playing with her doll, humming tunelessly. There was sadness in the face of Marie Menzinger. She would miss her little Resi, but she knew that she had no other choice. They could make the long trek to visit occasionally only, as it was difficult to travel there despite the relatively short distance. It was such a remote location. And it was even worse not to know how long Resi had to be hidden away. The Laumann family had to think about leaving. It was dusk, and they wanted to make it home before dark. Josef Menzinger shook Martin's hand. "I cannot really thank you enough for warning us, Martin. Let us hope for the best." They walked home with their full wagon. Mrs. Menzinger had added a bag of apples to the load, which smelled of fall and forest. The sky darkened to a crystalline azure, and in the quietness of the evening it was hard to imagine that the country was torn by war, hatred, and fanaticism. Martin Laumann had to think about that when a shooting star attracted his attention. Suddenly he had to think back to his childhood. He always had made a wish then. In a way there was still a bit of that youngster in him. Now he had to think of the Menzinger family and their difficulties, as he was hoping for a good outcome. He looked at the starry sky and listened to the quietness around. But there was also the knowledge that the peaceful stillness of this evening was something to be treasured. It would not stay this way for long.

Three

Destruction, Death And Violence

A Land Without Bridges - 1942 to 1945

Michael announced to his parents that he and his friend Peter would be staying in the city after school. There was this "must attend" meeting, and he knew that there would be the push to enlist the attending students into the SS. Nevertheless he tried to sound very casual about it, mentioning that he and his friend would be coming home once the event was finished. He saw the concern in the faces of his parents. His mother sounded almost resigned: "I guess there is not much you can do about it. If you don't show up, you'll just make it worse, and they'll come and get you at home." He hugged his mom and told her not to worry. He was determined to stay optimistic rather than to worry. There had to be a solution! His name had to be on the list as a sign that he had attended the meeting. But once his name was listed he had to find a way to leave. Peter was waiting for him after school. They had some time and sauntered through the downtown area. Nothing looked spectacular. The shop windows were nothing to get excited about, and war merchandise was not plentiful. Traffic was down as gas was rationed. They joked about the glorious country that looked somewhat inglorious, judging from the downtown area that was no longer attractive or vibrant. Together they walked to the large building that was generally a venue for concerts, meetings, and other public events. Flags were billowing in front of the building, and a crowd of students had gathered. Through a loudspeaker military marches reverberated across the square. Peter grinned at his friend. "Just look, what they have done to the Beethoven Hall! The composer would probably turn in his grave just listening to this musical mess they are playing right now!" Together they walked up to the second floor to the main auditorium. Michael's alert gray eyes quickly scanned the premises. The structure of the building showed that the caretaker's quarters as well as some small assembly rooms and washrooms were located on the ground floor. It was the upper floor that accommodated the large auditorium. He would have to check that out. He told his friend that he had to quickly go to the washroom, and he went down the steps and pressed the door handle. It was locked. He swore under his breath, but he did not give up. Swiftly he went to the caretaker's apartment and knocked at the door. A middle-aged woman opened, and a cat eyed him curiously. He requested to use the gentlemen's room, emphasizing his need to go by holding a hand on his stomach and showing a distressed expression on his face. The woman understood, nodded, and went to get a set of keys. Noticing that one key was gone, she mumbled something about the key being in the hands of the person who was in charge of the meeting. They should have left the door unlocked! She was annoyed but quickly handed the second key to Michael. "Here, you take it and go. Stupid people to lock the washroom! I can't be bothered! I am leaving right now, and I'm only back after they are done with their meeting. Just leave that key under the doormat. But don't forget it!" Michael thanked her and left. Looking around he noticed that a uniformed leader-type figure stood at the entrance of the building watching all the people who walked in. In the fraction of a second he registered what was happening. Whoever walked in here was intended to stay, and nobody would leave the premises. Quickly he unlocked the washroom and slunk in. He surveyed the tiny room and the adjacent two cubicles. There was a small window above the toilet. He looked out. It went down to the street, but it was not too high. The excitement seemed to make his guts hyperactive. To his own surprise he actually had to use the washroom, and he went out after washing his hands. In the mirror he saw a face that looked much older than the years it had seen. He noticed that a guard locked the door to the washroom after he had left, but Michael knew that he had the key to escape in his pocket. He and Peter would leave through the washroom window. It was their only chance. Quickly he went up the wide marble steps and looked for his friend who had posted himself by the door. Both were requested to put their names on a large list with many names, and they complied with the order. As they sat down, Michael whispered his observations to his friend: the place was supervised. Everybody had to register, and nobody would be let out. But he also mentioned that they would be waiting for a chance to escape through the washroom. Peter agreed. They could do this together!

The hall filled to the strains of a military march. Next a highly decorated officer stepped up to the lectern. His bellowing voice sounded through the hall. Everybody would be called to come forward, and those able bodied enough would be enrolled in the SS. A rambling account about the accomplishments of the party and of the SS followed. Michael listened closely. He and Peter were both able bodied, but they would have to get out of here before they were selected. If things got sticky they had to seek out one doctor in town who would certify them as "not suitable". People had whispered about that, but it was all kept under wraps, of course! An announcement followed. Those with the last names starting with the letters A to E were to come forward. Peter tugged at Michael's sleeve. Simultaneously they rose in the ensuing commotion and stepped towards an unsupervised exit door of the hall. They slipped into the vestibule and dodged behind one of the large marble pillars. Nobody had noticed them in the moving, milling crowd. The guard stood by another door with his back turned to them and prepared to go back into the hall. Noiselessly they crossed the hallway to the set of stairs and went down. Michael unlocked the washroom door, and they slipped inside and pulled the door closed. All of this had happened within less than half a minute. They hid in the cubicle and locked the door. Upstairs they heard a commotion of walking and commands. Cautiously Peter moved to the window. He pointed and grimaced. A guard was standing outside by the door right under their window. Even minutes seemed to be single eternities, but they could not do anything except wait. They could not leave, and they had to stay in the small room. After two long hours another marching tune was blaring through the loudspeakers upstairs. Countless feet stomped across the hall, and the clicking of heels was audible on the stairs. First there was silence, but shortly after authoritative voices sounded in the hallway, and heavy steps went by. Everybody had left. The entrance door was closed, and a key turned in the lock. They had been locked in the building, and they would leave through the washroom window, exactly what Michael had thought. They peered out of the window and saw a group of SS officers joined by other officials leave and disappear down the street. The person who previously guarded the entrance had also left. Michael cautioned his friend that they could not leave yet. They waited a little longer, as they wanted to play it safe, but there was nobody else. Michael slid out into the hall. He checked the front door. It was locked, and they could not exit here. Next he put the washroom key under the doormat at the caretaker's lodgings, after which they pushed the washroom window open. Peter lowered himself from the windowsill and jumped, landing hard but safely, and Michael followed. Through side streets they zigzagged their way to the tram stop, and after a tram ride in silence they hurried home. Peter was still concerned. "Do you think that they will get ahold of us?" Michael reminded him that they had put their names on the list. He reminded his friend that he as well as others could have been rejected because of a physical shortcoming. He shrugged his shoulders. "Just in case they come and ask more questions, I'll get a note from the doctor that I have flat feet and a crooked back. That should do it." Peter got the idea. "As of today my vision is lousy." He squinted at Michael. "Do I look convincing?" Michael nodded. "Sure, I know that you are as blind as a bat. Just get it all on paper in case somebody has any questions, and a pair of glasses may be another option. But I don't think that we have to worry!"

Both went home. Peter jumped the garden gate and quietly snuck into the house. Michael came home and heard a muted conversation in the kitchen. His mother's voice sounded anxious, but relief was in her eyes when she saw him. His father's eyes were questioning. Michael's own tension was almost forgotten. He told his parents about the happenings of the afternoon and how he and Peter had willingly put their names on the list of about two thousand students. He described how they had snuck out in the moving crowd of people who were called to come forward. Whoever was able bodied was to be enlisted with the SS. It had been easy to hide in the washroom, but he reported that getting the washroom key had been the tricky part, and next he might have to get a doctor's note to state that he was "not suitable". His father quietly thought about Michael's story. "Good work! You seemed to have gotten out of there all right. Let's hope that this will be the end of the story."

Nothing else transpired after this meeting, but news about destruction of large cities travelled through the radio and the newspapers, and a sense of profound unease descended over the population. The ugly specter of death and destruction became more present, as the highly industrialized Ruhr area further in the north of the country had been systematically attacked and destroyed. In the meantime nobody was under any illusion that their town in the south would be a safe haven in the future. Another frightening aspect was that old war technology had given way to new methods. It was the introduction of short-wave radar that facilitated attacks because it showed any target in remarkable detail. Not even a foggy night or poor visibility due to drizzle was a hindrance to hit a targeted area with cruel and powerful precision.

Sirens had sounded their menacing wail through a cool night in March 1943. The bright colored magnesium markers which people called "Christmas Trees" hung over the city center first, but a strong wind displaced them to the southwestern suburbs of the city. It was too late to run to the bomb shelter, and the Laumann family sought protection in the windowless room in the deepest part of the root cellar that served as a shelter in the house. They had taken water along and had a few towels that they could use to protect their faces from smoke or dust. After a short while the light flickered and went out. Electricity had failed, and they lit a candle. The barking of the anti-aircraft guns pierced the night, but above this sound the deep-throated roar of hundreds of airplane engines was droning. A terrifying thumping sound added even more noise to this cacophony. This was the sound of bombs that were landing closer and closer in intervals that were only seconds apart with loud thumping sounds. How long could it go on? Michael covered his ears with his hands but not for long. He needed the wet towel to cover his face next. The shock waves of the explosions had long blown out the candle, and they sat in the dark. The air became thick with mortar dust. They coughed and held wet towels over their faces in order to be able to breathe. After initially hearing the high pitched whine of falling bombs they now heard a deep roaring sound, and as it stopped, a shattering explosion rent the air. Everything seemed to shake, and it felt like the air had been sucked out of the shelter. How could they breathe? How long could they hold their breath? Michael's life seemed to flash by in fast motion: his time playing with his friends when he was small, his school days, saying good bye to Simon…He wondered whether this was how it felt before he would die. He and his parents were sitting huddled together, holding on to each other. It occurred to him that this was how they would suffocate together, and it would be the end. They gasped for air and thought that their lungs would burst. It was like a miracle that all of a sudden there was air and they could breathe again, greedily gulping for air. But the bombing fury continued. Even though it was over in less than half an hour, it felt like an eternity, an eternity they would never forget. Finally, when the sirens sounded their signal that the attack was over, they went upstairs. There was damage all over, but there were no fires in the house. The next morning dawned over a picture of destruction. The house where the Laumann's lived was not the only one that showed damages. The neighborhood houses had not escaped destruction either. Roof tiles were missing, and windows had been blown out. Nobody in the immediate neighborhood had been killed, but a few blocks away some houses had taken a direct hit. One building had collapsed, the residents had been trapped in the basement, and a water main had broken. All of them had drowned. Bomb splinters had hit some people, and they had bled to death. Some families had perished when explosions had burst their lungs. Next Michael went over to Peter's place. The house had some damages as well. One wall was close to collapsing. Peter and he went out to the field and the adjacent forest. At one point they had talked together about hiding in the forest during a bomb attack. They thought that it might be a safe area. What they saw after this air raid took their breath away. Nothing was sacred in a bomb attack, not even a serene forest. Bombs had struck the previously pristine wooded area, and large, old trees had been scattered around like lightweight sticks. It did not look like a forest anymore, rather like a bleak moon landscape. Not any living creature would have survived here! Bomb craters were everywhere. It occurred to them that there could be unexploded bombs after this attack. Quickly they went back. Grimly Michael walked through the neighboring area and saw what had happened during that night. He heard about the dead. They were all people he knew well. He walked through the swath of devastation that was just a few blocks away and saw the houses that were reduced to piles of debris covering the ground. He and his parents had survived, and he vowed to himself that he would leave this place as soon as the war would be over and the borders would be open again. Anything was better than living in a country like this, which had been destroyed and ravaged by war. He had only one goal: survive through all of this, and he did not even dare to think what else might be ahead. It occurred to him that even survival was uncertain after a night like this one!

In the meantime the damages had to be repaired. School had become erratic lately, and Michael helped neighbors repairing broken window frames and bracing sagging walls. Part of the brewery where Michael's father worked had had been bombed and suffered damage. Hastily operations were moved to undamaged buildings but this took time. For a while nobody could go to work, and Martin as well as Michael were becoming part of the neighborhood repair crew. It was tedious work to find roof tiles to replace the ones that had been damaged. Roofs had to be repaired first to protect the houses from rain. They collected roof tiles and carried them up to the roof; endless hours of walking up and down a ladder. Next it was like a jigsaw puzzle to place the tiles so they would fit. Replacing windows was out of the question. There were no replacements available. Instead large rolls of wire mesh that had been drawn through liquid glass were available. The material could be cut with large shears and was nailed to the window frames. Nobody had any concerns about curtains to protect the privacy of a room: the opaque material shut out the elements, kept the rooms bright, but nobody could look in or out. Work went on to enlarge the neighborhood bomb shelter. Michael and his dad worked with a heavy pneumatic hammer. The heavy vibrations followed them for hours after their work. It felt like their hands and arms were still shaking after having worked on a rock face like coal miners. The work gave them credit to stay in the shelter in case of a bomb attack. The structure had grown large enough to accommodate about thousand persons. When the sirens sounded they would sprint to the shelter. It was located in a hillside just a few minutes down the hill from their neighborhood. Sometimes the sirens sounded, but the neighborhood would not be affected. They went anyways. Nobody wanted to take a risk of staying at home, and interrupted nights became the norm. Some neighbors decided to camp out in the shelter. They were too unnerved to stay home and wait for the sirens. They would pack a bag for the night, some women even took their knitting, making themselves as comfortable as they could in an uncomfortable situation like that. It was not a place that instilled a sense of comfort. Anxious voices and crying children added to this impression of fear among the people who waited here for a bomb attack to end. But there was also the unease of what could happen, if a large bomb would fall and block the exit. There was only one exit that was secured with a heavy steel door. In the city people had sought refuge from a bomb attack in a tunnel, and a panic had broken out in which numerous persons had been trampled to death. All of these thoughts did not contribute to a feeling of being safe in a bomb shelter. It was rather a precarious sense of false security.

The entire summer was a frenzy to repair damages and make houses somewhat livable. Michael was working like the adults in the neighborhood, but in the middle of the work, a ladder slipped and he fell down several feet, landing on his left arm. This hurt, and he could not move the arm! His father went to the hospital with him. Michael disliked everything: the smell of disinfectant, the sterile white environment and the doctor's verdict that he had fractured his arm. Finally he could leave with his arm in a plaster cast. But this did not deter him from working. At least his right arm was useable. Another winter would be imminent, and shelter was of the utmost importance. It did not matter if inside walls were damaged or doors were broken. These repairs could wait; it was more important to be sheltered from the elements and have the outside walls and windows repaired.

Amongst the neighbors the mood had become more pessimistic. Only the hard-core Nazis were talking about victory and glory, but doubts were creeping in and were whispered about behind closed doors. The German Army had marched into Russia, and in a violent battle near Stalingrad the losses had been devastating. Even in the small suburb where the Laumann's lived, numerous families had lost their loved ones: young men, sons, brothers, fathers, and husbands. Yet fanatic voices still talked about sacrifice and patriotism. Nobody dared to voice a questioning opinion in public. The Gestapo, the secret police, had arrested those who had voiced overt doubts about the war and the actions of the party. Voices of resistance and acts of resistance had been blotted out forever. Those who dared to speak or those who rose up against the regime were arrested and brought to concentration camps. Executions of resistance groups who dared to actively oppose the leadership were common. Several resistance groups attempted to end the Hitler regime, but none of them had been successful. All of those who dared to resist had paid with their lives. Terror held the population in a stranglehold. And under this terror a sense of profound resignation was growing. For anybody who was objective and observant it had become very obvious that the battle of Stalingrad was a turning point in this war. There would be no victory, just a relentless downhill course and an uncertain future for the country. Ironic voices had coined the statement: "Enjoy the war, folks, because peace will be terrible!"

Destruction, Death And Violence

They had coped with winter, and everybody hoped for a better year, but during a cold night in March 1944- almost one year after the last devastating bomb raid- another assault followed that would wreak havoc in their neighborhood. Sirens had sent their wailing message through the cold night. Initially it seemed that the downtown area was targeted. The sky was virtually exploding into an ear splitting thunder of low flying four engine bombers. Massive explosions from a few miles away could be heard. A bright, gigantic flash lit up the sky, and it looked like a huge flash bulb had burst. The flash was followed by a deafening, booming sound. This sounded like the anti-aircraft guns had taken down a bomber. Martin was determined to stay in the house, and it did not take much to convince Louise and Michael to stay in the deep cellar, as the bombing carpet was approaching fast, moving closer and closer. They curled up in a heap in a corner of the basement bomb shelter that had withstood other attacks before. It was useless to light a candle; they knew that the explosions would snuff it out. All they could do was wait, holding wet towels against their faces to filter out the billowing dust. Also they listened for the string of explosions that were gradually moving further away from their house. As soon as the sirens sounded to announce the end of the raid and explosions could only be heard far in the distance, they ran up the stairs. Thankfully there were no fires in the house, but of course the windows were blown out, and the doors had been smashed. After all the repair work during the previous year they would have to do the same, tedious work all over again. They noticed that the house where Peter lived was burning, and the area was lit up in a ghostly, bright light. Phosphorus bombs had wreaked destruction.

Michael wanted to see that his friend was safe. He and his parents ran over to the house that resembled a flaming torch. Peter's family had escaped, but they heard screaming inside. Michael raced inside before his parents could stop him. The burning phosphorus was running down the walls, glaringly lighting up the inside. Despite the fire there was very little smoke in the house. In one hallway, a small figure staggered towards him. It was Rose, the nine-year-old daughter of the Kerner's, who lived here. She screamed and tried to beat out flames. Her hair was grotesquely singed. He beat out the flames with his hand. Flames were starting to lick on her sleeves and on her stockings. He beat out more flames, held her in his arms and covered her with his jacket to shelter her from the heat of the flames. She was small for her age, like a helpless little bird that he cradled against his chest. His clothes had caught on fire. He smelled burnt hair. His skin felt unbearably hot. Once he was outside he rolled on the grass and rolled her on the grass to extinguish the last flicker of fire. She was crying out in her distress and shook with fear, her eyes wide and filled with unspoken terror. Michael put his arms around her to console her, and she stopped shaking and was just quietly sobbing. It was like a miracle that she did not show any bad burn injury, as her escape had been fast enough. Mr. Kerner, her father, had also escaped unharmed. Frantically he wanted to go back into the house again, but a sea of fire had begun to rage like a storm, and his wife and his small son were trapped in the inferno. He had heard their screams, but shortly after the screams stopped, and the eerie roar of the blaze was the only sound in the night. Stubbornly he braved the fire, went back but came out of the house again. Neighbors screamed and tried to help him extinguish the flames on his hair and his clothing. His face showed an expression of disbelief, grief, and utter horror. Helplessly shaking his head he broke down in big, heaving sobs. His wife and his four-year-old son had perished. He had seen two burned bodies, a small one that clung to the body of an adult. When a neighbor tried to express his deep sympathy, he turned away. Distress, anger, and bitterness were in his face. It had not helped him to be a staunch supporter of the party. Part of him felt that his family had made the ultimate sacrifice for the country, but another part of him rebelled against his fate and against the world. He did not say a word to Michael, even though he had been the one who had rescued his daughter. His dislike for Michael and his friend Peter was deep and enduring. Also he

Destruction, Death And Violence

was in a state of utter shock, and he was too distraught and too stricken to express gratitude to anybody.

A large number of houses had been destroyed in this massive bombing raid. Peter's family moved their few belongings into a flat that had been abandoned. The previous tenants had fled the area and gone to relatives in the rural mountainous areas of Bavaria where bombs did not fall. They mentioned before that they would leave the area and move away, should there be any destruction. There were many others like them, displaced to another area of the country in the hope to escape the ravages of war.

Rose and her father occupied a flat in a house that had not sustained too much damage. Olga, a childless widow, who had lost her husband in the battles of Stalingrad, owned it and offered them this accommodation. Olga felt deep pity for Rose. She herself knew loss, and this poor child had lost her mother and her brother during one night of terror. It broke her heart to see the young girl that walked around in a daze of empty-eyed sadness and disbelief. She needed a home and help and most of all somebody who looked after her. Olga was a source of comfort and warmth to her, as the father was too hurt and too upset to think of anything else than the painful loss he had suffered. Rose grieved the loss of her mother and her brother, but she grew very fond of Olga, who was doing everything possible to care for her, and they developed a firm and loving bond. Rose's father was still the same awkward and grumpy man. He was even more taciturn than before, distraught and grieving the loss of his wife and his son. He was grateful for Olga's help, and under the rough surface was a good side, which he found difficult to show. He was a man of few words, but he repaired the damages on Olga's house and assumed all of the yard work to help her. Whenever she needed help he was there, doing his work quietly and refusing any payment. He did not want any thanks. After the night of destruction he found it even harder to show his feelings. It was also difficult for him to show love and affection to his daughter Rose. She reminded him of the night that had turned his life upside down, when he lost his wife and his son. His unresolved grief was like a wound that could not heal, and it was covered by a harsh surface. Olga was one of the few people who could see the good that was buried deep inside. She was not the submissive woman his late wife had been, who tolerated verbal abuse and had nothing to say for herself. Olga was feisty and assertive, spoke up and was never at a loss for words in verbal sparring rounds with him. In response to his grumbling and grousing she called him a "grumbly old bear", or in her direct, quick-witted way she reasoned things out with him. He, who was a difficult individual and did not listen to anybody, listened to her and respected her. In time she managed to tame him and even got him to smile, but most of the residents, who knew him from years past, were guarded about their awkward, silent neighbor.

The morning after the bombing the Laumann's heard steps outside, and there was a knock on the door. Josef Menzinger stood outside. He wanted to see whether they were safe, whether they would need any help. His wife had sent a pot of soup along, as she was certain that they would be homeless, and they feared for the worst. His farmstead had been spared, and things were going as well as they could. He was appalled when he saw the damage in this neighborhood. It was a miracle that the house, which resembled a ruin, was still fit for a human to live in. Quickly he looked around. One wall was not safe, and it had to be braced, preventing it from collapsing. He would come back and give his friends a hand. The houses that were damaged were a grotesque, almost apocalyptic sight. Walls had been blown out, and like in a doll's house the furnishings were standing in place, visible to anybody. Elsewhere charred skeletons of houses were still standing. In some cases all that was left of a house was a roof, which lay on the ground, as the walls had collapsed. Michael, Mr. Menzinger, and his dad went to work on the crooked wall. It did not look much better with the coarse beams that braced the wall in several spots, but at least it was safer, and they could continue to live there. They repaired the worst parts of the roof, once again scavenging the neighborhood for

Destruction, Death And Violence

roof tiles. Some windows were simply boarded up, as they could do without light in the smallest bedroom, which was Michael's room. Sheets of glass-coated wire mesh were installed once again like in the previous year, if daylight was needed in a room. The work did not seem to end, but neighbors helped each other, and everybody contributed with ideas and hard work to render a house livable again, if this was possible at all.

In the meantime it was known that the Allies had invaded Germany. It was just a matter of time that Germany would have to give up. Virtually every larger city had seen destruction, and invasion of foreign troops would be next. Martin Laumann read the newspaper and voiced his opinion that the country was doomed. Everybody who kept an open mind knew it too, and air raids continued with greater force than before. The area where the Laumann's lived had become quiet, but in other areas of the city the attacks continued. Many of them occurred during the night. On a beautiful July day during the same year a huge white cloud billowed over the valley where the city was located. The city had been bombed in a massive raid the day before. All public services had come to a halt, broken gas lines added to the fires, and due to broken water mains firefighters were left without water. Death had come for many of the city's residents in the most horrifying ways. Fires had consumed all oxygen, and thousands suffocated in the cellars where they had sought shelter. Those who had attempted to flee got trapped in the searing hot asphalt of the streets, slowly burning to death. For a while there had been no school, and Peter and Michael were curious to know whether the building of their high school was still standing. The trams had stopped running, so both got on their bicycles and made their way into town. It was easy enough to just roll the five miles downhill to their school. Coming back home would take much longer. The first part of their outing was easy, but as they got into the southern part of the city, they found that the road was impassable due to rubble from destroyed buildings. They pushed and carried their bikes to a side road, where it seemed to be easier to travel, but they were progressing at a snail's pace. Michael looked at his friend: "Do you want to go on, or should we just make our way back?" Peter was determined:" I'm not a slacker! We are going on. I want to see what happened to the school building!" In front of a row of large city buildings they spotted an unusual sight. They still were a distance away, and Peter shook his head:" Look at that! What have they done here? It looks like they piled up a bunch of logs!" Curiously they moved closer, and the smell of burnt flesh and rot that hung over the area was almost unbearable. Michael gasped, and his eyes turned wide. The pile of logs was not what he had expected. "Good God, Peter! They have piled up burnt corpses like cord wood!" The realization hit them and shook them up. They pedaled through a small square where the neighborhood had been severely bombed. To their astonishment they saw some figures lying on a sidewalk. There was no clothing store in the neighborhood but these figures looked like mannequins! Curiously they went closer, and to their shock they saw that the figures were dead people. There was death and destruction wherever they looked. The area of their high school came into sight. What used to be a school was now a burnt-out ruin. They realized that it would take a while till there would be any classes at all. They would have to take place at another location. Somehow they both found the demise of the structure strangely satisfying. During the last few years this institution had morphed into a tool to indoctrinate students and to make malleable yes-men out of them. The high school that had been meant to teach more knowledge had not reached a high, but had fallen low, using its influence to disseminate a godless and perverted ideology of hatred and injustice. As an institution of higher learning it had sorely failed. It seemed fitting that it had gone up in fire and smoke. At one point schools and lives would have to be rebuilt. But they did not know when this destruction would come to an end. Right now the city looked like a landscape of death and like a place without a future. They turned around and wheeled their bikes through another rubble-strewn street. Finally they got back to the road that was passable. They could not wait to get away from the area. The smell of fire and of decaying corpses followed them for a long time and had a haunting quality for them.

Summer had been overshadowed by the destruction of the city, and there seemed to be no end in sight. Bombing occurred relentlessly, but in the area where Peter and Michael were living no further airstrikes occurred. Nevertheless everybody knew how much other parts of the city had suffered. In the city center maybe half of the structures were left. Everything else was in ruins.

There was not much to celebrate for Michael and his parents about the New Year of 1945. The war continued, and life in the city had come to a standstill. The only reason to celebrate was the fact that so far everybody of the family had survived and even had been lucky enough to survive without a major injury. The only injury was a broken arm for Michael, when he fell off a ladder during one of the endless house repairs. It was not convenient, but in comparison to other war injuries this was harmless!

It was a relief that it was getting spring, which was a break from ice crystals on the walls and from the smoke of the kitchen stove that hung in the air because the window could not be opened. Now they could leave the door open and enjoy the warmer weather. Not everything was positive, of course. The war raged on, and the ruling party was insistent on carrying on with senseless fighting, even though it had become obvious that the war had been lost. The situation for the population was now desperate, and a new threat was the invasion of French troops into the area. They were feared, and Michael's parents had talked about murder, thefts, destruction, and other acts of violence that had been committed by the marauding soldiers in other towns close by. The inconvenience of living in a house that looked like a useless ruin became their salvation, as the soldiers did not even bother to break into such a decrepit structure. Surely nobody would be living there! Nevertheless Martin was worried about their safety.

They barricaded the door, and the nights were a time of fitful sleep. Any sound outside startled them. Once they heard steps of a group of people walking along the road, and they heard the voices of soldiers that were immersed in a conversation in French. "Rien ici! Allons!" Michael understood the simple statement. There was nothing here, they observed. They were leaving. Thank goodness, they were gone! From neighbors they heard that in another part of town the soldiers had gone on a rampage. Nobody had been killed like it happened in some other towns, but theft had been common, and many women of all age groups had been victims of violent rapes.

One evening towards the end of April it seemed to be safer again. Nobody had talked about violence, theft, or rapes. Louise was preparing to make her way to the orchard slope where the chicken coop was located. Martin did not want her to go alone, and he came along. They had to lock up the birds and give them food and water. Once they had neglected to close up the coop, and a weasel had killed some of their flock. Michael stayed home. He still had chores to do. Kindling wood was low, and his rabbits needed food and water. It was later today, as they had worked in the garden till dusk, digging up garden beds and getting them ready for planting. Spring was a busy time. Vegetables had been seeded, potatoes had to go in, bushes needed thinning out, and every hour of daylight was needed. The garden and its crops helped them to have food which otherwise would not be available. But it was spring. It had to get better. Despite the dire war situation they desperately wanted to have hope! A sun-filled spring day followed by a glorious sun set had turned into a beautiful warm evening with a crystal clear evening sky with the silver sickle of a half moon. It was getting darker as Louise and Martin walked along the field path to the apple orchard. The gate was ajar which was unusual. They were sure that they had closed it in the morning. A smell of wood smoke hung in the air. Inquisitively they walked down the hill, and near the chicken coop they found the remainder of what must have been a small fire. Some embers and ashes were still glowing. Martin went to get a bucket of water from the water pump close by. He extinguished the last bit of the fire and looked around. It looked like somebody had feasted here. He found chicken feathers, guts, and traces of blood in the grass. What happened? He looked into the chicken coop. Two birds were missing. Near the fire some leftover bones were lying around. Thieves! They had roasted two of their chickens for dinner. He swore under his breath. These prowlers had taken away part of their livelihood! A few empty liquor bottles had been left behind. Martin felt uneasy. There were some shady figures here in the neighborhood, when he thought that things were finally safe. Somebody had camped out here for the day, and it seemed to have been not just one person. Louise had collected some eggs and went outside the shed. Martin was still inside and closed the hatch. Within a split second Louise noticed a swift movement behind the trees. Three figures sprinted towards her. With a fluid, fast movement one of them jumped on her, smooth and almost animal-like. The impact made her lose her footing and threw her to the ground. Hands held her down like in a vise, and a voice shouted: "Jerome, vas-y! Une petite allemande pour toi!" She screamed and struggled, trying to free herself. She had understood the words "petite allemande"- a little German woman. They were after her! The person called "Jerome" joined the man who held her down. She yelled, kicked, scratched, and sank her teeth into a hand. Next she heard Martin's running steps and his furious shout: "No! Leave her alone!" But before he could intervene further, the third person of the group had given him a kick to his groin that sent him to his knees. His attacker wrestled him to the ground. Seething with fury Martin tried to get back on his feet. He would murder this bastard! A violent punch of a fist went square into his face. He heard bones crunch, and his head exploded into lightning bolts of pain. Blood was running into his eyes. Blows of fists hailed down on him, heavy boots kicked him into his back, and darkness enveloped him next.

Louise heard the sounds of a violent struggle, sounds of groans, kicks, and punches, and at the same time the man called Jerome, who had joined her attacker, grabbed her, ripped her clothes, and tore away her underwear. Rough fingers fumbled and groped her private parts, and she felt how his body was painfully forced into hers. Her screams of terror and Martin's shouts pierced the air. Desperately she fought and yelled, but the man's rapid thrusts did not stop. Her fighting back seemed to make him even more excited. He groaned and panted, intent on getting his sense of satisfaction. A yelled remark and raucous laughter from one of the soldiers encouraged her attacker: "Amuse-toi bien, Jerome!" His hand held her mouth closed and covered her nose. She could not scream, and she could not breathe. Everything seemed to spin in circles and sink into a swirling fog. A violent thud and a yelp of agony from Martin was the last thing she heard. She did not know how long she lay there. The hand was gone. Her head stopped spinning. She could breathe again. The smell of acrid tobacco smoke from her attacker assailed her nostrils, and she caught a strong odor of alcohol from his breath. Finally he finished, stood up, buttoned up his trousers and swiftly walked away, followed by the other two shadow-like figures. For a moment she sat on the grass, too shaken, too stunned. She felt a sticky liquid on her thighs. Was she bleeding? She squinted in the fading light. No, at least there was no blood! With a feeling of confusion that escalated into panic she looked around. Where was Martin? Then she saw him, a crumpled figure on the grass nearby, and quickly she stepped over to him. She was sobbing: "Martin, Martin!" She touched him and shook his arm, terrified that he might be dead. He groaned, turned around, and slowly attempted to sit up. He was bleeding from his nose, and he held his head. A bleeding gash was on his forehead, and his face was covered with blood. His one eye was closed shut. His head, groin, and back caused him excruciating pain. Laboriously he got up. Louise looked at him with alarm. He was badly hurt. They would have to go to the hospital. She did not even want to think about herself and what procedures she would have to endure. Both were too stricken to speak, and they left to go home.

Destruction, Death And Violence

At home Michael looked at the kitchen clock. It was getting darker, and his parents were still not back. They had never been so late. His unease grew. He had to go and see where they were. Something must have happened. His apprehension made him move as fast as he could. He jogged along the field path, and next he saw his parents approach slowly. His father was limping. Even in the falling darkness he could see his father's blood-covered face, his bleeding nose and forehead, and the swollen-shut eye. Martin's face was reflecting the terror they had gone through. "There were three of them that attacked us." The expression on his mother's face filled him with anguish. Oh God! His poor mom! His dad had obviously tried to come to her defense, but it had been impossible, and both had been victims. At the same time he felt a sense of impotent rage at the perpetrators who had violated her and injured his dad. The same thoughts he had had a year earlier came back: after living through hell in this country he would leave as soon as he could manage to do it. When? He did not know that, but he was determined now even more than before.

Louise and Martin walked to the small local hospital. They were told to sit in the waiting area, which was lit by a single, dim light bulb. The walls were damaged, and it was a makeshift facility. Other people sat and waited, their faces closed and dull. They were asked for their personal information, and a nurse ushered them into a small cubicle. A doctor entered the tiny space. The man looked tired. He still cared, but he was reaching the limit of what he could do. A constant, seemingly endless stream of patients had walked in during the day, and it had been always the same: attacks by soldiers, injuries, and rapes, some of them so violent that the women needed surgery. He examined Martin first. His injuries looked like they needed attention. He needed sutures on his forehead, and his nose was broken. He would have to be seen by a surgeon who would give him a shot of freezing, close the gash on his forehead, and reposition his fractured nose. He could go home after that, but it would take a while. Martin was beyond caring what would happen to him. Worriedly he looked over to Louise.

Christina Schilling

"What about my wife, doctor?" The doctor asked him to leave the cubicle. He needed to examine her and decide on a treatment. Louise had to answer to questions of a very private nature. She felt uncomfortable. Sexual matters were something no real lady should even think about without blushing! These were topics she found improper and too embarrassing to discuss with anybody, but here was the doctor factually asking those questions that made her cringe. When was her last period? When did she last have marital relations with her husband? Was there any pregnancy except the one that resulted in the birth of her son? Did she or her husband use any precautions? Did she or her husband ever have a venereal disease? How could she discuss such matters and look into the face of a man, even if he was a physician? She was mortified, feeling like she was naked and exposed, having lost her last bit of privacy. Outwardly she tried to maintain a stoic dignity. She struggled to overcome her embarrassment and answered as factually as she could. No, they had not used any precautions as they had tried to have more children, but it had never worked, and now she was at the end of her thirties. Yes, she still had her menstrual periods. She had relations with her husband on a regular basis; two days ago was the last time. Good heavens, how could she even talk about topics like that! Even worse: how could she talk about them after the events of this evening! Shame flooded her face like a fiery wave. She started to shake violently, when the doctor began to examine her, and his hand explored her genitals. The terror came back and jumped at her like a vicious animal. Her breathing was rapid and shallow, and she felt like she would pass out next. The physician called a nurse to stand by her side, talk to her, and hold her hand. He examined her carefully and told her that she was lucky to have no injuries. All the same he was concerned that she could have been exposed to a venereal disease. A nurse would administer a treatment in the hope to prevent this. Otherwise she should wait for her period. If it would not occur, she should present herself again at the hospital. In view that she never got pregnant after having had one child he was not even concerned about pregnancy. Now she was in her late thirties, and pregnancy was even less likely. In any event she should come back to be checked in a month or so, whether there would be any venereal disease, or whether she had stayed healthy. The doctor walked out, and a nurse came in. Louise felt calmer. The worst seemed to be over. She felt a liquid that had a chemical smell, which was used to rinse and clean her, and a soft cloth drying her. In a way it was a relief; she felt soiled before. Now she wanted wait for Martin, till they could finally go home.

With a dull feeling of exhaustion she sat in the waiting area. A hand touched her shoulder. Josef and Marie Menzinger, her friends, had entered the waiting area. Marie was unsteady on her feet and deadly pale. She seemed to be in pain, and her eyes were distraught. Josef looked somber. Marie was crying: "Oh Louise, it is too much to bear!" The two women were sobbing and falling into each other's arms. Marie too was a rape victim. Two soldiers had assaulted her in her kitchen, while her husband was outside in the barn. They were both together in their own world of suffering, and they understood each other in their distress. After a long wait Martin came back. His wound had received stitches, and his nose was no longer bleeding, but his face looked swollen and disfigured. It was close to midnight when they walked home supporting each other, but sleep would not come. The last night traumatized them deeply and had distressing and haunting qualities for both of them.

May would normally be the glorious month of spring, a time of new life, flowering gardens and the beauty of nature. For the population of Germany May 1945 was the month where their country had seen the end. Hitler's much-touted "thousand year reign" had ceased, submerged in tears and blood. Hitler had committed suicide on April 30, and on May 8 the country capitulated. The war was officially over. After the fact that fifty million people had lost their lives in the countries that were affected by this war, which a dictator had instigated six years earlier, the people in Germany were burdened by the knowledge that the hatred of the world would be directed against them. Many now despised the people of Germany that were previously admired. They would be contemptuously called "Nazis" for generations to come, even including those who had refused to embrace Hitler's ideology. Michael's family and the people around them were aware of the burden of guilt that would never leave them. They were trying to exist in a country that had been bled to death. Everybody had experienced losses, and it did not look like there would be any promising future. Even with the war being over it was still a matter of surviving a time that held no promises, just more deprivation. They all would be paying dearly, many of them forever marked by physical and emotional scars.

Martin Laumann and his wife felt the depressed and dark mood as much as everybody else. They were alive but living a life of uncertainty. To witness the profound sense of hopelessness and despair among some neighbors was heartbreaking. In short succession three persons in the neighborhood had committed suicide. One was a young woman who had lost her entire family in the war. She had lost her husband in the last days of war. Her parents had been killed during a bomb raid, and her baby succumbed to pneumonia during the winter months before the war ended. She did not see a future any more, and she was found in the forest where she had hanged herself. An old man was the next victim. He had swallowed rat poison. Age was not a factor for those who killed themselves. Even for a young twenty-year old life had lost its meaning. A farmer found him dead in the neighborhood pond one morning. The neighbors had known all those people. Three funerals took place within less than two weeks and left the people shaken.

Josef Menzinger and his wife Marie were burdened by the same trauma as Martin and Louise Laumann. They were grateful that they had experienced no other injuries in their family and no damages to their place, but Marie was struggling. She felt anxious and depressed. After the assault she needed surgery, had lost a lot of blood and had been diagnosed with a venereal disease. She had to return to the hospital for repeated antibiotic injections and felt like an untouchable person, which distressed her greatly. Josef, her husband, was a rock of strength and loving support to her. Louise went to see her often and helped her with some of her work, so she could rest and recover. Both had to see beyond the one day that had violated them and distressed them beyond belief. At one point they sat together and looked at their lives, at all the good they had experienced. It was difficult to count blessings, but they were both determined to see the positives. They had survived, and their families had survived, which was more than many people in this town could say. From here on it was like a journey of taking one day at a time. There were setbacks but also better days. For Marie Menzinger the sense of depression and doom started to lift after she and her husband made their way to their relatives in the Black Forest. They had not been able to see their daughter Resi for quite a while due to the turmoil of bomb alarms and attacks in the area. Now they went to see her. She was overjoyed. Even though she had been happy at her aunt's farm, she wanted to go home. She said that she missed Hans, her brother, and her parents, and she wanted to sit on the bench in the kitchen and help her mom fold laundry. Her aunt had taught her that and other simple household duties. When she heard that she would go to school she was excited and happy. She had grown, but she was the same sweet child that always would be child-like and would never grow up to be an adult. Her parents felt immense gratitude to their relatives who had sheltered her and the happiness to have her back home again.

For the Menzinger family it was a day of great joy and relief, when Josef's brother Leo came back from the war later in the year. They had not heard from him, and not knowing his fate had been a heavy load on their minds. When he stood at the door, his brother and the family barely recognized him. He looked like a vagrant with long, matted hair and an untidy, overgrown beard. He had lost a lot of weight, and his hair, clothes and skin were crawling with lice. He refused to enter the house, but soaked himself in the watering trough outside and scrubbed himself with laundry soap and disinfectant to get rid of the crawling pests first before setting foot into the house. Leo had survived fierce fighting in Russia and had laboriously made his way back on foot from Russia to Germany, tenaciously covering the thousands of miles. He knew that he had to go west; he walked during the night and slept in abandoned buildings during the day. Sometimes he had the chance to jump onto a slow- moving westbound train, and he got a break from the arduous walking. People in remote villages were not hostile towards him. In his years in Russia he had very quickly picked up the basics of the language. Sometimes he got some food in exchange for farm work. At other times he subsisted on fruit or vegetables he found growing in orchards and fields. He watched out for soldiers, as there was the risk of being caught and imprisoned as a prisoner of war. War prisoners could be sent to Siberia, and he heard enough terrible stories. What saved him was the fact that he had always been tough and a survivor. He realized that he could not be seen in a German uniform. In a destroyed village he came upon numerous dead people, and with a quick decision he swapped his German uniform for the clothes of one of the dead. A shot had grazed his right leg, and in the murderously cold winter near Stalingrad he had lost three of his toes, but otherwise he was unhurt. His truck had been confiscated during the war, and as a result of that he was now out of work. But he was resourceful, took any available odd job to make some money, and otherwise he was grateful to be back. Like before he made himself useful at his brother's farm, helping with all the work. In time he would find work in an automobile factory close by like so many other men in this area. The time of spring and the promising signs of new life was still a time of gratitude and relief, but it was also interwoven with despair and death, a difficult and challenging time for everybody in the country.

Destruction, Death And Violence

As always, Martin was studying the political events in the newspaper, and Michael usually picked up the paper when his dad was finished reading. He was already well informed by listening to various radio stations, but one day he spotted headlines in the paper. "Dachau Finally Liberated By US Troops". He had heard the name before. It was one of the facilities, called "KZ" or concentration camp that the government had opened up immediately after seizing power well over ten years ago. Michael heard stories that were relayed in hushed tones: this camp and many others housed prisoners. Dachau was the oldest camp, and it was associated with a string of other names: Bergen-Belsen, Mauthausen, Auschwitz, Buchenwald and many more. All of those were places where people had been incarcerated that were either inconvenient to the government or not fitting the norm. Many of them were people from other countries: Roma gypsies were one group, and large groups were Jews. Others were people with mental disorders, but outspoken priests and nuns were also incarcerated and killed. These camps had not been prison facilities only. Michael heard that many of the prisoners simply disappeared, never to be seen again. Due to the secrecy of the government details were scarce, but horror stories were circulating in the population. The inmates of these concentration camps were systematically worked to death. Others were shot or herded into gas chambers and killed, and their remains were either dumped into mass graves or cremated. Neighbors mentioned that the prisoners were used for the most inhumane and cruel medical experiments. All this sounded terrifying enough for Michael, but the newspaper article described details that were so disturbing that he found it difficult to finish reading the article. And there were the pictures! Even though they were just black and white photos of the camp at the time of its liberation, these pictures revealed in stark, graphic detail what unbelievable atrocities had been committed. Michael saw hollow-eyed, emaciated faces staring from behind barbed wire fences. He saw pictures of persons, their heads shaved, looking like walking skeletons, looking more dead than alive. One picture showed a close up shot of the gas chamber and a pile of clothes and boots in front of it, clothes of the prisoners who had perished here at the command of a perverted government that took satisfaction in killing and torturing innocent people. On one photo he saw a boy, holding on to his mother's hand, a young face marked by hunger and deprivation, the dark eyes sunken deep in their sockets. The eyes looked like Simon's eyes, and the woman could have been his mother. No, it could not be! Simon and his family had left. For a moment fear put him almost in a stranglehold. He hoped that his friend's family was safe, but of course he never heard from them. He tried to reason that there was war action and no overseas mail. But there were so many others like the Hoffer's, incredible numbers of people who were imprisoned, tortured, killed, and their ashes were scattered like dust in the wind. Thinking about this was unbearable. Michael could not look at the article and the pictures any more. He folded up the paper and put it in a corner where he did not see it. It was time to settle down for the night. After a while he fell into a fitful sleep, but the pictures followed him into violent dreams. He saw his friend Simon and his mother behind a prison fence. Their heads were shaved, and they screamed for help and waved their arms. He had to run and help them escape…with a start he woke up. The scream had been his scream. His mother stood by his bed, touching his forehead. He was drenched in sweat and shook uncontrollably. She held his hands. "Wake up! You are having a bad dream." She had a damp cloth in her hand and sponged off his face. Both parents looked at Michael with a question in their eyes. Michael sat up. "Mom, Dad, I'm not sick! I just read something in the paper, and I dreamed something terrible." Martin nodded thoughtfully. "I know what you mean. I saw it too. It's the article about Dachau and the pictures. Yes, it is a nightmare. This is a nightmare that is going to haunt us, the German people. Go back to sleep now. Let's be grateful that your friend and his family are out of the country." Michael's face was still reflecting the terror of his dream. "I dreamed about them. They were in this nightmare.

They were prisoners behind a barbed wire fence." Louise shook her head: "No, Michael, they are safe. Just trust. At one point you may hear from your friend, but this can take a long time with this country being in shambles as it is. There is barely any mail service." Quietly Martin and Louise went back to their bedroom. Martin sighed. His poor wife was still haunted by the violence she had experienced, and it affected him just as much. His facial wounds had healed, and the scar on his forehead did not bother him too much, but he still had throbbing headaches. Now his son had read a disturbing report about the atrocities that had been committed and could not sleep. The war might be over, but the pain was not over. They all had lived through a nightmare and had to recover, but he also knew that they had a long way to go.

Connections and communications with relatives in other parts of the country had been lost during the war. The country was not a country that was whole any more. It had been divided into various zones by the occupying forces. Its capital, Berlin, had been divided into four parts as well. American forces occupied the Southern part of Germany where the Laumann's lived. Further southwest French forces were the occupants, whereas the British were in the north of the country. The Russians had occupied the eastern part. Postal services had failed to operate, and they were still erratic now. Even though Louise's relationship with her sister Alma had not been close due to tensions over different political opinions, Louise decided to write a note to the family. They lived in the area of Dresden, once a beautiful city that had been entirely destroyed. She was uncertain whether she would even hear from them. But she had to try, as she wanted to know what had happened. It took a long time till she received an answer in the mail. The letter had been forwarded several times to other addresses in an effort to locate the family. Alma and her daughter Hilda were the only survivors of the family. Alma's husband was killed during the last war year.

The Russian forces shot Albert, her son, a proud member of the SS. Members of the SS had immediately been marked as enemies that deserved to die. She and her daughter had lost their home and all their belongings in the devastating bombings of February 1945. It was a miracle that they could flee towards an outlying area during the first parts of the bombing raids. There were estimates that more than hundred thousand people had perished in the bombing that had virtually erased an entire city from the map. They had found temporary shelter in a neighboring small town, where they lived in an unheated garret. There was no kitchen, no washroom, and no running water. They had to rely on the help of other people in the house to meet their needs. She mentioned that life in the Russian occupied zone was not easy. She closed the letter mentioning her last visit with Louise and her family, and she hoped that despite the differences of the past they would be able to reconnect again. She realized that she had been wrong in many ways, following a leader that had plunged the country into an abyss of disaster. Louise felt the pain of her sister Alma. She lost everything: her home, her belongings, and worst of all two of her loved ones were dead. What Alma had endured was even worse than what they had been going through. She tried to comfort her sister in the letter she wrote as an answer back and promised to keep in touch. She had finished her letter and read through it once more. Like an uncomfortable undercurrent she still felt the events that had overshadowed her life at the end of the war. She could not write about them to her sister, as she still felt haunted by them. The days were getting better, but the nights tortured her with terrifying dreams. Martin understood her and tried to calm her down, telling her that life had to go on. They had survived together, which was the most important thing, and they hoped they would be able to put this evening of horror behind themselves too, but it was a struggle.

Four

Hardship And Survival

Rebuilding Bridges - 1945 to 1950

*M*ichael woke up in the middle of the night. An anguished, moaning sound made him shudder. His mother still had nightmares from the evening that had left his parents shaken and distraught. He heard the quiet voice of his father, as he was trying to calm her down, telling her that she had a bad dream. Michael felt helpless. He tried to help more around the house, seeing how tired and worn out his mother looked. There was no talk about the day that had darkened the recent past so much and that was still like a heavy load on his parents. He fell asleep again, precious sleep, as he had to get up early. He as well as his father had resumed their familiar routines. School was back in session, and Martin Laumann was back at work.

Louise was at home alone with her thoughts. She felt relieved. After having been reexamined by a doctor at the hospital she had been told that she was healthy, and there was no sign of disease. She felt reassured when she detected some traces of blood, showing her that she seemed to get her monthlies as usual. They were later and weaker than usual, but this seemed to be still normal for her. The next month was similar except there was just a tiny trace of blood. She paid her doctor a quick visit. He offered reassurance.

She was at the end of her thirties, but due to the deprivations of the war and starvation she could very well be entering the change of life. Aside from this she seemed to be healthy. He did not need to examine her at this point. This was his opinion. She trusted his judgment, as he was a physician who would know more about health than she did and went home feeling relieved. All the same she continued to feel out of sorts. Usually she was busy with her work all day, but lately her energy seemed to be drained, and she had lost her taste for her food. The most distressing problems were the nightmares that continued to reoccur and woke her up. She attributed her tiredness and lack of energy to a chronic lack of sleep.

It was time to go to the bakery to stand in line for a loaf of bread. With some luck she would also get some brown flour, maybe some oats too. Despite the ration cards there were always line-ups, and getting the groceries was a long, tedious affair. Today it felt even more tiring for her to wait in line. Her feet felt like lead. She was chatting with Peter's mom, when she felt her legs buckle, and the world seemed to start turning around her. Some helpful arms held her and lowered her to the floor, after which everything went blank. When she opened her eyes, the kind wife of the baker ushered her to the living room that was next to the store. She told her to rest on the couch for a while, gave her a cup of warm herb tea with honey and offered her a piece of bread. She was concerned that she did not have much to eat for breakfast like most everybody. Food had been in short supply for so long. Of course this was true. Louise had given most of her share of breakfast to Michael. He was still growing; he needed it more than she did, and she did not feel like eating anyways. After doing her errands she went home exhausted. She slept for an hour, but after waking up a bout of nausea came over her, and later she merely dragged herself through the day. It was disturbing. Louise had not been sick in years, and this was summer, when people would not have to fight colds and flus. A feeling of unease crept up in her. They had survived the war. She could not turn sick now. There was so much work in the garden in summer, and her family needed her!

In the evening she mentioned to Martin that she had fainted. He was concerned and also noticed that Louise only picked at her food. She said that it made her feel sick to her stomach. Something was not right. He insisted that they would go to the small local hospital together. The physician on call asked them to step into the tiny room. Louise felt her hands turn sweaty, and she started to shake. It was like a flashback: she had been in such a small room just a few months back, had endured the questions, the exam, and the treatment. Martin understood. He held her hand, feeling helpless in his efforts to comfort her. The physician was a calm man, and his quiet manner instilled trust in Louise and Martin. He took time, and he listened to the concerns of the couple. He acknowledged that she had been raped, but her periods seemed to have returned after that, though they had been much weaker, and now they had stopped altogether. She was free of venereal disease. Here was a patient who had always enjoyed good health, even in the trying time of war, but now she was feeling unwell. He listened to the opinion, which his colleague had voiced: menopause. But his colleague had not even examined the patient! The doctor saw the look of worry in the face of his patient, and he tried to reassure her. He knew that it was not comfortable for her, and he would be as careful as possible, but he needed to examine her now. Martin noticed a look of surprised concern in the face of the doctor, when he came out of the examining area. He was waiting for an answer. He could not remember having seen his wife so unwell, and he was worried. If Louise would only get better! The doctor faced them both. "There is no doubt after having examined you that you are pregnant, Mrs. Laumann." The news hit them like a lightning bolt. Louise shook her head incredulously. "What about menopause?" He shook his head. This was not menopause. She was definitely pregnant, but he could not tell her with certainty how far along she was. There were inconsistencies in the dates. But he mentioned that judging from his findings she was close to four months pregnant. This meant that she would feel the baby move in a few weeks. They left the hospital in a state of shock. Louise felt dull, walking automatically, her eyes not seeing, just staring ahead. This was too much! How could they go on? She felt Martin's hand holding hers. He was silent, and she was too stunned to speak. They arrived home. They sat down, holding on to each other. Both of them were crying. At least Michael was not home. He was at his friend's place. Martin's face was somber. His thoughts were racing. Almost four months! This was already a tiny child with a beating heart, with hands, feet, eyes, and a mouth that in the future would say "Daddy" or "Mama". It occurred to him that most likely he was not the father, but the thought of seeking out a doctor and asking for an abortion was even more distressing. This was like asking for the execution of a helpless, innocent person. His voice betrayed his distress: "What can we do? We cannot get rid of it." She burst into tears: "Martin, I could never do this! There is also the possibility that this is our child, yours as well as mine. We don't know! Oh God, what can we do?" He shook his head sadly. "I'm sorry, Louise, I should not even have said 'it'. This is a human being, and half of this baby is from you. I just feel like a load of rocks has hit us." They prepared to settle down to sleep. He wanted to pull her in his arms, wanted to make love, desperately trying to find consolation, but Louise was crying and turned away from him. Since the assault she tensed up, when he wanted to touch her, and it left him with an aching feeling of frustration.

Michael eyed his parents. A sense of unease was almost palpable. Usually Sunday mornings were cheerful and relaxing. Today was different. Both parents did not have much to say and looked like they had not slept all night. He looked at his mother. She did not look well, and today she did not only look sick but sad as well. His father was stone-faced and sat slumped over at the table. It was his father who broke the silence. "You may as well know, Michael. Mom went to the hospital yesterday night." Michael bit his lip. Hospitals generally were bad news, at least for him. He had broken an arm two years ago, and it had not been pleasant to go to the hospital. Louise nodded. "Yes, the doctor told me that we are going to have a child." Michael swallowed. This piece of news was unexpected. He would have a brother or a sister! In the past he thought that it would be nice to have a playmate, but this never happened. At one point he heard from his parents that a doctor was of the opinion that they seemed to be unable to have more children. And now he was hearing news like that! His parents were older, his mom going on thirty-eight and his dad over forty-four already. Good Lord, and now a baby! Why not earlier? He stopped himself quickly before putting his thoughts into words. A thought had come up in the back of his mind, and it went back to the distressing evening a few months back. With it the realization hit him that this was not happy news for his parents. But the least he could do was being a helpful big brother in the future. Right now it was awkward, as he could not smile or say 'congratulations'. Cautiously he voiced his thoughts:

"I'm just glad, that you are not sick, mom. You had me worried." His father looked at him gravely. "You are absolutely right, but I can't see anything else that is positive!" He had to think how multifaceted life could be: there was gratitude for Louise's health, but at the same time he felt apprehension over the arrival of a new life in a time where the future was uncertain. Even more there was the sober, painful realization that very likely he was not even the father of this child. Raging fury boiled in him about the one person who had violated his wife and him as well. He felt a flood of anger that he had no choice in a situation beyond his control. All of these emotions seemed to assault him simultaneously. It was too much! Martin's face betrayed his inner distress, and abruptly he got up. "I can't take it! I have to get out of here."

He got his jacket and left the house leaving Louise and Michael in tense silence. He walked aimlessly for hours, and his mind was in turmoil. Louise would have a child. After years of wanting another child she was now pregnant. Normally he should be happy, but of course neither he nor Louise could feel happiness about the news, as this new life was most likely the result of a rape, and he was not the father of this child. And yet, could he be certain? Louise had reminded him that they did not know. She felt as helpless as he did. What if the child, that had been fathered by a man who had no morals and no conscience, would turn into a person like this father, a person with asocial behavior, as violent and devoid of any conscience? What could he do to change this, and could he do anything at all to prevent this from happening? He realized that life was uncertain, now and in the future. He did not have control over everything. Martin did not know how long he had walked. In the meantime it had turned dark. He went through a forest trail with the moonlight helping him to find his way, but he could not bring himself to go home. He had a fleeting, irrational thought of running away, going anywhere to escape a situation that was overwhelming. But he also realized that he could never abandon Louise, his wife. And there was Michael, his son. He could not destroy his family with his behavior. As he leaned against a tree, an outburst of crying and a spasm of sobbing shook him. After a long time he turned around and started to walk back to the area where his and Louise's lives had been shaken up and altered forever. He had to face the place and think. He did not know what time it was, and time was something immaterial to him right now. Finally, hours later he arrived back at the familiar orchard slope, exhausted and thirsty. He opened the gate, made his way to the water pump and drank the water in big gulps. Under one of the apples trees he let himself fall into the grass. His mind was still going in circles, but some thoughts became clearer. Some time by next January he would be a father. Being a father meant that he would be entrusted with a new life that needed him as a source of strength and support, of love and guidance. Half of this baby was coming from his wife, and it would be up to him and to her to love this child unconditionally, help him or her to grow up, and be the guides on his or her way. A child could be only guided with steadiness and love, and their love as parents could overcome many obstacles. But first he had to make the decision to love this child! Could he do this? He wanted to love, but showing love was an enormous task. All his life he had struggled with this. Louise seemed to understand that he was a silent, unemotional man. Love for him meant being there and providing for her and their son, but displaying love in words or other ways was not his strength. Showing tender emotions had never been on his agenda. He had always dismissed it as useless and sentimental. Now he had the uncomfortable feeling that he needed to learn more about a subject that did not come easy to him. Deep down he knew that love was stronger than the evil that had affected his wife and him. With this thought came the realization how easy it was to fail to love. How often had he failed? He had to think about Louise. What he did to her yesterday, walking away and not even returning at night was one of the worst things he could have done. What had happened to staying with her for better and for worse? Would she be able to forgive him at all after he hurt her like this? Oh God! Here he was, a supposedly mature, middle-aged man, who had to learn so much more about love. Could he learn at all, and would he ever learn? Maybe the child that Louise was carrying was meant to teach him, an older father, more about love. He felt a flicker of hope, but exhaustion overwhelmed him. The first grey morning light was dawning. He was spent, mentally drained, tired beyond belief, and his head sank forward on his chest, as he sat slumped over under the tree.

Michael quietly sat with his mother. He told her to rest, and she gave him a grateful look. Both of them felt a painful void. Michael quickly stepped out and told his friend Peter that his mother needed his help, and they could not do anything together today. He went back home to help with the daily work. Martin did not return at lunchtime. His chair at the table was empty at suppertime too. The morning left Michael stunned. His dad had left. He had never walked out of the house like that before. Going for a quick walk to clear his mind was something he would do, but not that! Night fell, and his mother had gone to bed. She was quiet, but he heard how she cried herself to sleep, and finally exhaustion had taken over. Michael was tired but could not sleep; he tossed and turned. Where was his father? A terrible thought went through his mind: what, if he never came back, what if he had harmed himself? Suicide had become rampant. Recently he heard about a neighbor whose house had burned down during the war. The man could not cope with the distress of war, and seeing no hope for himself, he had jumped off the railway bridge. And he was not the only one. Just a couple of weeks ago yet another person had been found drowned in the river. Michael felt the load of responsibility on his shoulders, knowing that he needed to be there for his mother and a baby. It felt like a heavy load. He was only fifteen years old, but he had to grow up even faster. Finally tiredness took over, and he fell asleep.

Hardship And Survival

Monday morning dawned in a dull, overcast light. Louise got up, mechanically going through the motions of her early morning work. She prepared breakfast for the family. With a sting of pain she noticed that she had also put a plate for Martin on the table. But he was not here. She sat at the kitchen table for some time and let her tears flow. How much more could she endure? Michael had left for school. She had to walk over to the field in order to quickly let out the chickens and give them water. Normally Martin would do this. Ever since she had been assaulted there, she could not bring herself to walk along the field path and the grassy orchard slope. It filled her with panic. Now she had to go there. Her breathing was rapid, she was shaky, and she broke out in cold sweat. Next she opened the rusty gate and saw a hunched-over figure sitting on the grassy knoll under one of the apple trees. Cautiously she went closer. She saw Martin and called his name. He was startled, like he had woken up from his sleep, and slowly he turned his head. She saw his eyes, weary to the soul, the eyes of a broken man. Martin got up and walked towards her. His face was tear- streaked. He fell to his knees in front of her and held on to her. "Louise, I do not think that you can ever forgive me. Now I have hurt you even more by just walking away." In his eyes was a silent scream for help. She bent down, held his head and stroked his hair. "Let us go home, Martin; please come home. There is nothing to forgive; life will go on. You have always told me that. I know how hurt and upset you are. It is hard for both of us, but together we can go on." He nodded and went back to the house with her. Quietly they sat together. He took her hand, and a question was in his eyes. She gave him a gentle kiss and stroked his face. "I love you Martin; we still have each other. I'm so glad that you are home." He noticed that she had set the table with a plate for him earlier. "You were expecting me, Louise?" She looked at him seriously. "Yes, Martin, I hoped. I could not just give up hope." He saw that she was fighting back tears. He took her in his arms and felt her unfailing love for him, feeling humble and grateful. "I should have told you yesterday that I love you, and I failed. Forgive me, please;

I hope it is not too late today to tell you that I love you, Louise." He shook with emotion as he was holding her. She had never seen him like that. Martin usually was stoic, quiet and unemotional. He heard her calming voice: "No, it's never too late. It's for better or worse; and it will get better, Martin." She smiled through her tears and pushed away the breakfast dishes. It was not important to sit at the table. They went into their bedroom, and he held her in his arms. Usually he was impatient and hurried, but today he realized how precious Louise was to him. They were partners, and their bond had lasted through many struggles in life, and they would overcome the difficulties of this tumultuous time too. They had survived, and they would persist. With love they could do it.

Summer slipped into fall. They had harvested fruit and vegetables from the garden and Louise had canned as much as possible for winter. It was a generous crop, and they were grateful. Martin had piled up firewood. Nevertheless it was an ongoing struggle to get food. The Menzinger's helped wherever they could, but they also had their own family to feed. Out in the country farms were larger and more prosperous. On one Sunday in late fall they walked along the country road to a village, pulling their small, rattling wagon behind them. They had taken anything that had trading value. Farmers would accept table linens, bedding, and carpets and offer food in return. Alcohol and tobacco were other items that were desirable. They walked into a farmstead and to the door, and they felt like beggars. The farmer's wife was just returning home from church. Would she be interested to trade food for a lace tablecloth? The woman scrutinized them. No, she was not interested. She mentioned that she had everything she wanted, but pointed to the floor. "This is kind of bare here. An oriental carpet would be nice." Cool eyes looked at them without the faintest trace of compassion. "You are people from the city. Yes, there will be a lot of people dying of hunger in the cities." She talked like she was mentioning a rainstorm, when she was in a house that was warm and dry. Next she closed the door into their faces. For her they were an inconvenience on a Sunday morning. For them it was another disappointment. Wearily they walked on. Another farmer leaned over his gate watching them. He beckoned them to come in. The family was sitting around the table having a midday meal. A few chairs were pulled up, and gratefully they sat down. A steaming bowl of soup was put in front of them, they were invited to partake, and the farmer traded goods with them and invited them back. These were different people on the same day in the same village. It was lifting their spirits that despite all the hardship there was still compassion. It was not easily found everywhere, but they had found it today.

Louise woke up in the night. It happened more often now than usual. The baby was kicking, and she had woken up from the movement. Martin felt her turning over in bed. His hand reached for hers; he was concerned about her. "Are you all right, Louise?" She reassured him that she was fine. She did not have nightmares any more. She just had woken up, and she took his hand and placed it on her belly. He felt the kicks of the unborn, and he heaved a sigh. He did not know what he could say. Right now he could not express joy, even though that here was a small human being moving and making his or her presence known. For him it was just like another kick the enemy was giving him. At times the memories assaulted him like a vicious beast that jumped on him. The scene in the orchard still haunted him. In April they had kicked him in the head, in the groin and in the back. At times he still had bad headaches. Now it was October. He was being kicked again. It felt like the pain was mercilessly repeating itself, a constant and relentless reminder of the evening in April. Oh God, when would these memories stop? He could not say anything like that to his wife. She needed rest; he lay alone with his anguish, and his pillow felt damp from his tears. It was a relief to cry. Cautiously her hand reached for him. "I want the child to have your name, Martin." He bent over to kiss her. Through his tears a small laugh rose in his throat. "What will we do if it is a girl?" She seemed to be so sure that it would be a boy. Her answer came fast. "I still want the child to have your name. What about Martine?" He was touched by her answer. He was very likely not the father of the baby, but Louise trusted him to be a loving father all the same. He agreed: "Yes, that would be nice." He was quiet after that and had to think that here was a human being that did not know anything of war and violence. This was not the vicious kick of an enemy but the movement of a small and helpless child that would come into the world needing his help and his protection. Louise, the mother, would love this child, and she was the woman he had vowed to love and to honor. Louise's child needed him as well, needing him as a helping and guiding father, regardless whether he was the biological father or not. This was his role in the life of this child that one day would say "I love you, daddy" with the deep trust that he, the father, would love him or her as much. As he had these thoughts his mind was getting calmer. Love was a decision, and he had decided during that one sleepless night in the orchard to love the child that Louise was carrying. He bent over to his wife and kissed her. Gently he caressed her swollen belly like he wanted to calm the unborn, and holding on to Louise's hand he could feel calm and fell asleep.

The year was coming to a close, a difficult year, which was a constant struggle to obtain the most basic necessities to live. It was also a time marked by emotional turmoil. The war had ended, but it was a matter of hanging on and surviving. Winter had arrived, and it had become bitter cold. Louise's pregnancy was very advanced, but with the warm, bulky winter clothes she was wearing it was barely showing that she was in her last month of her pregnancy. Her tiredness had long disappeared, and she was her usual self again, healthy and always busy with her work. Christmas was behind them. It had been a quiet celebration with the little they had, and the days between the old and the New Year were a time of rest.

Two days before New Years Eve Louise and her friend Marie Menzinger finished the washing for the week. Marie came over once a week, as she wanted to help Louise with the chores that were too cumbersome for her now. Marie said good-bye after lunch and left for her home through densely falling snow. Martin and Michael washed the dishes, and Louise got busy ironing a load of laundry, when she felt a wave of discomfort in her belly. It came and went. Martin was outside getting more firewood for the stove that heated the living room. She dismissed the discomfort. It would settle. But the waves came back, and they became stronger. After several episodes that were just a few minutes apart she could no longer deny that she was about to give birth. Her voice had a calm urgency: "I have to go. The baby..." Two pairs of anxious eyes stared at her. The baby was at least three weeks earlier than expected! There was no midwife in the suburb. And how could they even get her to the hospital? It was snowing heavily. Michael ran out of the house. One neighbor at the end of the road owned an old car. He had offered to help should they need transportation, but they should bring some gasoline which was still rationed. Martin had bought a few liters, and it was stored in the tool shed. Fingers crossed that the old clunker would start! Michael was relieved that the neighbor was home. The man eyed the falling snow, got his coat, and went with Michael. "At least it is not far", he muttered. He tried to sound optimistic, poured some gas into the tank and started the vehicle. It sputtered for a while due to the cold weather, but after a few wheezy puffs the engine caught. They helped Michael's mother into the car. The neighbor drove, and Martin and Michael stayed behind.

They were startled when the phone rang later in the evening. A nurse was calling. Louise had given birth to a healthy girl.

Martin and Michael decided to walk the three kilometers to the hospital, even though it was late. The snow had stopped, and they entered the building. It had sustained damages during the war, and some areas were still under construction. They entered a room with unfinished floors and unpainted walls. Louise looked tired but relieved and happy. She was holding the newborn that was swaddled in a towel. Michael saw a tiny, wrinkled, red face with a nose that looked like it had been squished and eyes that were just slits. The mouth seemed much too big for the little face, and this baby had a shock of the darkest auburn hair he had ever seen. Only a mother could love that face, he had to think! And she was small too, a little something that looked almost fragile. The neighbor's tomcat was about her size. Normally he would have said that this was not a pretty looking baby, and he quietly wondered whether he had looked so ugly too when he was born. But of course he could not say anything like that, as it would upset his mom. He grinned and looked at the little face. "Hi Martine! You look so funny!" Martin stepped closer and hugged his wife; he stroked the baby's face, and all of a sudden the eyes opened, large baby-blue eyes. Small arms were flailing, and he touched a tiny hand that seemed not larger than a large rosebud. A small fist closed around his finger, a sensation that went right to his heart. His reaction was unexpected and sudden. He started to cry and looked at his wife and the newborn. "Louise and Martine! I love you so, my two girls!" It was a bond that was instant and lasting.

Michael had to think that life was not the same with a baby in the house. Martine slept in a small wicker basket in the living room. It was the only room that was warm. Despite her small size she managed to let the world know that she was a force to be reckoned with. Her small whimper quickly escalated to a full-blown wail, and Louise picked her up to let her nurse. Peace seemed to be restored, but not for long. Michael picked up his little sister and rocked her, but this did not help. How could such a tiny scrap of humanity make so much noise! Wrinkling his nose he quickly handed her back to mother. He decided that babies did not always smell sweet! In an effort to focus on his homework he plugged his ears. At this point Martin arrived at home. The evening paper was in his hand, and he also held a letter. It was an envelope that looked creased from a long journey, and it bore foreign stamps. It was addressed to the Laumann family. He opened it and shook his head in wonder. "Michael, you won't believe this!" He handed the envelope to his son. It was a long letter from Simon Hoffer. It had been mailed three months ago. Michael's old friend had kept his promise. He had written, hoping that they would receive his news. It was a report about a trip hidden in a drafty cargo hold of the truck to Italy. After this there had been a stormy trip across the Atlantic, and they all had been violently seasick. Next was the arrival in Montréal and a train trip to Toronto. It was like a kaleidoscope of light and dark, a collection of months and years. Simon had written an incredible account of struggles to get a foothold in a new country and efforts to learn a language as fast as possible. It sounded like the family had jumped into the deep end of a pool, first just barely keeping afloat. But within a year Paul Hoffer, Simon's father, had steady work at the firm of an architect and was now preparing to open his own office. Ruth, his wife, had taken up her artwork again. Her work was finding recognition, and she was selling pieces through local galleries. Simon had thrown himself into English studies, and otherwise schoolwork was unproblematic. The letter was written in German, but Simon also mentioned that he planned to write more in English in the future. It was his biggest wish to receive news as soon as possible. He really wanted to know that they were all safe.

Michael wrote back. He warned him that the letter would not be pretty, as he was describing the war years in it. He wrote about the death of the neighbor, Mrs. Kerner, and her small boy in a bomb blast, but he did not want to describe the terrifying details of this night of horror. He just mentioned that he managed to rescue Rose, the little nine-year-old girl, from the flames. He told him that the school had burnt down, but he did not go into details, when Peter and he went through this neighborhood seeing corpses lying in the street. It had been too gut wrenching. He described the constant struggle for food, jokingly comparing it to the hunters and gatherers: sometimes they would be lucky to eat, but at other times the pickings were slim. Michael decided to write that he had a baby sister, mentioning that she was a "surprise", but he did mention the details that were still having a haunting quality. At one point in the future he would tell his friend the story about Martine and about the harrowing experience of his parents. Winter was wearing on, a long, cold winter, even though the calendar said March. In the night ice crystals were forming on the walls of Michael's room. He bundled up some more, as he did not want to sleep in the warmer living room where his little sister was sleeping in her basket. The baby would wake up and cry, and he really wanted his sleep. At one point it would get warmer. He thought of spring and summer. It would get easier, not everything, but there was hope.

Louise was sitting and knitting socks for her husband and her son. She had unraveled a sweater that she could spare. They needed warm socks for next winter more than she needed the extra sweater. It was an old sweater, but the wool was still useable. Beside her lay an old flannel bed sheet. The baby needed diapers, and she cut out a few squares from the partially torn fabric. Later in the evening she planned to work on the sewing. Otherwise there was never a shortage of work. Food was still scarce, but she managed to feed the baby. Marie Menzinger often came by and brought some precious goats milk for the baby, and she and her husband just lived with their meager dinners consisting of boiled potatoes and vegetables, if they were available. It could happen that they went to bed hungry. They were lucky to get eggs from their chickens. Other people who could not keep a garden were much worse off. At least she did not have to worry so much about her eldest one any more. It helped that he was receiving a meal at the school like all the students. School meals were a relief effort by the occupying American forces to feed the youngsters at school. A ring at the doorbell surprised her. A postman was outside. "A parcel for Laumann!" It was a large box, and it was fairly heavy. She was taken aback. Why a parcel? They did not expect any parcel. There was no birthday, and it was not Christmas! And who would have money for sending parcels anyways? It was wrapped in brown paper, which was tattered at the edges, showing the wear and tear of a long journey. With large letters "Care Package" was written on top of the box. She noticed that it was clearly addressed to the family. Incredulously she read the name of the sender: Paul Hoffer. A street address followed. It came from Toronto in Canada. She had to sit down. This was unexpected, almost unreal. With a sense of disbelief she touched the package. This was not an apparition; it was a parcel that had travelled from half a world away. Louise decided not to open it but wait for everybody to be home. They would open it together. After Martin and Michael were home, they unwrapped the box. They felt overwhelmed. Louise could not help it but cry. What riches were in that parcel! There were cans of meat, blocks of margarine, a bag of sugar, a tub of honey, raisins, egg powder, milk powder, and a tin of real coffee with a scribbled note on top: "We remember how much you like your daily brew- enjoy!" Warm winter gloves for the adults, a baby quilt, a cozy little pink jacket, and a small rag doll completed this wonderful and entirely unexpected gift. They all sat in stunned surprise. It was hard to believe that they had received such a generous gift. But it did not end there, as several months later another package arrived, and yet more parcels arrived over time. They wrote letters to the Hoffer's, letters that showed their immense gratitude for their generosity. How could they ever thank them enough!

The war was over, but life had its ups and downs, and changes were brewing in a country that had to be rebuilt after years of destruction and deprivation. Everybody was aware that Germany was no longer a whole country but a nation divided into sectors. For Michael and his family it was not a source of concern, and life went on for them. Their relative Alma who lived in the Russian occupied zone reported that for her life was still very restricted and difficult. The Laumann's lived in the sector that was occupied by American forces. Michael practiced his English with some of the soldiers. They were easy-going, friendly fellows, and most of them did not mind chatting with a local who spoke English. They did not speak German, and many people of the population did not speak English, but simple gestures and friendliness brought down language barriers. They stood at a street corner, offered him a piece of chewing gum, and they talked about their hometowns far away. They were on duty in a country that was foreign to them, and for some it was like an adventure, but for others it was a source of homesickness. The population got used to American soldiers driving huge, chrome-gleaming automobiles through the small streets. No, they had not seen such flashy vehicles before! Often there was the incongruous mix of a horse- drawn farmer's wagon sharing the village street with a large turquoise Ford with big tail fins, which was not an ordinary every-day sight. The population still struggled to buy necessary goods. Money seemed to be worth only a fraction of what it used to be worth, and nobody had accumulated any riches. Things started to look up when a new currency was introduced which replaced the old unstable "Reichsmark". Everybody received a starter amount, and whoever had any of the old money, needed to go through the process of applying for a conversion. Martin sighed. He had seen the big inflation in the 1920's when his savings had disintegrated into nothing. Now he found himself at a similar point of starting all over again. With the stabilization of the currency and the new "Deutsche Mark" all of a sudden the stores had merchandise to offer. Theoretically people could now purchase what they needed, but reality was different: nobody had huge bank accounts and fat wallets. It was a gradual process of getting ahead. The daily needs could be met, but this was a far cry from luxuries and affluence! The Laumann's thought that life was starting to get better for them, but the next setback for them came shortly after.

In the meantime a steady stream of refugees had flooded the country. People arrived from the easternmost areas of what had been Germany, areas that had been taken by Russia. Refugees left their homes often just carrying their meager belongings in a small wagon, which they pulled. They endured terror and hardship. Those who survived often had endured acts of unspeakable violence. After the bombing there were no homes available to house the refugees, and the local authorities took a hard look at the situation. Anybody who had space to spare had to accommodate a person or a family. The Laumann's were told that their four- room flat would be spacious enough to accommodate another family. They just had an almost grown up son, who was close to finishing school and a toddler. Besides that there would be an attic chamber for them to use. As a result they were required to share their flat with a refugee family of four, father, mother, and two infants. They were incredulous. They would be losing part of their home. The attic chamber was a room under the roof that was not fit to accommodate any person in colder weather. It was not insulated and the wind blew in through the roof tiles. Nobody in the house could use this space for any other purpose than storage. It was useless to object. Police arrived and accompanied the family that was about to move in to make certain that there would not be any resistance. Live became cramped and narrow. All they had left now was their previous bedroom and a small living room. The kitchen was still theirs, and they had a bathroom. The toilet had to be shared with the new residents of this flat. Eight people were housed in these cramped conditions. Each year they hoped that the family that lived in their flat would finally find alternative accommodation. Each year was a new disappointment. After the destruction of the country it was taking a long time to rebuild.

Over the years apartment blocks sprung up at the edge of the outskirts, ungainly structures that looked like blocks of concrete that had been dumped into the landscape. Many refugees found new homes there. For the Laumann's it took six years till the family that lived in their flat moved out into one of the new apartment blocks, and they finally got their living space back!

Michael finished grammar school. He wanted to pursue his interest in drafting and designing and attended courses for two years at a technical school. His teacher recommended him as a very competent student to a local architect. But he was still learning. He felt that he was only scratching the surface. During the days he worked. At night he took additional courses. Peter had started an apprenticeship as a mechanic. They were still buddies, but both were busy, did not have much free time on hand, and money did not grow on trees either. Michael sank his money into further courses; Peter found that apprenticeship only yielded some pocket money, but no big riches.

Michael sat at the table and waded through his course materials. It was difficult to study at home. His little sister followed him like a puppy wherever he went. She was almost four. He had to acknowledge that she was not the ugly little thing that she had been at birth; she was a pretty little girl now. When he went for a walk with her, admiring glances from the neighbors followed her. But he also picked up whispered comments. The word "French soldier" had fallen. Of course the people in this close-knit neighborhood knew what happened, and rumors made their rounds. Michael felt bad for his parents. He would stare those whispering neighbors down to express his disgust with their hurtful gossip. His caustic comments to improper remarks were already known in the neighborhood. Some nosy individuals had been put in their place by his sarcastic one-liners in a way that made them cringe with embarrassment, wishing that they had kept their mouths shut. As a result one look from the young Laumann was often enough to silence them. Michael also noticed that there was nothing left of the relatively peaceful baby his sister had been. To the contrary: this little girl was a small ball of fire with nothing of her mother's gentle dignity and of course nothing of Martin's quietness! She still had the shock of straight, deep auburn hair that was now tied into two perky pigtails. Little Martine did not have the pebble-grey Laumann eyes or Louise light blue eyes. Her previously baby-blue eyes had changed to a green that looked like a dark pine forest. She stuck out in the Laumann family because of her looks starting with her hair being a dark auburn, which was different from the straight medium blond hair of her brother or father, different too from her mother's light brown locks. She did not have Michael's thousand freckles but Louise's soft complexion, and she had Louise's heart-shaped face and her straight, finely shaped nose. But the high arching, strong eyebrows, the soft, round mouth, and the small ears were different from anybody else in the family. She was a horse of a different color in every way, and that included her temperament.

At times Louise looked at her little girl and sighed. She was such a loveable, cuddly, happy little thing. At the same time she was also a bundle of boundless energy with a mind of her own, and this child put her to the test. Michael had rarely gotten into mischief, but this little girl did all the things Michael had never even thought of doing. She was not the delicate little girl that that she had envisaged, a girl that liked to sit quietly and play with her dolls and who loved ruffled dresses or bows in her hair. Sometimes she could drive her parents and her brother to distraction with her ideas. She grabbed a rabbit from its hutch and wanted to take it into bed with her, insisting that it was cold and lonely, and there were big tears when the parents said a firm "no". It was after Easter, and Louise found a stuffed toy Easter bunny in a store, which was on the clearance table, and it became a much loved bedtime companion for the little girl. She came home with slimy garden snails in her pockets, proudly brought mud pies into the freshly cleaned living room, and was squealing with delight, when she caught a large, ugly looking beetle in the tool shed. One day she climbed into the cherry tree and swung from a branch so vigorously that it snapped. To everybody's relief she was unhurt, as she took a soft landing in the smelly compost pile full of chicken and rabbit manure. The one person who had a seemingly endless supply of patience with her was Martin. When she cried after this adventure, he told her that he would build her a swing in the garden, but no more swinging from trees, or she would not get any cherries or other fruit from the trees. Her special bond with him showed early, as her first word was a loud "ba-ba", calling for her father. Saying "Mama" came next, and she followed her mother around like a constant shadow of curiosity with most of her questions starting "Why? Why Mama?" And now she was after Michael. She called him "Micky". She wanted to play ball in the garden with him. Michael got up from his books. It was of no use to tell her that he would play with her later. His little sister knew what she wanted: Martine wanted to play ball, and she wanted it right now! Eventually she would be tuckered out and go to sleep. He could continue to study later in the evening.

The person who had the qualities of a little friend to Martine was Rose, the young girl of the Kerner's. After her little brother and her mother had been killed so suddenly in the bomb attack that had devastated so many houses, the girl was the only child. She felt alone and lost. Rose had mourned the loss, and it was not something that was easily forgotten. The traumatic event was only a few years ago. She still remembered the haunting night when the neighborhood had seemingly exploded into fire, and flames had licked on her legs, on her arms, and had singed her hair. But she also remembered the reassuring arms of Michael, when he pulled her out of the inferno. Ever since she had seen Louise taking tiny Martine out in the small old baby carriage, she admired the baby and was eager to watch over her and to wheel her around in the neighborhood. It was not a little brother. She was aware that she would never have another sibling, but it was a baby to love. Even though her father did not like to see her go to the Laumann's home, Olga, her stepmom, pointed out to him that it would be good for Rose, and she would be less lonely. She had lost her brother and was now the only child in the company of adults. Grudgingly he relented. The two, Rose and little Martine, were like sisters and were great friends. Rose patiently drew pictures for Martine, whose little hands tried to copy the artwork. She cut out paper dolls for her, or they glued colorful pictures of sun, moon and stars on a piece of paper or decorated a paper shopping bag. For Christmas they cut out paper stars and snowflakes; for Easter they colored Easter eggs together.

It was summer. Martine and Rose went out into the backyard together with Martine's mother to pick berries. Rose was fourteen now. She loved children and wanted to become a nursery school teacher. Michael had come home, and he saw the three between the bushes and went to join them. He liked Rose. An easy friendship had started to develop between them. They had gone on bike rides together, and sometimes they walked in the fields. Both were watchful. They knew that Rose's dad did not like Michael, a dislike that went back to the time when Mr. Kerner had been high on Hitler and the Nazis. It had been the time when Michael and Peter were not respectful enough for his liking and refused to be pliable material to his pressure to be loyal youth party members. He was quieter after the war, of course. After the war was over nobody liked the old Nazis any more! But his dislike for Michael and Peter remained. People stopped calling him "Little Adolf", but they were not quite able to forget his fanatic attitude of the past and were on guard. He was known as the awkward neighborhood grump. Everybody found it hard to understand why his new wife had married him at all. When the war was over he quietly got married to Olga, the war widow, who had taken him and his daughter into her house. Rose loved her, as she was such a warm and caring woman. The neighbors shook their heads and wondered how two people who were so different from each other could get along at all. Olga certainly knew how to handle him, but the neighbors were at a loss to comprehend how these two became a couple! This was the most unlikely match! But it was none of their business, and at least the young girl Rose had a good stepmother.

After helping with the berry crop, Rose and Michael walked along the field path. She still had a few years of school ahead of herself. He asked her what she wanted to do afterwards. She still wanted to be a nursery school teacher. What about him, she wondered. He told her that he was working to become a draftsman, a designer, and ultimately he wanted to leave the country. Her eyes were sad. "I'll miss you." He nodded. "Yes, I'll miss you too, Rose." He stopped and held her hands, shyly pulling her closer to him. "Wouldn't you want to leave too? I mean, not next year when I'll be leaving, but maybe later?" Her eyes had become soft, caught in thoughts about her future, a future that seemed far away and yet so close. He saw her face, the dream in her eyes, and he kissed her on her lips, a shy first kiss. She looked at him. It was a happy look, but a shadow went over her face next. "I'm not even fifteen, and I know that my dad will never let me go. If he catches me walking with you, he is going to throw a fit, and I'll be grounded." She gave him a shy kiss. "I guess it's a bit like being in jail. Yes, I want to leave, but I can't. I have to do time before I can get out."

They walked back, carefully parting ways before they came close to the house where she lived.

With fall approaching the time to spend outside was more limited, but Peter and Michael had planned an outing together. The last fall days beckoned with blue skies and golden leaves. They were biking along a forest path close to the city. They still loved their time outdoors. Fall in the forest meant also foraging for wild mushrooms. They enjoyed the small joys and simple pleasures of a time, where money was not plentiful, but survival had become less of a struggle, life had become easier, and their future seemed more secure. Peter would finish his mechanic's training soon. A local garage had offered him work as well. They parked their bikes near a forest trail and started walking. Michael saw that the trail was forking, and he took the one branch whereas his friend took the other one. They were looking for forest mushrooms hoping to be successful. The weather had been promising. Some rain had fallen a little while back, which should make for a good crop. They would communicate by shouting to each other through the quiet forest. Michael found a few chanterelles, those tasty, wild yellow mushrooms. Nice! He walked on and saw a small pond, but he gave it a wide berth. These water holes in the forest in this area were not good news. Ponds in this area of the forest were uncommon. Mostly these water holes were huge indentations that a bomb had left behind. It could be deceiving. Under the surface of stagnant water could be an unexploded bomb. His father had warned him about those.

The forest was silent like a natural sanctuary. Only the sweet song of a blackbird sounded through the stillness, and a brisk fall wind was sweeping the leaves off the trees. In the distance he heard Peter shout: "Hi-ho! I have found something, Michael!" Michael wanted to respond, but before he could, a deafening explosion rent the air. It felt like every tree was shaking, and the ground under him was vibrating. "Peter!" He shouted his friend's name. "Peter!" He followed the direction of the noise, walking cautiously, watching every step he took. His heart was pounding like a hammer. He screamed his friend's name, again and again. There was only silence, even the birdsong had stopped, and the stillness seemed to choke him. Then he saw it, a picture that would follow him and haunt him in many dreams. His friend's body was lying on the mossy ground. It was mutilated beyond description, arms and legs missing, blood was everywhere, a face no longer recognizable.

Michael screamed and raced back to his bike, furiously pedaling away from the forest, racing back towards the town.

He was arriving at the police station, pale, sweaty and shaking. The officer stood up from his desk and looked at him with alarm. "My friend," Michael gasped, his face a mask of unspeakable horror. "In the forest…he must have stepped on a bomb. We were picking mushrooms." He broke down, shaken by sobs. "Oh God! Peter is dead." The officer made him sit down and put his hand on his shoulder. "You will have to show us the location. I will call two colleagues. I'm so sorry, and I can only offer my condolences. But I will need your report. This has happened too often already. It's still happening, even though the war has been over for almost five years." Silently the somber-faced officer picked up a piece of paper and started writing a report following Michael's halting description. Two other officers appeared, and Michael went with them to the forest area. He felt like he was walking through a nightmarish movie in which he was condemned to be an actor. The nightmare continued, when they went to the house and rang the doorbell to notify Peter's parents. He would never forget the shock and grief in their faces. Their son, their only child was dead! They sat down together silently. It was like a dark cloud that hovered over the entire neighborhood. Everybody had known Peter. In a way he was yet another victim of the war, another senseless loss of life. They had all returned from the funeral and gathered at the place of Peter's parents. The small living room was crowded. They looked at pictures and thought back. It was time for remembrance of a life that had been much too short, a reminder of how fragile and how precious life was, and also the knowledge of the impact that the war had left. There was also the sobering realization how this war and other wars had made life cheap, something that was destroyed and discarded at will. War had extinguished and desecrated lives, trampled over people's lives and uprooted them, and it had spat into the face of human dignity and justice. This was recent history, and past history was full of it as well. Michael went home. He had to write a letter to his friend in Canada. They would bear the burden together. They had thought that they were still the three friends that had survived the war, had planned on meeting sometime in the future, a reunion of survivors; but this was not to be. His closest neighborhood friend was dead, and his loyal buddy, who had not forgotten him, was half a world away. He mailed the letter with a heavy heart.

Michael made a trip to the Canadian embassy in a neighboring town. He had to take a train trip, but luckily it was just a short day trip. He had filled out an application to immigrate into Canada. His decision to leave the country never left him ever since that evening of the war, when he and his parents sat in the deep cellar under the house. It was a night, when none of them knew whether they would survive the bombing that was destroying the area. His resolve of leaving became even stronger after the night when he witnessed the terrible death of Mrs. Kerner and her boy and when he dragged Rose out of the flames. The violence at the end of the war and the trauma to his parents was yet another impulse. Now Peter's death was the last blow. He received a sorrowful letter from Simon after his communication regarding Peter's death. At the same time Simon wrote to him that it might be time for him to consider a new start. Michael was amazed how his friend expressed these thoughts. He had mentioned to Simon some time back that he contemplated leaving Germany, but he was still not sure about all the details. It was typical for Simon to think further about Michael's plans. On an extra sheet of paper Simon's father had written him a message as well. It was a message that reflected the kindness and warmth that he had always seen in Simon's parents. Paul Hoffer impressed on him, that he should seriously consider coming to Canada. He explained in his note that there would be work for him at his office. They needed a draftsperson, as the workload had been growing steadily after the war. At the same time he cautioned him that life in Toronto was not a fancy affair; Montreal would be the larger city. But he would have work, and he would have a place to stay at their home after his arrival. He did not want to push him, but he wanted him to know that there was a landing spot for him in Toronto, should he decide to immigrate into Canada.

Michael shared the news with his parents. They were not surprised; he had talked about his future plans often enough. Michael would be turning twenty-one next year, and he had said it before that he planned on leaving the country. The parents listened, their faces grave. In contrast to the quiet, subdued mood in the living room the sound of children's laughter drifted in from the garden. Martine was outside with her neighborhood friends, a group of chatty five-year-old girls. They were without a care, playing with a skipping rope, chanting and laughing. Summer was easy, they did not go to school yet, and they did not have to face any hard decisions in their own cheery little world. Michael looked out at the playing children. "Let's hope that they will know more peace than we have had." His parents were fervently hoping for the same.

It seemed to be getting better for everybody in the neighborhood, and the daily struggle for survival had become less arduous, but another enemy was lurking. It was no longer war and famine but instead diseases that became rampant. First a wave of parasite infestation swept through the population. People worried that the food would be infested, and nobody knew the source of the problem. A few neighbors died, and everybody took the problem seriously enough after that. The drugstore sold a deworming medication. Michael swallowed the bad tasting liquid and the dosage of castor oil that tasted even worse. Martine fought, cried, and swallowed more tears than medication, but it had to be. It seemed that everybody in the neighborhood had worms, children and adults alike, pinworms, spool worms, and the much-feared tapeworms.

Hardship And Survival

Next many children, but also adults, came down with whooping cough, and there was no protection from it. Martine got sick, and Louise felt helpless, when she held her little daughter who was shaken by spasms of coughing and retching. Martin sat up beside her during the night, watching over her that she would not choke. After a few days their doctor told them that there was something new to help. He administered some injections. Martine screamed, terrified of the needle that went into her behind, but the disease seemed to break. She was slowly recovering.

However, the troubles were far from over. Even though it was spring and not usually a time of illnesses, the next epidemic came at the heels of whooping cough. The word "polio" filled people with dread. Several neighborhood children became sick. Two of Martine's little friends died. To protect their daughter from exposure to the disease the parents kept her home. She could not go out and play with the neighborhood children, as nobody knew who would be affected next. She was upset, but she understood what was happening. There was the tall, gaunt man who came walking down the road with a large pushcart. He went into the houses where her friends had died. He came out, wheeling a plain wooden coffin that was covered with a cloth, and the cart left with its ominous rumbling sound. The man looked almost like death himself, all skin and bones, and Martine asked her mother what he was doing. Louise told her that this was the person who was sent from the cemetery to pick up people who had passed away. She looked at her mother with wide-eyed horror, and she cried bitterly about losing two of her friends. The next time they went to the doctor's office she did not even wince, when she was told that she was getting a shot that would stop her from getting sick from polio. It was new, and it would help. The shot hurt! She bit so hard into her sleeve that her bite left a hole behind in the fabric, but she did not want to get sick or die. She was only sad that her friends did not have a chance to get the same new medicine that would protect so many others from this illness.

Summer was slipping into another fall. Michael had met with his old school friends and friends from his work. It was time to say good-bye. The mood was a strange mix. On the one hand there was regret from his friends to see him go, on the other hand there was excitement and enthusiasm. Some of them were thrilled and wanted to do the same as he, go to another country, do something new and different. Rose had joined the group. She had slipped away from her place. Her dad was not home. Her stepmom knew about her plan and encouraged her to go and say good-bye. After the group of friends had left, Michael and Rose went for a walk. They sat down on a grassy hill that overlooked the valley. Michael held her hand. She looked at him through tears. "It is sad that you are leaving, but I understand you." Michael looked at her and gave her a hug. "It's not easy for me either. Oh Rose, I wish you could come!" Sadly she shook her head. "You know that it won't work. I'm too young." She tried to smile a brave, little smile and continued, "But I still think about leaving once I'm of legal age. I'll write to you." He nodded seriously. "I want to keep you as my friend. You remember, when you were nine, I pulled you out from that burning house. You were just like a scared little bird, and I held you close to my heart." He pulled her closer and kissed her. "You are still close to my heart, and you will always be, Rose. I just can't pull you out of the house now, and it hurts." She knew. It was hard to be only seventeen.

Five

Hope For The Better

A Bridge for Michael - 1951 to 1955

The family stood at the railroad station. Michael carried a large travel chest. He was ready to go on his long trip. It was a brisk, sunny October day, which was like an encouragement for a safe journey and a start into a bright future. The parents wished the best for their son. He would travel far away, but they were optimistic. It was a new start, and he was spreading his wings. Martine eyed him curiously. "When will you come back?" Michael's smile was uneasy. He could not tell her lies. This kid had a memory like an elephant! If he promised her anything in the past, she remembered every detail. "I don't know when, Martine." She nodded in agreement. "Will you tell me if you know?" "I promise, I will." He lifted her up and whirled her around. She giggled cheerfully and planted a kiss on his nose. "Have fun on your trip, Micky." There were no tears from this little girl that only saw the excitement and fun of a trip! She looked at life through the eyes of child that was not quite six years old. He was a young adult, and he had seen years filled with struggle and toil. For him it meant the new start he wanted so much, but he was under no illusions: the roads on the new continent were not paved with gold, and life was not a picnic in the park. He was glad when the train was pulling out of the station. Hands were waving and handkerchiefs were being waved at the travellers from the distance. Long good-byes and tears were painful. Boarding the steamship at the harbor town by the North Sea was the next step. He had bought a ticket for steerage at a price that had cost him a small fortune of two hundred and fifteen dollars. With the help of Simon's dad he had opened a bank account to pay the amount in US Dollars. It had been complicated, but it was done! With a throng of other travellers that were Canada-bound he went through the necessary checks: he was healthy, was not on a list of wanted individuals, was not penniless, he had a clear travel destination, and a job was waiting for him. He heard that the good ship "Canberra" had been built some forty years ago. It certainly did not look remotely like a luxury cruise liner from the movies but rather like a very utilitarian, aging vessel. He boarded with the crowd, glad in a way that there was nobody to see him sail away. There were heart-wrenching scenes of farewell between loved ones. Standing by the railing he saw the coastline get smaller in the distance. The waves had picked up, and as he tried to negotiate the narrow and steep steps that led down to the dormitory, he had trouble getting a foothold on the pitching vessel. He did not have much to eat except some cookies and a cup of tea, and he felt his stomach lurch. But there was no need for embarrassment, as he was not the only one with the predicament of seasickness. Another hapless landlubber was holding on to the railing beside him, violently heaving. The dormitory was a spartan and uninviting affair: three double bunks with high metal railings occupied the room. The railings were meant to keep the occupants safe during storms. This area was located on the D-deck, three floors down from the main deck. It felt like being deep down in the cellar with the bilges underneath.

The next day at sea brought sunshine. Another stop was made in Southampton, the last port in England, where a crowd of passengers boarded. While initially it looked like there would be a sense of spaciousness on board, the scenario now had drastically changed. The craft seemed to be like a teeming ant heap. There was something disconcerting about being the human cargo of an overloaded ship. But then nobody here was in for a luxurious journey. England had been left behind, and there was nothing but the wide, blue, seemingly endless Atlantic. After four days the journey became difficult. The waters turned into a violently churning dark gray threat. The old ship was pummeled incessantly by high waves. One of the engines failed, and the journey became painfully slow. The crew tried to dispel the concerns of the passengers, but a sense of unease and fear was almost palpable. Howling storm gales reached a wind speed over 60 miles per hour, and high seas were constantly breaking over the foredeck.

Seasickness was very real for most of the passengers. Michael forced himself to eat, as an empty stomach made things worse. After a day he managed to keep his food down. The dining room was empty, as a lot of passengers did not appear for meals. Food was plentiful, and he dug in. He could feel some sympathy for one of his bunkmates whose constant groans filled the dormitory. But it became difficult to sleep to the litany of his constant moaning: "What do they do to me if I die?" Another passenger was running out of patience and shouted a gruff: "Shut up, man! They'll feed you to the fish; what else?" The storm had not settled, but the seasick bunkmate decided to keep it quiet from then on and suffered in silence. Due to the storm the journey had been an agonizingly slow ten days. The winds finally died down, and the passengers were elated when the high cliffs of Newfoundland and Labrador were rising from the dark waters. As sunlight filled the skies, the passengers emerged from their bunks to sit on deck chairs and breathe in the fresh, bracing air. Many of them looked more like haggard survivors after a harrowing journey during which they had been ill for over a week. They were ghostly pale, and many walked gingerly on the deck, more like ailing, frail convalescents than travellers. The quiet landscape along the St. Lawrence River was gliding by, and finally the ship arrived below the Citadel of Quebec City. Michael stepped on Canadian soil on the pier. He was receiving the small yellow card that certified him as a "Landed Immigrant". It was real. He was ready for a new beginning on a new continent. The next harbor was Montreal, and for most of the passengers it was the end of their journey. It looked like a large city. For Michael a lengthy train trip was next. Finally he had made it to Toronto. Wearily he collected his travel chest. He had not slept in 24 hours, had not washed himself in two days, and with his beard stubble he looked like an unkempt vagrant. He had to look twice, when he caught his disheveled reflection in a shop window. This was he after a trip, but things would improve. His mind was made up: he was determined to make himself at home. Tomorrow he wanted to look less bedraggled and a little more respectable. He knew that it took time to get settled.

Simon had drawn him a detailed map describing to him a tramline from the railway station to the Hoffer's home. It was easy to follow these instructions. Simon asked him to call from a phone booth close to the stop. They knew when he had boarded the ship, but nobody could possibly know his exact time of arrival. Michael watched attentively, as the tram rattled along the streets. There were rows of houses, a small corner store, and a grocery market. For a larger city it looked rather plain, entirely different from the city where he had grown up. It was twilight, and the streetlights were illumining the road. It had been a long day. Here was the tram stop where he had to get off! The helpful driver shouted the name of the street and motioned to him to get off the tram. A phone booth was on the street corner opposite, exactly as Simon described it in his letter. He dropped the coin into the slot and dialed the number, looking at the sheet of paper in his hand. The phone was ringing, and a girl's voice at the other end said "Hello". All of a sudden he found it difficult to speak. "Yes, hello, this is Michael Laumann." A pause followed, then a shout: "Simon, quick! Your friend has arrived." Simon came to the phone. "Wait for me. I'm five minutes away, and I'll be right over. You are at the tram stop, right?" There was a click in the line, and he was gone. Michael saw the short, trim figure of his friend jogging along the road and walked towards him with his travel chest. It was an exuberant greeting, clapping on the shoulders and a bear hug. Simon was thrilled that his friend had arrived: "So good that you made it in one piece!" Simon looked at Michael. He still saw the Michael he had known, but a lot taller now, of course. But he saw the same observant eyes and the same hair. He looked almost like the younger edition of his father, a tall and wide shouldered young man. Michael studied his friend. Yes, it was Simon, a grown up version of the friend he had known. They had exchanged photographs in their letters. Even though Simon had been the taller one of them in the past, he now was much shorter than Michael. He still had the face of a thinker, and he took after his mother having inherited her medium frame, her dark, expressive eyes, and dark, wavy hair. Otherwise he had his dad's straight, proud nose, sensitive mouth, and strong chin, but he looked much younger and more boyish than his friend. Despite all those years, despite all the changes, they both had the feeling that not much had changed between them. Theirs had been a lasting friendship, past and present were connecting, and they made their way to the house, hauling Michael's travel chest between them.

Work at the Hoffer office was busy, but Michael had to quickly relearn, as he was facing measurements of feet and inches instead of metric measurements. It was a hurdle, but then he expected hurdle races. Simon was still studying in preparation to become an architect and to follow into the footsteps of his father. It was the profession he always had wanted to pursue. As before he breezed through his studies, and he worked in his father's office whenever he could. They exchanged ideas and absorbed more knowledge, and Michael was doggedly working his way into his new workplace. It did not matter to him that his days could be longer. He was pleased with his pay of forty dollars every week, but after a month he insisted that he needed to find his own place to live. Simon's parents had been more than hospitable. They did not mind that he was staying in one of the little rooms in the basement of their house, but they understood that he wanted his independence, and so he moved.

One of his co-workers had a neighbor, who had a room for rent. It was west of Spadina Ave. and close to the bus. This was in an area where immigrants from Italy had made their homes. Michael arrived at the street corner, where a sign said "Tony's Market". Tony was the owner of a grocery and produce store, which he operated together with his wife Jadwiga. He had come from Italy a long time ago; she had emigrated from Poland. They had a spare room in their flat above the store. It looked a bit like a small, old-fashioned living room from Europe with a small couch, Jadwiga's crocheted covers, a bed and a table with an embroidered tablecloth. It felt like a comforting little piece of home in a new city. Michael found himself in a language medley of Italian, Polish, and English. At the home of Simon's parents he heard mostly English, except Simon's mother would sometimes throw a few Yiddish words into her sentences. And on rare occasions Simon's Dad could utter a string of choice, familiar swearwords in German, if he was upset. A language mosaic like this could be confusing, but it worked anyways. Smiles and gestures filled in the communication gaps. He was part of Tony's and Jadwiga's household, and for ten dollars per week he had a plain but comfortable room, got his laundry done, and got breakfast every day; and Jadwiga made sure that he got a big breakfast. She felt that she had to mother him: here was this tall young guy, who in her opinion was way too skinny! Lunch would never cost him more than fifty cents, and the streetcar or bus cost him ten cents per trip. He was frugal and wanted to save his money. Often he was invited to join the Hoffer's, and he brought along some fruit or vegetables that Tony, his landlord, was giving away, as in his judgment they were not fresh enough to be sellable. But the Hoffer family happily accepted these offerings. There were not only Simon and his sister Sarah, but also often some of Simon's friends from university or Sarah's teenage girlfriends at the dinner table. It was a cheerful clan, and even though winter had arrived with snow and freezing rain, they had a home that exuded warmth and happiness; everybody was welcome. Christmas was coming close, and Michael got swept up in celebrations of Hanukkah first, as this feast was as important to them as Christmas. Simon's mom was Jewish, and everybody in the family celebrated Hanukkah, the feast of lights. Christmas was next, and it was as joyfully celebrated as Hanukkah. The Christmas tree and the Menorah illumined the living room. He sat together with the Hoffer's, and their thoughts went back to Europe. For them so many years had gone by. They had settled into a comfortable life of work and enjoyed leisurely times as well. Simon was still studying, and his sister was still in high school.

The thoughts of all of them went back to Michael's family. Michael told them that they were doing well. Things were getting better after the war. They expressed their surprise that he had a young sister. Michael realized that it was time to tell them that

Martine was not simply a surprise. The pregnancy had been a shock to his parents, and it was very obvious that his sister was the result of a rape by a French soldier. The Hoffer's were taken aback by this story, as they had not known all the hardship Michael's family had to endure at the end of the war. Simon was the one who expressed his thoughts: "This has been incredibly hard for your parents, and it must have been terrible for you to witness such a difficult time. But when I see the photos now, I don't see the hardship any more. They look so happy together, and her life is like a gift. She looks like a bright, little spark that lights up the lives of your parents. And that's important for them now that you are away, Michael. What would their lives be like without her?" Michael had to agree, and often his thoughts wandered back across the ocean. He had written to his parents. He had also written to Rose. He got a reply from her to his first letter, but she did not answer his second letter, and he only received a Christmas card where she wrote that she missed him.

One evening his landlord Tony approached Michael. He had too much work. Would Michael mind helping him out? He had some grocery orders that needed delivery. He let him drive the old rusty Ford that still had the proud sign "Tony's' Market" lettered on the side, and after a few evening rounds together, Michael slipped into the role of the delivery driver. He did not mind it, as he picked up driving and Tony paid him for his help. Some grateful customers also gave him the occasional tip. It all added up. Michael quietly wondered about rules and regulations like a driver's license, but Tony waved away his concern. In time he would get it! The big day eventually came. Tony mentioned to him, that he had almost driven twenty thousand miles, and he should go to the licensing office to get his official license. Michael entered a cramped office space, and standing at the wicket he was expecting a test, questions or forms. The employee cast him a quick glance. "Coming for your license?" When Michael acknowledged, he got up and reached for a form. It was filled in with all the necessary information: name, date of birth, address, and some other points. Another questioning look by the man followed. "So you figure that you have driven approximately twenty thousand miles?" Michael nodded. "Yes, close to it anyways." The employee reached for a black book that looked like thousands of clean and not so clean hands had handled it over the years. Solemnly he put it on the counter in front of Michael. "So I ask you to swear on this Holy Bible that you have indeed driven the amount of miles you have stated to me." Michael's hand was on the book. "I swear on this book." A short nod on the other side of the wicket was the answer. "Very well; here is your license." He signed and stamped the document and handed it to Michael. He thanked the employee, paid the fee, and left. He had just cleared yet another set of hurdles, as now he had a driver's license! If only all hurdles would be that easy!

He found that communication was the biggest hurdle. At times he missed his family, his father's biting remarks about politics, his mother's calming voice and the happy chatter of Martine. He wrote to them and included pictures he had taken. Rose's letters were sporadic. More than once he had noticed that she had not answered to questions in his letters, and she described just what she was doing. It was puzzling to him how difficult it was to stay in touch. Was it the distance, or were they simply drifting apart? She still wrote at the end of her notes "I miss you so much." It sounded sincere, but he found it difficult to understand that she did not seem to find it necessary to reply to his letters. The last communication had been a Christmas card. The ending sounded painful and sad. "It has been lonely. You are a friend I miss, and I hope it is not a bother to you that I write a note to you." He shook his head. She had never been a bother; he loved it when he received any news from her at all, but the letters had become less and less frequent. He felt that they were losing each other. He did not know why this had to be, and it hurt.

Work in the meantime had become familiar and easy. One morning Simon's dad asked him to come over to his office. He wanted to discuss an idea with him. Michael wondered whether his work was to his satisfaction, and he laughed his big laugh. "Look, Michael, you are actually too gifted to be stuck with the work you are doing." He suggested to him to further upgrade his training. The step to become a structural engineer would not be impossible. He had all the practical experience already. There were day or evening courses. Wouldn't he want to continue? He still could work part time at the office, maybe putting in a few extra hours with the same salary. Michael's thoughts were racing. He had just been thrown a lifesaver. His job was secure, and he had saved money. Would it work? Simon's father nodded an encouragement. He should consider it. And if he was in a pinch for a meal, he was always welcome to join them. It did not take much to convince Michael. Tony, his landlord, understood that his career as a delivery driver in the evening was over. For Michael it meant that he was going back to school and to studying. He still worked four days a week, putting in extra hours. During two days he sat in lectures. On some evenings he had some additional courses, and he also had to study. Sometimes the evenings were long and extended into the early morning hours. He opened the window to his room to let the cold air in and put his feet into a bucket of cold water to stay awake. It was a grueling schedule, but he persisted. He wrote more letters to his parents and to Rose. There was always a reply from his parents, but the only note he had received from Rose was a birthday card. It was hurting him to see a friendship come to an end like a tiny, flickering flame on the Christmas tree that had finally stopped flickering and went out.

Contrary to this personal disappointment his courses were successful, and the highlight was the receipt of his engineering certificate. He felt like he finally had an extra set of wings to spread out and to soar. Now he finally could afford to take some time off on weekends. Simon, Simon's sister Sarah, some other friends and he went to the parks. They played ball, took a picnic, walked by the lakeshore, and enjoyed the early spring sunshine. They called it "spring fever". Winter had been a long five months, and a Sunday out was a day of golden freedom. Sarah was usually a cheerful spirit, but lately she had been subdued and quiet. A close girl friend of hers had recently moved far away to the West Coast. She had hoped to maintain the close friendship they had enjoyed, but for some or other reason it fizzled out. It was a sober realization that one-sided friendships were not working. Michael tried to comfort her. He told her that he had a similar experience with a girl in Germany. She smiled a sad smile and nodded. In some ways she was similar to Rose with her even-tempered disposition. But from her appearance she was a striking mix: she had her father's dark blond hair and the dark, expressive eyes of her mother, different from Rose's golden blond hair and cornflower-blue eyes. She was almost twenty, studying to become an art teacher, and she enjoyed her classes. She planned to graduate next year.

Over time she and Michael spent some of their free time together. They went for walks and talked endlessly about their past experiences, his life back in Germany, and her life in Canada. He laughed when he reminded her that her brother had called her a crybaby when she was five and told her about the trip in the cargo truck. She remembered that journey, but she laughed out loud, when he told her about Menzinger's beer that had put her to sleep and stopped her from crying and fussing during the trip in the truck. This was a story she did not remember! He turned to her and laughed back: "You are not a crybaby now. I love it the way you laugh!" She smiled at him. "And I love it when you make me laugh!" He had kissed her, and she had kissed him back. It became a summer they would remember. They went to dances together, and he walked her home. Her parents liked Michael. He had been almost like one of their family since his arrival. They went out and watched the occasional movie together, and in the dark of the movie house they sat close together, their arms around each other. Summer slipped into fall. One day they walked in the warm fall sunshine. The leaves were turning color in the brilliant shades of orange, yellow, and the darkest red. She admired the colors and wanted to take the landscape as a model for an aquarelle picture she was planning to do in art college. They were sitting between the tall grasses away from a trail of a conservation area. He took her into his arms. "You are all the color I want in my life. I love your pictures, but most of all I love you, Sarah." They lay on the bed of dry leaves in a passionate embrace, her body close to his, both wrapped in a symphony of orange, red, and yellow fall colors with the brilliant blue fall sky above them. Like in a dream they got up, and walked back. The late afternoon turned into a crisp evening, and they stood in their sheltering embrace in front of the door for a long time before they parted. Winter announced itself with frosty days. Michael and Sarah met at her parents' home; they spent their Sundays together with the family. Often they escaped for a quiet walk in the neighborhood. He held her and sheltered her in his winter parka. They were warm together despite the colder weather, and their loving embraces made them forget that it was winter. It was like the colorful, passionate fall day was still surrounding them.

Hanukkah and Christmas were coming closer. Darkness came early, and colorful store decorations and twinkling lights announced the upcoming holidays. After work Michael went through the shopping area close to his work place. He had already bought small gifts for Simon and his parents, and he was thinking of a special gift for Sarah. He wanted to give her a ring, a small diamond with her birthstone and could hardly wait to see her eyes, when she opened the box!

One evening Michael was at his small place relaxing and listening to the radio, when somebody knocked at the door. He stood in surprise to see Sarah. She had never come to his place before. This was later after her classes were finished.
She held a rolled up canvas in her hand. "Michael, I simply had to come by after classes. I just finished the painting I talked about a while back in fall. Remember?" She gave the rolled up tube to

him. "It is for you, because you were part of that day and part of that picture." He embraced her and unrolled her artwork, a brilliant aquarelle of fall in a forest, breathtakingly beautiful in its colors. His thoughts went back to the afternoon of them lying between the tall grasses in the fallen leaves. It all came back, a passionate feeling that had yet been unfulfilled. He could not let her go. She whispered:" I'm still dreaming of that day, Michael." He saw her face, her yearning for him, for more than the passionate embrace on the dry leaves. She saw his want for her, the same feeling that was pulling them together like a powerful current. Like in a dream they went to the bed, their hands caressing each other. Except this was not a dream. It was not the symphony of colorful fall leaves and warm fall sunshine, just their bodies in the symphony of making love and the heat of their desire that finally was fulfilled.

After a long time he released her from his arms. She smiled, a loving, warm smile, full of happiness. "I hate to leave, but I have to make it home." She put on her winter jacket. He got dressed, and they walked together to the tram stop. He gave her another kiss. It was hard for him to say good-bye. "When do I see you again?" She smiled her tender smile that held a promise. "I'll come to your place tomorrow after evening class." He went back to his place. The bed was still warm from the warmth of their bodies, and he went to sleep.

The next day brought work with its usual demands, and after work he went home, feverishly waiting for her. It had been after eight yesterday when she arrived. Now it was nine. Any sound made him wonder and listen closer, whether she was coming up the stairs. No, he was wrong. Tony, his landlord knocked at his door at ten o' clock. "Sorry, Michael, there is a phone call for you." He went with him. He had to think that this could be Sarah; maybe she was not able to come over, as it was late. The radio was playing in the living room; Jadwiga was doing some needlework, smiled at him, and invited him in. Simon was at the other end of the line. "Michael, is Sarah at your place? We are a bit concerned because it has started to snow." Michael took a deep breath. He told Simon that she had been at his place the evening before. "No, Simon, she wanted to come after classes today, but she has not arrived here. I thought it was she who was calling." He picked up on the worried note in Simon's voice. "Would you please call me, once she is home? You got me concerned now too." Simon reassured him: "Yes, I will, Michael. Talk to you later." The line clicked. Michael apologized for the late phone call, but Tony and his wife were unconcerned: "Don't worry, we are awake anyways." They stayed up long. It was a long day, and he fell asleep to the hypnotizing ticking of his clock.

He felt like a diver surfacing from the depth, when a loud knock on his door made him jump up. "Michael! Telephone for you." Tony's voice had a disconcerting urgency to it. He hurried out of bed, grabbing his clothes and quickly glanced at the clock. It was just past midnight. Tony was still in his day clothes. He was a night owl. Michael picked up the receiver. He heard Simon's choked voice. "Oh Michael…it's about Sarah. Michael, I can't…" He heard a heart-wrenching sob from his friend. "Sarah is dead!" His world seemed to shake and then disintegrate. He clenched the phone cord in his fist and held on to the table. His voice was part gasp, part a cry like from a tortured animal. "No!" His landlord looked over, alarm in his eyes. He grabbed a chair for him, and Michael sat down heavily. "What? When? Where are you, Simon?" His friend was crying and could barely speak: "A drunk driver hit her, when she walked from her evening class to the bus stop. We are all at St. Michael's Hospital." Michael's voice broke. "I am coming right now. I get a taxi." He felt Tony's hand on his shoulder. "No taxi. I'll drive you." Jadwiga looked distraught and close to tears. "Any time you need help Michael, we are there."

Silently the two men drove through the night. Michael went through the emergency department. A nurse escorted him to the small cubicle, where the family was crowded together, Simon, his father, and his mother. They were too shocked to have tears. Arm in arm they stood together looking at Sarah's body. They were all united in their disbelief, anguish, and grief. Mercifully she was not disfigured. Together they walked out into the dark grey wintry pre-dawn.

It was a workday. Michael went through the motions of work like walking through fog. Only willpower held him up. Simon's dad looked at him and told him to go home early. They all could not cope with more. It was exhaustion that allowed them some sleep. The next days had nightmarish qualities: the flowers that filled the room, friends that came to call, the burial, the Shiva, the condolences, concerned faces, and sympathetic voices. And ten days later the holidays started. They could remember, they could celebrate a life that had been much too short, but they could not see the happiness of previous holidays. They lit the candles on the Menorah and later on the Christmas tree. Sarah would have wanted to see the candles being lit. Looking at the flickering lights they had to think of light, of hope, but they sat together in the dull darkness that enveloped them emotionally. Joy had united them in previous years during the holidays, but now they held together in mourning. New Year's was somber and quiet. Michael did not feel like celebrating his birthday and could not bring himself to write to his family overseas. He did not want to burden them, and they did not know about his love, Sarah. He wanted to tell them at Christmas, but this was now a shattered dream. The ring he had bought was lying in its heart shaped velvet box in his dresser. He could not look at it, and he could not bear to keep it. One day he walked to the jeweler's store to return it. The jeweler looked at him questioningly. "I would need a bill for the return." Michael shook his head. "I'm sorry, I did not keep it." His voice broke. "I cannot use it. My girlfriend, who would have been the recipient of this gift, was killed in an accident before Christmas." The shopkeeper's face showed shock and sorrow. He probably did not hear that too often. He took the ring back and refunded the money. Michael put the bills into his wallet, anonymous bills in company with other anonymous bills. They did not remind him of the ring.

First he could not bear to look at Sarah's aquarelle and wanted to put the picture away in a closet. But later he decided to hang up the artwork above his bed. It was like a shrine of remembrance for him, as he had nothing else. Winter slipped into the days of grey clouds and melting slow. Snow was no longer the soft, forgiving cover of trees. The stark, bare shapes in the monochromatic landscape reflected what Michael and the Hoffer's felt inside. The light and the color had vanished and given way to a harsh, unforgiving reality.

Spring arrived. They went to enjoy the outdoors. It seemed to get easier except for Michael. Dutifully and punctually he went to work, but life had become empty, cold and hopeless. One day he decided to walk to the lake. He hoped that the soothing lapping of the waves would be a source of serenity to calm his mind. Automatically he walked up to the pier and sat down. He looked at the almost hypnotizing lapping of the waves and noticed the stillness around. But the stillness did not feel calming. Today it felt like death. The water was deep and still winter-cold. It would be so easy to simply slide into the depth, and it would not take long. With a start he realized what he was doing. No, he had survived so much in the past! His life was not finished. It was like he would be throwing out an uncut precious stone, a gift that he had been given. He almost ran, leaving the pier and the lake behind. Now he was scared and horrified of what he might do. And he had not been scared often in his life. The realization came to him that he needed to talk to his friend. There was nobody else he could confide in. He took the tram and went to the Hoffer's place. Simon was home. He was engrossed in reading a new book, which he quickly put away, when he saw the expression in his friend's face. Simon's eyes were somber with worry. "Michael, something terrible has happened to you. It shows in your face, and I feel it. Please, let's talk about it." Michael told him about his afternoon, his thoughts on the pier by the lake. Simon listened quietly without interrupting him, before he spoke: "Michael, I know what went through your mind, but you cannot do that. You still have our family here and your family across the ocean. Together we can get through this time. Remember? We are survivors, and this has been a gift to both of us. We need to talk some more, anytime you want. I don't care whether you call me at three in the morning. Promise?" He nodded: "Yes, Simon, I promise". Later in the evening he went back to his room. Simon, his faithful friend, had reminded him about the gift of having survived war and hardship.

 The face of Josef Menzinger, the farmer in his old home town, appeared in front of his inner eye, and he remembered the one sentence he had said to him, when they did not know about Simon's future: "Living is about the courage to trust and carry on." This was a powerful reminder: courage…trust…carry on. He remembered his family, and he felt a longing for all of them; and there was Rose. She was still in his heart, his friend, his first love, a love that had just started before he left. It did not have a chance to grow. He felt the anguish about this loss and the other losses in his life. Despite the fact that he had not heard from her, he decided to write one final note. He told her about his life, that life had been a trying stretch of ups and downs. It was his work that was holding him up, but he described that his friend Sarah had died, and that it was a blow that had made the year dark and sad. He wanted Rose to know that he wished her well for this new year, hopefully a better year than the year he was having. He also asked in this letter whether she had received any of his letters, as he never got an answer to them, and he found it puzzling.

 The year 1955 seemed to be a year of trials. Even though the area around showed signs of growth and new affluence after the war and Michael's parents found that life had become easier, not all was well. Louise Laumann was accompanying Martin to the doctor. He had been feeling unwell, and this had been going on for a while. They were sent to the hospital for blood tests. The news was devastating to them. Martin had received a diagnosis of leukemia. The doctor mentioned that the type of disease he had would generally respond well to treatment, but he could not predict the long-term outlook and was guarded. The word "cancer" was a threat, no matter what. They would both fight, but they did not know the outcome. And Martine was just nine years old! She needed her father.

One day they received a letter from Martine's teacher in the mail. The teacher wrote that Martine was a seriously disturbed and violent child. Louise was incredulous when she read the teacher' note. Martine had never been violent to anybody. She was temperamental and talkative, but violent? They had to address the problem. The teacher invited them into the office and reported to them what had happened. A boy in a higher grade, who was the son of the principal, apparently teased Martine during recess in the classroom, and a group of kids laughed and made fun of the situation. She was furious and hit the boy over the head with a ruler. The boy screamed and had a big blue mark on his head. The teacher commented that she did not witness the incident. Louise was thinking and spoke up. Why wouldn't the teacher get the two students and ask them what exactly had transpired? They stood there, an eleven year-old boy, indifferent, with a smirk on his face, with his hands in his pockets and nine year- old Martine, her face angry and her arms defiantly crossed in front of her. The story unfolded. He admitted that he had taken away her crayons, broken them and thrown them into the garbage can. It was just a joke. She had been upset, cried, and called him a mean, bad boy. The teacher asked what happened next. Martine's face was contorted with rage. "First he broke my crayons, and I can't use them anymore. And my dad and mom don't have so much money that we can buy new stuff all the time! Yes, it is true that I called him a mean and rotten boy. Next he called me a bunch of bad names like a mishap, a stupid French bastard, and a fatherless brat." The children in the room laughed, and she had taken the next available thing, a ruler, and hit him over the head once. There was shocked silence from the side of the adults. The teacher remarked: "So, this boy called you names, and this got you angry?" Martine had tears in her eyes and nodded. "He has said things like that many times before, but I did not say anything. He is saying bad words to me all the time, and now I'm really mad at him." The teacher asked the boy: "Why would you say such ugly things to Martine?" Defiantly he looked back. "It's true, because my dad says so too; that's why I called her like that." The teacher turned to the boy. "Back to your room! We are not finished; I'll see you after school." Martine went back to her classroom too. There was silence. Finally Martin looked up, a hard look on his face. "If you ask me, this boy deserved everything what he got. Too bad that the father of the boy did not get hit over the head, as he seems to be the instigator in this! I'm not condoning the behavior of my daughter though." The teacher's face showed embarrassment. "I'm very sorry. This boy's behavior is shocking and unacceptable." Louise's face was determined. "I refuse to accept that my child is now labeled as disturbed and violent. Knowing the full truth leaves me shocked." She turned to leave. "In my opinion the root of the problem is the behavior of the boy's father. We just heard it that he is the one who put these thoughts into his son's head! It makes it even worse that a man with this attitude is in a leadership position at this school. And I will take it upon myself to go to the school board and file a complaint about this happening. I expect an apology! Have a good morning."

Martine came home when school was over. She was quiet, seemed to be preoccupied and was not her usual bubbly self. Louise knew that her young daughter had questions that would need answers after this incident at school. The prospect of talking about it filled her with some apprehension. What would she tell her? "Something is bothering you, Martine. Is it about school?" The girl nodded seriously. "Yes, but It's something that has to wait till daddy is home. I have to ask him something really important."

Louise felt relief. It was probably better that she did not say anything else. If only Martin would come home soon! Martine did her homework and looked out of the window, waiting for her father to come home from work. Martin arrived and sat down with his evening paper, but he did not have a chance to read it. Martine sat perched on the armrest of his chair, and he looked into two serious, questioning eyes. "Daddy, this boy at school called me a fatherless brat. I'm really angry with him. But you are my dad, aren't you?" Martin put his arm around his daughter. "I know you are angry with him! So, what do you think, Martine? Tell me what makes me your dad!" She looked at him with the deep trust of a child. "Well, I know that you must be my dad! You are always there when Mama or when I need you. Only dads do this. When I was sick, you stayed up in the night and watched me. When I ask you a question, you never say that it is a stupid question. You always have an answer. I remember, when I fell into the pile of stinky stuff, when I broke a branch from a tree. You told me that I did something wrong, but you were not mad at me for a long time, and you built me a swing. If you were not my dad you would have never done that! If I need my scooter fixed, you do it, even if it is evening already and you are tired. You always told me that I'm your little girl and that you love me. Nobody except a mom or a dad would say that." For a moment she had to think. "I believe that dads are also there when their baby is born. You were there when I was born, weren't you?" Martin nodded and smiled at her. "Yes, I remember that day. I was there. You were very small, and when I touched your little hand, you made a fist and grabbed my finger." She giggled happily. The memory was still touching him now, and he had tears in his eyes. "I was happy to say hello to you, our little girl, and your Mama and I have loved you from this minute on." Martine gave him a kiss on his cheek. "Nobody else can ever be like you, daddy. I love you. This dumb boy can fly a kite! Maybe he does not have a good dad like I do, and he is jealous. I know that you are my dad. Nobody else can be it." Martin hugged his daughter tenderly. Her reasoning had been the uncomplicated reasoning of a child. Louise and he had not told her everything about the facts of life yet, but she knew that babies grew in their mommies' tummies and that the father had the seed for the baby to grow. But she did not know anything about the complicated variations fatherhood could take. At one point they would talk about it more. He had to think that in a way she was right with her simple logic. He was the father who loved her, and she knew it with unshakable certainty. This certainty was what she needed right now. At this point in her life any other explanation would be confusing and unsettling to her. For her the father was the person who had always loved her and was there for her and who also loved her mother. The shadowy figure in the orchard had been a biological means to start a life, but this was far removed from being a father who loved and protected his child and the loving bond between them. She would understand the biological aspect later as she was growing up, even though it would be painful and disturbing to hear about the beginning of her life. Louise sat down beside them, and Martin put his other arm around her. His two girls! Both of them were a blessing in his life. His life would not be fulfilled without them.

The school incident was behind them, but they did not want their daughter to be exposed to more harassment. They went and filed a complaint. After a while an apologetic, rather generic letter was in their mailbox, more a symbolic act, but not an apology that sounded sincere. The boy who had loudly called her names before was now whispering to the children that Martine was a stupid girl, and her parents were dumb people too. Martin and Louise had enough. They decided to send Martine to another school. They had to recover from another blow. It was difficult for them to see an attitude of callous contempt and mean spirited gossip even now. And that was ten years after their initial plight!

Rose walked to her workplace at a nursery school with a heavy heart. The exuberant celebrations of Carnival were over. It had been a time of fun, of dancing, and Thomas, the young man who had befriended her earlier in the year, had taken her to a few dances. She had forgotten about all the grinding daily routines, her father's unsmiling face, and she had tried to forget the fact that she had not had a note from Michael for over a year.

Thomas was a few years older than her and had a way to steal her heart. He was charming, witty and attentive, and she had flourished. It was a feeling of simply being happy after a time of doubts and questions. Michael did not seem to think of her, but here was a good-looking, attentive man, who said that he loved her! Only her stepmother knew about her new relationship. She encouraged her to get out of the house, to enjoy going out dancing, and to have fun. It had been a happy three months of feeling carefree and looking forward to developing a friendship that would grow. They spent the one evening at a dance, but he went with her to his place after that. He kissed her, and she could not help it, but return his kisses and felt his embrace that became more demanding. He said that he loved her, and he wanted her. It was a dizzying, intoxicating feeling, and she cast any other thoughts aside. It was the feeling of being loved that made her fly high. They made love this evening. It was fast, uncomfortable, and anything but loving or beautiful. For her it was a sobering experience, and he shrugged his shoulders indifferently. It did not seem to be his concern that her first time had been a disappointment. This was her problem. He had gotten what he wanted. He mentioned that none of the other girls he knew had ever complained that he was not good in bed. She sadly realized that she was just another one in a lineup of many. After that he called her a few times, but she did not want to go back with him to his room, and his attention seemed to fade into nothing. He stopped calling. Rose met Thomas on the road once, and he nodded to her like she was a stranger. She went to her workplace. The children played, and as she picked up a puppet, which one of the children had thrown into a corner, she felt a keen sense of pain. She had been like a puppet too to a man who had used her and then just lost interest, except he was an adult. It was easier to understand the behavior of a child that got bored with a toy. And she had been stupid enough to be his toy! She was angry with herself, angry at her naivety and gullibility. Soberly she realized that she had not been loved at all. It had been a sorry mix-up between love and lust, and this did not feel good.

One bright spot in her life was a close contact she had kept with one of her colleagues, also a nursery school teacher. Monica had gone to Toronto by invitation of her aunt and found a workplace as a nanny in the house of a lawyer. He was widowed and had eleven-year-old twins, a boy and a girl. Monica, her colleague, was leaving the workplace, as she was getting married and would be moving to another city, and her employer had asked, whether she knew somebody who could take on her work. She recommended her friend, and Rose's mind was made up. She was turning twenty-one this summer. She wanted to apply for a visa, buy a steerage ticket and leave. It had been her wish to leave the country anyways.

Now it was evening, and she came home from work. Olga, her stepmom, greeted her at the door. She handed an envelope to Rose. She was puzzled, when Olga told her that she had found the envelope when she cleaned up the bedside table drawer of Rose's father. Rose's hands were trembling when she saw the name of the sender. This letter came from Michael. But the stamp bore a date, which went several months back. A sudden suspicion assailed her. She tore open the envelope and read. The final question in Michael's letter confirmed her suspicion. Over time he had written many letters to her, and she realized that it was her father who had intercepted them. She never received any of them. Hot fury boiled in her. Her father had deceived her, and another man had used her. This was too much! She was not going to take any more abuse! She was short and terse with her statement, when she talked to her father: "You have withheld letters from me, and I'm not taking this any more. I'm leaving." Scornfully he laughed: "Sure!

Not before you have my consent. I'm still your father." Her voice sounded calm but determined: "I won't need your consent much longer. This has been like doing time. I'll be twenty-one soon!" She went out of the room leaving him alone with his thoughts. The same evening she wrote a letter to Michael and told him about her own plans, a concise, factual letter. She was hesitant to even think about any feelings that he might still have for her. After reading his letter she knew that there had been a friend by the name Sarah, and she wondered what she had been to him. He had moved on with his life. Probably she, Rose, had receded into the distance, just a pretty picture from way back, but nothing more. It was painful to accept the end of a friendship. The only thing she wanted to do now was move forward with her plans and get away from a place that held too many painful memories for her.

Six

Love Built And Trust Destroyed

A Bridge for Rose. Simon's Disappointment - 1955 to 1961

The end of May had all the signs of spring slipping into summer, bright and sunny. Michael joined Simon and his parents on Sundays. They were united as a new family, holding together, carrying on, and trying to come to terms with the aching gap that Sarah's death had left behind. Overall it seemed like they were recovering gradually. It took time, but they had always been a family that could face adversity and carry on in difficult times.

One evening after work, Michael went home. The familiar airmail envelope was in his mail slot with the handwriting of his mother, and the connection comforted him. He sat down to read, but after a few lines he put down the letter. The writing became blurry in front of him. He was too stunned to grasp it all. His dad had been diagnosed with leukemia, and the future was uncertain. He had to think about his mother and his sister. They had lived through difficulties and deprivation together in the past, but now he felt the painful cleft of being on another continent. He felt helpless, and at the same time he grieved about all those who death had taken away: there was the neighbor woman and the helpless little boy that he could not save. He had not been there, when his parents had been attacked, he had witnessed the horrifying death of his friend Peter, and he felt the sense of loss and mourning for his love, Sarah. And it did not seem to stop here. It would be only a matter of time, and he would lose his father too. Work was the only distraction, but he worked like an automated device. Restless sleep was barely a reprieve. Simon looked over to him from his desk. He saw that his friend seemed to be getting more taciturn, and he looked tired. He was silent during the lunch break, and Simon decided to let him talk. "Michael?" Michael looked up and saw deep concern in his friend's face. "Michael, I'm worried about you."

Michael sighed. "Yes, I'm worried myself. It's not getting better as I had hoped; it is getting worse. I had a letter from my mother. My dad has been diagnosed with leukemia." They sat together in silence. Simon thought aloud. "What you really need to do is go and see your dad. Not knowing how he is makes it worse for you. And not going and then receiving more bad news would be devastating. It is also important for you to see your mom and your sister. They are having a difficult time. You should go." Michael agreed, but his face had an expression of resignation. "You know, Simon, you are right in a way. But in my situation it won't work. I have to take the boat. Steerage last time cost me plenty, and even though I am saving like a squirrel before winter, I won't have enough for the trip and time away from work. Yes, and there is the work...you know how much it is. I can't let you down." Simon nodded, seemingly in agreement, but he was having his own thoughts.

On the weekend Simon suggested that Michael should join his family for lunch. Paul Hoffer waited till after lunch, but then he spoke up. "Michael, this year has been hard on all of us, but we know that things are even worse for you. Listen, you cannot carry on the way you do. You work like a horse; you look like sleep has become something from a foreign language dictionary to you. A few hours on Sundays have been all your time off. You are burning the candle on both ends." Michael shook his head. "I can't just stop. You know that I love my work. It has been the one thing that has stopped me from going insane." Simon's mom agreed. "Yes, I do know that work can help. It has been therapeutic for me. But you are dealing with the uncertainty about your dad, which has added even more to the load. Don't wait for more bad news. Go and see your dad and your family. It's important for them and for you." Simon's father went over to him and put his hand on his shoulder. "You are like another son to me. I have to look after you now." He put an envelope on the table in front of him. "Here is a ticket for the trip. I'm not sending you away. Your work will be waiting for you. But go, see your family, walk a bit down memory lane, and start to live again. We need you back here in one piece." Michael stared at the ticket and at Michael's father. "Yes, Dad and Mom Hoffer. I will pay you back." Ruth Hoffer shook her head. "No, you won't! Let us not even talk about that, Michael."

The trip became imminent. He did not travel with a travel chest this time. Michael packed a suitcase with some clothing. He planned to be away for no longer than six weeks. He was all set and ready to leave, when he saw another letter in the mail slot. It was an airmail envelope. He heaved a sigh, hoping that there would not be more bad news about his father, but the handwriting was different. He was stunned to see Rose's writing. Why was she writing now? His last note had been more than three months back, and he had never heard from her. And there was nothing he could do now, as he was getting on his way to the train and next to the boat, which was leaving out of Montreal. After getting settled in his seat on the train he started reading the letter. He realized what had happened over the years. Any communication with her had been actively undermined by Rose's father. In the beginning she had received the very occasional note from him that Olga had found in the mail, and otherwise her father had made it his business to intercept anything he had taken out of the mailbox. As a result she had believed that Michael no longer wanted to communicate with her. It sounded like Rose had made her own plans now. She was determined to leave, and she had a job as a nanny in Toronto.

She was still living at her father's place but was ready to leave as soon as she would be turning twenty-one. Michael stared at the letter. Over the last four years he had lost connection with Rose, the friend he had, and six month ago he had lost Sarah. These two losses caused him so much pain that it was hard to bear. He had to think that fate was cruel.

He boarded the "Fair Sea" on a calm June evening. After his previous experience at sea he was guarded about the trip and cautiously looked at the sky. But there was no cloud, and the ocean was calm. Memories of the raging, howling winds came back making him almost feel queasy to his stomach. There was none of that at all. Some winds blew before they came to the coast near England, but the entire journey had been calm and had only taken seven days in comparison to the ten grueling days at sea four years back.

He boarded a train in the harbor town. It would take him a full day to travel to southern Germany. He did not tell his parents about his arrival, and he made his way through the city that once had been familiar to him. It was gratifying to see that many ruins that the war had left behind were no longer visible. New buildings had sprung up virtually everywhere. Shop windows were nicely decorated, street side cafes were busy, a sign of new affluence and the economic upswing that happened in the country. He read about it in newspapers. They called it the "Economical Miracle" or "Wirtschaftswunder". The country had reaped big benefits from foreign help. The progress was amazing, but it also spoke of an enormous amount of resilience and hard work of the people to get out of the rubble and ashes that the war had left behind. Fewer scars of the war were visible in a city that had seen so much destruction and damage, but he knew that it was the people who were still affected by the memories. Any survivor would have his own scars-small or larger- as a result of the war. The familiar street looked unchanged and yet different. He was used to the wider streets in Toronto. Everything looked so small in comparison to Toronto, almost cramped, with the narrow streets and the houses standing so close together. The houses in the old neighborhood had been painted, and everything looked renewed and fresh.

He put down his suitcase by the door and rang the bell. Fast steps were heard inside, and the door flew open. A young girl with dark auburn hair that she wore in a short ponytail stood rooted in her steps and looked at him curiously. "Micky? How did you get here?" She turned around and shouted excitedly: "Mama, can you please come quick?" Louise approached from the hallway and stood speechless first. "Mother, I came to see all of you. Your letter started it." Martine eyed him thoughtfully. "You promised that you would tell me when you would come back, but you didn't!" He grinned at her and pulled her ponytail. "You have a good memory! But I had no time. My friends told me to get on my trip really quick." They stood together in a big hug, sat in the living room next and talked for hours. Martin Laumann was still in hospital. The last few weeks had been uncertain and precarious. The doctors had doubts whether he would survive. Since a few days they were cautiously optimistic about his condition. Michael planned to visit him the following day. He wondered about the neighbors and heard that Rose was working as a nursery school teacher not far away from this neighborhood. Quietly he decided to go to her workplace. He would see her there, when she got off after work.

On the next day he walked down the sterile, white hospital corridor. His father was resting. He looked at Michael like he was seeing an apparition and sat up. He was weak and his skin color was very pale, but the same spark that Michael remembered was still in his bright, grey eyes. "I never imagined that you would come. It's too far to travel. What happened?" Michael held the hands of his dad. "It's a long story, dad. Mom wrote that you were not well. Mr. Hoffer told me to get going and see you. It was an order. He paid for my steerage. I know that he was right." Martin

Christina Schilling

smiled. He looked tired, but he had the face of a fighter. "It's good that you came, Michael. Tell the Hoffer's how much this means to me. I'll do my best to get better. The rest is up to a higher power." Michael requested to talk to the treating doctor. He explained to him that his father had a form of leukemia that was treatable. He had shown signs of improvement, and the disease could show signs of remission for years. There was no certain cure, but he would be able to live with the condition and be able to control it. It sounded encouraging, and it was a relief for Michael to listen to the doctor's opinion.

Next he made his way to the nursery school. He waited for Rose. She was leaving after the group of children had left and stopped abruptly when she spotted Michael. Slowly they walked towards each other, both unable to say a word. He held her hands. "I had to come and see you. It has been a long time, Rose." Her smile was cautious, subdued, and insecure, as she answered: "Yes, and our lives have been going on." Together they walked beside each other, first in awkward silence. Next they talked, trying to bridge the past with the present and stopped in front of the house where she lived. She looked at him. "I wrote you a letter about my plans. I had enough. You know what my father is like. You may remember that I always wanted to leave, but I couldn't. Finally I can do it." She had just turned twenty-one, and the ship would be leaving in less than a month.

The front door of the house opened. Mr. Kerner, Rose's father, stood and glared at Michael and his daughter. "I thought that you had finally disappeared from here!" Turning to his daughter he yelled: "Get the hell into the house! I never want to see you in the company of this fellow again. You know it!" He wanted to grab her arm, but she pulled away. "Leave me alone! " She stared him down; her young face was now angry, hard, and fiercely determined. "I told you before, that I'm not taking it any more. You have forgotten that I've turned twenty-one a week ago." Michael took her hand. "Maybe we should go, Rose." She walked with him. The last they heard was a furious shout from her father. "You can just go to hell!" Michael turned around and stared at the man. His eyes were like slivers of ice. "After you, Mr. Kerner!" They walked to his parents' place. Rose was crying. Michael's mother listened to Rose's story. She put her arm around the distraught young woman. "You can stay with us, Rose. I never knew how bad it has been for you." It was a bit less spacious in the flat. Martine and Michael shared Martine's room, Rose slept in the living room, but there was peace and no more interference from Rose's father. She went to work. Michael saw his old friends, visited his father, talked with his mother, and together they walked through town. One evening he was at home with Martine. Louise was at the hospital visiting Martin, and they were alone. Martine scurried around in the kitchen and insisted that she was in charge of supper. She wanted to surprise her brother. He noted that the old wood stove had given way to a new gas stove and oven. There was a new fridge in the kitchen and a washing machine in the corner. He had to think back how his mother had to slave over the washtub in the basement in the past and how the search for dry kindling wood had been an ongoing chore. Years had gone by, and progress was making life easier. Amusedly he watched his sister bustling around, setting the table, going out into the garden and getting some flowers, which she put into a vase. It was funny to observe that she was still the little ball of fire that he knew from four years ago, always busy doing something, always having her own ideas. But she also was very competent for her nine and one half years. They sat and consumed a supper of spaghetti and tomato sauce, which she had heated up, and they drank some grape juice that she had found in the root cellar. When they were finished, Michael told her that he and Rose were planning to leave for Canada soon. She looked at him, her eyes serious and full of tears. "This time it is even worse! Rose has told me already that she will be leaving too. Now it's only Mama and I. Daddy is sick in the hospital, and I don't even know when he will come back. It is not fair!" She gesticulated, and her head sank on the dining table. The grape juice bottle took a tumble, and a rivulet of dark red juice ran under the table. Now she was even more upset. "Oh no! What will Mama say? She told me not to make a mess, and now all the juice is gone too!" Michael got up and cleaned up the juice puddle from the floor. Poor Martine! It hurt to see her so unhappy. He sat down beside her and rocked her in his arms. He told her that he would buy another bottle of juice. After all, his announcement of Rose and him leaving had contributed to the mess! He hoped that his next piece of news would comfort her a bit: "Listen, I'll see you again Martine! Please, don't cry so much. And dad will come home from the hospital soon. He is a lot better." Her face brightened up, when she heard that her father was getting better. She looked at Michael with the critical eyes of a child that was able to think about her future. "I saw daddy in the hospital, and it was so bad! There were not many people to take care of him. The nurses had way too much work." She sniffed, wiped her face with her sleeve, and continued emphatically: "I'll be a nurse one day, so I can take care of daddy or other people who are sick. And I really, really want you to come back to see us! Do you promise that?" He smiled. "Yes, for sure, but it will take me some time to save money for another trip. And I will write letters to you. All right?" Eagerly she agreed: "Yes, I can write too, and next year I'll start taking English at school. You just wait! I'll write to you in English!" He was not surprised. He knew how determined his young sister could be. When would he see her and his parents again? It hurt that distance was such a limiting factor.

Rose had arranged for her steerage ticket some time back. It turned out that she as well as Michael would be taking the same ship to Montreal. Quietly she went back to her father's place and quickly packed her few belongings. Her father was out, and Olga, her stepmother, helped her pack the two suitcases. They parted. It was a sad good-bye. The two women hugged. They wanted to stay in touch. Michael stayed at his parents' place, and he was still seeing the homecoming of his father. He was convalescing and it was a brittle balance, but at least he was getting better. On the last day Rose and he went for a walk through the neighborhood. It was a good-bye to the place that was familiar to both, more to her than to him. Cautiously he held Rose's hand, as they were walking. Thoughtfully she looked at him. "We went for a walk four years ago, when you said good-bye." His face was serious. "Yes, it was difficult." She sighed. "It is difficult now. We are still the same people a few years later, but it feels like we have to get to know to each other again." He stood still and put his arms around her. "Rose, if you want it, I still want to be your friend." He saw tears in her eyes. She turned to him, and he saw doubt and profound sadness in her face, as she looked at him. "I don't even know where I stand. You wrote about Sarah. She was your love, and I don't know how I can fit in. I can never replace the person you have lost." He held her in a comforting embrace. "Rose, remember what I said four years ago. I told you then that I carried you out of that burning house in the war, and you were like the little bird that I held close to my heart. I told you then that you would always be close to my heart. We tried writing to each other, and any chance of staying close was undermined. It hurt a lot because I thought that I had lost you. And yet, you have never stopped being in my heart." She nodded under tears: "Yes, I believe that I know what you mean. It has been the same for me." She cried, and he tried to console her, stroking her hair and wiping away her tears with his handkerchief. "We need time, Rose, both of us." Michael's parents and Martine saw them off at the railroad station, and Rose's stepmother had come as well. After the train ride they boarded the large "Fair Sea" in the harbor city. The ship left the coast in the evening dusk. Four days were pleasant and uneventful. For Rose the trip was something new and fascinating; for Michael the trip by boat was more familiar. Michael and her talked about the last years. It was like a bridge that was being built to connect the past with the present. During the next days the sea got choppy, and larger waves made the vessel pitch and roll. Rose was out on the deck, and she found it thrilling to stand outside by the railing. She was watching the churning waves, holding on like being on a wild ride, but after a while the thrill was over, and seasickness took over. Michael comforted her, telling her that he had experienced the same on his trip. He held her head and offered her his handkerchief. She smiled an embarrassed smile: "I'm sorry that I look like a wimp. The way I have been using your handkerchief lately, I owe you two new ones sometime!" He looked at her pensively. "You are not a wimp, Rose." He had to think that she was anything but a wimp. Rose had been struggling for the last four years, fighting the unsupportive attitude of her father and the daily drudgery. Only her stepmother had been steadfastly supporting her to become a nursery school teacher. Her father had told her that it would be a waste and told her to get a job at the local garment factory or find work in a store and make money. During the day she went to college classes, and after classes she cleaned houses, which helped her to pay for her courses. Olga slipped her some money whenever she could manage to do it. She had carried on with the goal of leaving the joyless setting. Olga knew about her plans and supported her. Rose's face had a determined edge, and there was a steely will under her quiet demeanor. Michael also noticed that her blue eyes had lost their trusting expression, and it had been replaced by hurt. He wondered, what had happened in her life. They sat on a bench on the deck watching the sun disappear into the ocean after two days of strong winds were over. They were both silent. Rose broke the silence. "I don't know whether you want to talk about your life. But you wrote about the death of Sarah. It must have been devastating to lose her." He looked up. "No, I can talk about it now, and you should know my story to understand this part of my life." He looked into the distance and told her about the time with her; it had not even been a year. He told her, what she was like, what she loved doing, that art had been her passion. He described the shock of losing her, the mourning and grief of her family, all of that due to a drunk driver just before Christmas.

Rose understood. "This is awfully sad. But it is a great comfort to you that you have been loved so much by her. She must have been a beautiful person. Be grateful for the time you had, Michael." Her comment left him in deep thought. She was right. He had been so fortunate to know Sarah. He had to think that Rose did not look like she had been dealt happiness or love. It was written in her face. He knew about her father's attitude, knew already how much she had struggled to get as far as she had come. But he also had to wonder whether there had been even more abuse and hurt. "Tell me about your life, Rose. It would help me to understand you. What happened to you?" She looked into his face, and he saw pain in her eyes. Haltingly she answered: "I haven't experienced death, but something in me has died, which is my ability to trust. My father has deceived me and made it impossible for me to keep in touch with you. It was Olga, who found your last letter and gave it to me. For years it has been a fight to make my way, but it was worth it. Otherwise I have been used instead of loved. It happened last February. It was a young man, who made friends with me. He said that he loved me, but I was no more than part of his trophy collection. He was just a player, and I was like a toy. At times I'm still angry and mostly angry at myself that I was naïve and stupid." She looked away. "It did not feel good, and it is over, but there is always the thought in the back of my mind, how many other players like that are around. It is a scary thought." Michael calmly took her hand. "Rose, look at me, please." She gave him an insecure, timid smile, and he realized that she was still laboring under the past experience. He continued: "I'm thankful to you that you told me about that. I feel terrible about all you had to go through, and I only know now how much you have been hurt. Yes, I understand you. It will take time for you to trust again. But you need to know one thing about me, Rose: I'm not a player." She felt his kiss, and she did not turn away, but shyly she kissed him back. Quietly they sat together on the bench and looked into the sunset.

After their train trip to Toronto things went very fast. Her girlfriend had asked her to call her after her arrival. She wanted to come, pick her up and bring her to her new workplace. Michael waited with her; he wanted to be certain that the meeting would take place and she would be safely on her way. They had exchanged addresses and telephone numbers earlier, as they wanted to stay in touch now. Rose's friend Monica arrived. There were fast hellos and introductions, and after that the two girls went on their way together. Michael went back to the office. He had sent a telegram before he boarded the ship, telling his friends that he would be back soon. Nobody had expected him to arrive back after being away for just a month. It had been a whirlwind trip. The Hoffer's were happy to see him back. They had missed him, he felt their warm welcome, and he knew that he was back home. This was home for him now. Europe was far away. He told them that his old neighborhood friend had arrived and was working in Toronto as a nanny, and they were pleased for her, having heard the story Michael told them about the difficulties she had endured. It would be a positive change for her. When they heard that she was working in the Forest Hills neighborhood they were impressed. This was a posh area with beautiful homes, and her friend who had worked there before had been pleased with her workplace. Things should be looking up for her.

Rose was quickly familiarizing herself with her new work situation. Her employer was a tall, pleasant and good-looking gentleman who was in his early forties. He appeared very correct and coolly reserved. In a fairly formal fashion he introduced Andrew and Donna, the eleven-year-old twins, to her. The children eyed her curiously. Donna was the one who had a happy smile for her; Andrew appeared guarded and awkwardly shook hands with her. Rose looked at the two siblings that were so very different from each other. The children had their summer vacation, and she was in charge of them during the day. Once school was starting, she would be in charge of getting them ready for school, preparing their lunches, bringing them to school, picking them up from school later, and supervising them with their homework. She was also put in charge of their suppers. Generally her evenings would be free, but at times she might have to stay, when their father had an evening commitment. Rose was confident. She would be able to do her work and hopefully do it well. She had a small room beside the children's rooms with a bed, an armchair and even a radio on a small bookshelf. Her room at home had been a sparse affair with a creaky metal bedstead and a chair. This here was almost luxury! It helped that her friend Monica showed her around for a week. She quickly got to know to the neighborhood places, the corner store, the bus stop, and the children's school.

She took the two to the beach, and they went to the park together. Even rainy days were fun, as Rose did crafts with them. Andrew loved painting. Donna was still the one who easily accepted Rose as the new nanny. Andrew looked at her with caution. He had the same coolly reserved manner as his father. One day he eyed Rose with defiance. She had told him to clean up after his painting. He sulked and stated: "You can't tell me anything. You are not my mom." Rose reminded him, that she was not even old enough to be his mom. She was twenty-one, and he was eleven. He grinned an awkward grin, and her comment seemed to settle him down.

Michael called her after a few days. He wanted to know, how she was doing at her new work place. She told him that she would have an evening off. He came and picked her up, and they took the bus to bring them downtown. They wanted to walk through the shopping area of the city. Rose admired the displays. She was happy to spend an evening out. He told her about his work. Both of them led busy lives, but they enjoyed it to spend time together, even just walking or going to the park. Summer had arrived with hot, humid days, and when they had time off on weekends, they went swimming and took a picnic along. Fall was coming closer. They strolled through farmers' markets or they went out, watched the occasional movie or went dancing. It was an easy and undemanding friendship that they could never develop before. The most important point for them was being able to talk about their lives. It was like an intricate web that bridged the past years with the present. It became also a journey to rediscover each other. They had met in front of Rose's workplace almost being strangers, but they were growing together as friends. Thanksgiving was spent with Michael's friends, and the Hoffer family warmly welcomed Rose. Ruth Hoffer enjoyed it to have another young woman in her circle of friends. Rose celebrated Hanukkah and Christmas with them, and it was like she was getting an adoptive new family. They celebrated the present and they remembered Sarah. Rose had made candles for the family, helped Ruth with the holiday preparations and helped to decorate the house. She had knitted a sweater for Michael, and he gave her a cozy fur hat. They exchanged their gifts in the warmth of the Hoffer's living room. When Michael brought her back to her workplace, he gave her a hug and smiled. "It seems that we want to keep each other warm." She snuggled into his embrace. "Yes, winter is cold here." He pulled her closer. She did not resist, and he kissed her, and his kisses became more passionate. She clasped her hands behind his neck, felt his warmth and saw love and devotion to her in his eyes. "Rose, you are so much more than a friend now." He felt her hold on to him and heard her breathe his name. He kissed her, and she heard him say: "I love you, Rose." She responded to his tenderness and whispered into his ear. "Michael, I love you so much." They did not feel the cold of winter, just the warmth of Christmas and the love that had been growing between them.

Valentine's Day came closer. For Rose it was something new. She did not know much about it, but the children were eager to make Valentine's cards for their friends, and she got swept up in their happy excitement. She and the children were sitting together

Love Built And Trust Destroyed

making cards, when their father came into the room. He watched them as they were laughing together, happily working on their project. They looked like a perfect family. Rose looked up and caught his glance. It was more than just friendly interest, and she blushed uncomfortably. He handed her a bouquet of pink roses, a box of chocolates and a Valentine's card. She thanked him and insisted to share the treats with the family. His smile was benevolent, but the cool expression in his face made it appear less cordial than what he intended it to be. When the children had left the room, he looked at her thoughtfully. "I saw you and the children sit together, and it is wonderful to see how you are caring for them." Rose agreed: "Yes, they both are a joy to look after." She mentioned that Andrew seemed to have more difficulties to accept her presence than his sister Donna. In response he smiled his cool smile. "I think that he should get used to you. I have been thinking about their future. They need a mother. I wanted to propose marriage to you, Rose." She stared at him feeling disconcerted. This could not be true! This man had never shown any sign of affection to her, and she had never been anything more than friendly but professional towards him. It occurred to her that all of this seemed to be like a calculated, unemotional move. She certainly could not see more in him than the person who had hired her to look after his children. He always had been very correct, very formal, and had never displayed any other feelings except a cool, reserved distance. Even in his behavior towards his children he had never come across as a warm and loving father. His face was serious, as he continued. "I can offer you anything a wife would want, security, the carefree life a lady deserves, and you certainly would always be taken care of." Rose looked back at him, silent for a moment, but next she found her voice, answering in the same cool, measured manner. "I feel very honored by your proposal, and I am moved by your generosity. But I have to say no. I cannot make such a commitment, even though I value you as a generous and kind man. I have a friend who loves me, and my heart belongs to him." She smiled at him. "I can be like a big sister to your children, and I am truly fond of them. But I cannot be their mother, and I cannot be your wife." He raised his eyebrows and smiled, somewhat disappointed. "I respect your decision, Rose." She found it incredible, how this man seemed to be devoid of any emotion. This had been like a business proposal. He wanted the best for his children and had offered her financial security in return. It was sobering to see how love and affection did not seem to be part of the equation at all. She felt uneasy. For now she would make sure that the children were happy and knew care and affection, but in time she would have to look for another work situation. Valentine's Day fell on a Thursday, and Michael and Rose were not off work, but Michael picked up Rose after work. The children were at a Valentine's Day party at a friend's place. Michael wanted to take her out for an early dinner in Chinatown, something new and unfamiliar to her. It was still daylight, and they walked through a small neighborhood of comfortable looking older homes that had small tidy front yards and fenced backyards. Rose had never been there before. She admired the area: "It is so nice here. Everything looks so tidy." Michael agreed. He knew the area well and liked it. They stopped in front of an older, white bungalow with a large front porch. "Yes, it's nice here, " he replied. This was the house that his landlord Tony owned. He mentioned to Michael that he wanted to sell, and he was willing to accept a low, very reasonable offer, as it was an older place that needed work.

Michael and Rose walked around the white picket fence to the side, and he put his arm around her. "Would you like to live here? It is an older house, but it could be comfortable with a bit of work." She looked at him, speechless for a moment. He bent over her face and kissed her. "Michael, you mean…" she hesitated, and his kisses stopped her from saying more. He held her in a firm and warm embrace. "Yes Rose, I mean it. I love you! I want us to get married. I don't have a bouquet of roses, I don't have a ring, and I don't even have a Valentine's card, but I wanted to ask you today. Do you want your old friend with an old house?" She held on to him, felt his kisses, and felt his hands that caressed her face. She felt loved, and she had so much love to give. "Yes, oh yes, Michael!" She was laughing and crying at the same time. Then she looked at him with a happy smile. "I have no card for you either, and I almost forgot to give you something for Valentine's Day. I made it. It is nothing fancy, but it's going back to the time, when you gave me your handkerchief when I cried. Next you gave me another one on the ship, when I was seasick. I told you that I owed you two new ones." He looked puzzled and unwrapped the small package. She had embroidered two soft batiste handkerchiefs with his initials. In the corner he saw a tiny embroidered heart. He smiled at her lovingly. "Oh Rose, you have a way to make memories come alive! Let us make memories together for a lifetime." They stood in their warm embrace, as the February breeze ruffled their hair. Next they went to Tony's store. He was still busy with customers. Michael introduced Rose to him and told him that he was interested in buying the house. Tony smiled at them with his big, hearty smile. "This is great news. Congratulations! Let's have a glass of wine on that together." He hung the "Closed" sign on the door of the market and took them to the apartment above the store. "Jadwiga, bring out some glasses and the wine. We have something to celebrate." They sat together and toasted to the future of the new owners of his place and to their life together.

Afterwards Michael and Rose went to his room together. He opened the door and smiled at Rose. "How about celebrating some more, Rose?" She flew into his arms, and he carried her to his bed. With a sense of wonder he realized that the connection between him and her had turned from friendship and tender love into passion that they would finally see fulfilled. She was still his little bird, the girl he had cautiously carried out of the flames so long ago. He wanted to take her along to Canada, when he first left, and it hurt that he could not follow his heart then. Their lives had taken a circuitous route, and yet they had found back to each other. There was no shyness from her. She had waited for him for so long, and she knew how much he loved her, and with this knowledge there was nothing awkward and uncomfortable about her intimacy with him, but a joyful feeling of fulfillment and happiness. Passionately he gave himself over to his desire for her and a love that he had carried within himself for years. He had thought that he had lost her, but now he felt the overpowering joy of finally being one with her. They got married on a bright spring day, and the wedding celebration was in the backyard of the Hoffer's. Their friends had gathered for a party, and they went to Niagara Falls afterwards for a few days. Rose's stepmother sent them a parcel with a tablecloth and serviettes she had made herself. To their surprise her father had made a wooden serving tray for them. It was beautifully done like he had put his heart into it, but he was still the same man who struggled with words and emotions. All he had managed to write was a "Congratulations!" at the end of Olga's letter. Michael's parents sent a parcel with flatware, and Martine made them a picture. It was a beautiful painting of a vase with summer flowers, unbelievably mature for a girl that was just over ten years old. Michael shook his head in surprise: she did not have her artistic gift from her mother; his sister was so very different! They felt the love of their parents from a distance, a bittersweet note to their happiness. Distance could hurt, but for Michael it was a comfort that he had seen his father when he had been so ill, and he felt thankful about his recovery. They had received a letter telling them that Martin's illness was now in remission.

During the celebration some of the Hoffer's relatives were present as well. They were a cheerful, talkative group. One of Simon's aunts, a sister of his mother, joked with Simon that he would be the next one to tie the knot, but Simon waved away her suggestion. "No rush, Aunt Miriam! In time I'll find that special someone." She teased him some more: "Well, you cannot expect her to be delivered to your doorstep." He laughed and shook his head. His aunt was always outspoken and direct, and good-naturedly he put up with her joking remarks.

Time flew by for Michael and Simon during the busy days at work. After a while Rose found a work place at a nearby daycare center, which was closer to her home. After work Michael and Rose worked together on their house. It was a lot of work to renovate the old house, but as they fixed it up and repainted it inside and out, it became their comfortable, cozy home, which they enjoyed. Summer evenings on the new front porch that Michael had built, or barbecues in the backyard became social gathering spots for them and their friends. Their happiness was complete, when their little son Christopher was born two years later. Michael and Rose asked Simon to be his godfather, and Simon was thrilled. He mentioned that at one point he hoped to have his own family, but for now he doted on his new godson and was happy to watch over him when his parents needed a few hours off.

Simon found a small apartment close to his workplace. He needed his own space, and he enjoyed his privacy. One Sunday, when he was visiting at his parents' home, his aunt and her husband were visiting there as well. Aunt Miriam seemed to have an ability to remember old topics, even if they were going quite a while back. She turned to her nephew. "Simon, you have to listen to me! I told you some time back that nice girls are not just appearing at your doorstep, but I think there is a very nice young lady that you should meet. She is the daughter of my best friend. Her name is Stella." Simon was mildly interested. If his aunt thought that she was a nice girl, why not? Sometimes it was best to humor a person. An evening out could be fun, and he was open to meet new friends, male or female. "What can you tell me about her?" He smiled at his excitable aunt. She was really in her element now and described the young lady. She was vivacious, very sociable, loved to go out, came from a prominent family, and was the only daughter. His aunt enthusiastically continued: "Oh, and not enough that she comes from a family with lots of money! She is also a sight to behold. What a beauty!" With her hands she drew the figure of an hourglass in the air. Simon was amused at his aunt. " You are really describing her in glowing colors! I trust your recommendation, auntie! " His aunt invited him as well as his parents to her place. They would meet informally for coffee next Sunday afternoon.

Simon and his parents arrived at the home of his aunt and his uncle. They heard chatter and laughter in the living room and the clinking of glasses. A group of people was sitting together over coffee and drinks, immersed in an animated conversation. Simon only knew his relatives. There were introductions and handshakes. His relatives introduced their friends. "Meet our very good friends, Mr. and Mrs. Morgan and their lovely daughter Stella." Simon looked at a young woman, who gave him a radiant smile. His aunt certainly had been right. She was a very attractive young lady. He looked into the bluest eyes he had ever seen, and her sapphire necklace matched the color of her eyes. Her fair complexion was a striking contrast to her inky black, shoulder long hair. Warmly she clasped his hands and looked at him. "I am so very pleased to meet you, Simon." He smiled at her. "The pleasure is mine as well. It is so nice to meet you, Stella." It sounded like a very formal introduction to him, but his uncle and aunt were more formal and surrounded themselves with more formal, if not classy company than the easy-going Hoffer's.

They started to talk about their daily lives. Stella looked at him with astonishment, when he told her that he was working as an architect together with his father. "Oh, this is so interesting." Her father, an elegantly dressed gentleman, stood close by and listened. Coolly he eyed Simon. He wanted to know more about his work and how the business was doing. As he commented on Simon's work, he seemed to be mainly concerned that it might not be enough work to support a family comfortably. Simon felt annoyed. What a condescending snob! He was not about to give this man an account of his monthly earnings just because he wanted to go out with his daughter! Nevertheless he stayed calm and polite. "I'm doing very well, sir, and this is also work that gives me a lot of satisfaction," he replied evenly. After having been scrutinized by Stella's father once again, he was tempted to ask whether he had passed inspection, but he decided to swallow his remarks. This was not the circle of people he normally felt comfortable in. He invited Stella for an outing the next Sunday, and she was eager to join him. They would discuss during the week where they would be going. She promised to call him. Simon got her phone call a few days later. She sounded chipper and upbeat. Simon suggested a day trip to Niagara Falls. It was a beautiful venue in early summer. Her response was an unenthusiastic sigh, when he suggested leaving early enough in the morning. "Don't even wake me up before ten", was her answer. They settled for a picnic on Toronto Island.

Simon took a picnic basket and borrowed his father's car. He wanted to pick up Stella at her place. She lived in a fashionable apartment overlooking the Don River. She came to the door in a bright, low cut summer dress and high-heeled shoes. She looked like she was going to a party, and it occurred to Simon, that this might not be the most comfortable pair of shoes for the trails on Toronto Island, but she dispelled his concerns. No, she liked these shoes, and she was used to wearing them, but she did not like going on long walks anyways. They took the ferry and walked through the area. Close to the beach they found a picnic area with benches. Simon brought a picnic blanket and everything for a leisurely Sunday lunch. She sat down, making sure that her skirt slipped a bit higher, showing off her shapely legs. Simon observed her quietly. She certainly had her charms, and she also was making every effort to play them up. His smile was a bit ironic when he acknowledged: "Nice legs!" He saw her blue eyes sparkle and observed the flutter of her long black eyelashes. Her voice had a sultry and seductive note. "Yes, and you are even allowed to touch them." He was cautious with his answer: "Not so fast, Stella." A pouty smile was her answer. He felt observed by her. Was he a target or was she just trying to be funny and flirtatious? After lunch they sat back and talked. She was twenty-eight and worked part time at her father's company. Simon wondered about the part time situation. She explained that she did not like to do more work. She had other interests, and she was not in need of any money, as her father supported her. It sounded like she enjoyed it being a lady of leisure. She liked to go golfing and play tennis. Somehow she came from a different part of society than he did. He invited her to a concert by the symphony, but she did not seem to relate to that; so he looked for other entertainment. There was an advertisement for an evening of music from Broadway musicals. He picked her up, and the concert venue was just a bus stop away from her place. As they walked she looked at him disconcertedly. "Where is your car?" He mentioned that he used his father's car for the few times when he could not take the tram or the bus. It helped that he lived close to his workplace, and for him it was a priority to save his money because he planned to buy a house. She made a face. "What if it rains? I just had my hair done, and it will get ruined." He thought that she was making a joke and grinned at her. "It is unlikely today; not a cloud in the sky, and we are not made out of sugar." The concert was enjoyable for him, and she seemed to have had a good time as well. He brought her home to her place. She eyed him with a coquet smile. "Do you want to come up for a drink?" He smiled at her and shook his head. It was late, and he needed to be at work early. Somehow he had the uncomfortable feeling of being a target again. She was nice enough, but he felt that kissing her good night was as far as he wanted to go. She kissed him and tickled him at the nape of his neck with a slight but deliberately seductive touch that gave him goose bumps. "Too bad for you and too bad for me! We are missing all the fun!" She laughed at him with a little silvery laugh, turned around on her heels, and went into the building.

He shared with Michael that he had started to see Stella. Michael listened and had to think about what Simon told him. This young lady seemed to be a real flirt! It sounded like she wanted to move fast-forward with her relationship, faster than his friend was prepared to go. He decided to speak his mind as usual: "Well, pal, she seems to come from a different segment of society, but it's a big world out there. Everybody is different. You are the quiet and cautious sort, and she seems to be the extrovert who wants to have fun!" Thoughtfully he looked at his friend. Simon had never been in a close relationship with a young woman. He had his work, his hobbies, and chasing and seducing girls was simply not on his agenda. He was confident that at one point in time he would find his soul mate. Judging from Simon's description of her, Stella seemed to hardly fit the criteria of a soul mate, even though Simon's aunt had so warmly recommended her to her nephew. He had the uneasy feeling that his friend, who was inexperienced and trusting, could be sailing into troubled waters. He was gentle and kind-hearted, looking for a lasting friendship and ultimately a life partner, whereas she was coming across as refined, cunning, and intent on leading him on. Michael observed: "From what you are telling me though, she seems to like playing a role of the seductress, and she is good at it too. Since your aunt seems to know her, I hate to think that she is a floozy! The way she is acting it sounds to me like she has been around playing the field, and she has her routines with guys. So, watch out for what you are getting yourself into!" Michael paused. He knew that his friend was quiet and private, and he was reluctant to say more, but he did not trust the situation his friend had described to him. He decided to caution him anyways. "Simon, I know, that you don't talk about private matters. So, don't get mad at me now. But here it is: getting the clap or knocking her up isn't anything you need in your life! For heaven's sake buy some protection at a drugstore before you hop into bed with her." Simon shook his head. "I'm glad that you are your direct self, buddy. No, I'm not mad at all. I'm not even sure that I should go that far. I don't know."

Simon and Stella had gone into the main shopping area of the city. It had been her idea. She said that she loved shopping. Simon walked along. Shopping was not a big item on his agenda. He went shopping if he was buying birthday gifts, and he went shopping for Christmas, but shopping for entertainment was not one of his hobbies. Before last Christmas he had bought himself a suit for more formal occasions, and he bought presents for the family. It was interesting to look at the displays at the Eaton's store. She was absorbed with looking through various outfits. With winter approaching she wanted to have clothes to go to parties. She had told Simon that she loved parties. Finally she stepped out in a swingy polka dot skirt with a matching top. She twirled around and smiled. "How is that? Do you like it?" He acknowledged that it suited her well. They went out for lunch together. Simon wondered what her hobbies were. Going to parties was one; going shopping was another one on her list. She liked popular music. Books were not on her list of favorites, but new movies were something she enjoyed. Simon asked her whether she had friends. She had a few girlfriends. They usually went to parties together. She had a number of boyfriends in the past, but she commented that they were humorless or otherwise boring. She hurried to give him a warm glance. "You are different. You are such a nice guy!" The way it came out he was not sure whether it was a put-on or a sincere statement. Later that week he called her, intending to surprise her with a spontaneous invitation for dinner. The phone rang endlessly, and he thought that she was not home. When he was about to give up, somebody picked up the phone. First there was no answer, and the receiver was put down. He heard a murmured conversation on the other end and a male voice. Strange! He just wanted to hang up, when he heard her say a breathless "Hello".

When she recognized his voice, she seemed uncomfortable that he had called. He apologized for disturbing. Immediately she assured him, that he had not disturbed her. He thought that she had company, but in her response she was almost defensive. No, the radio was on, and there was nobody at her place. And she was not really in the mood to go out this evening; she was busy. He wished her a good evening and hung up. All of this was very vague, and he was almost certain that she lied to him, as there was a male voice in the background. Was he just jealous for no reason? After this call he decided to let things cool down a bit, and he did not call her for two weeks. She called him instead. "I have missed you. Are we going out somewhere?" He agreed. This time they went to the movies together. She snuggled up to him, and he put his arm around her. At her place she invited him upstairs, and he went with her. Somehow Michael's warning was in the back of his mind. He had no intention to get more intimate. She offered him a drink, but he just had half of it. They sat together, and she looked at him with her sexy come-hither smile. "You have a way of turning me on, Simon!" He kissed her, and her mouth and her tongue invited and aroused him, but he was on guard. She pouted. "Aren't we going on to the next chapter?" Her voice was sultry, and her eyes had an expectant sparkle. His smile was friendly but determined: "I has been a lovely evening! I had plans to say good night and go home." Again he felt that she was trying to play games with him, trying to nudge him to go further. It showed in her face that she felt like a sore loser, when he was not game to her plan. "You are a coward or a fag", she hissed, when he went to the door after kissing her good night. After that evening he did not feel like calling her. He had no appetite to be on the receiving end for more derogative remarks from her. It seemed that she had her mind set on dragging him into bed. And if things did not go her way she got snarky. After a little more than a week later she was on the phone sounding distressed, tearful and contrite. "I feel so bad about last time. I feel terrible about the things I said! What I said when you left was unacceptable and really mean. Please forgive me, Simon. I don't know what came over me." He decided to let it go. Sometimes people said hurtful things. Maybe she had a bad day. He thought that nobody was perfect, and she also seemed to be truly sorry. All the same he decided to not let his guard down. They spent more Saturdays together, going to movies, going out shopping, going out for lunch. She enjoyed it and was her usual self, lively, talkative, fun loving, flirtatious, and she hung on every word he uttered with interest and undivided attention. She seemed to be genuinely interested in him and enjoyed his company. Every time they met she was very affectionate towards him, and he truly looked forward to their time together.

Winter and time for parties was approaching. She asked him to escort her to one of the parties she wanted to attend. He accepted. It was a Friday night. He came in time to pick her up. She invited him to come upstairs to her apartment. By the looks of it she was just getting ready and opened the door with a towel wrapped around her. Her eyes had the teasing, tempting expression he knew from before, but he did not feel like taking the bait. He eyed her speculatively and wondered about the party. Her answer had a suggestive quality. "We can go now, or we can go later. What is your pleasure?" She emphasized the word "pleasure" with a coy smile. "We are going now," was his determined reply. She heaved a sigh and went to the other room to get dressed. He stayed back and waited, even though she had left the door wide open in a non-verbal invitation for him to come in. She was walking around half naked in full view of him. He had few misgivings about her state of undress, but he did have misgivings that he was quite obviously her target in this strip show. This was not a girl who was harmlessly picking out her clothes to get dressed. She was deliberately posing to tease him some more and push him over the edge. It was exciting and uncomfortable at the same time. For a few moments he watched her, but it felt like he was being dragged into a cheap and tawdry strip joint, and he looked away. This was going under his skin, and he almost felt like walking out. Her seductive behavior was starting to undermine his defenses. In a way he liked her. She was a fun-loving, attractive young woman, however he felt an uneasy undercurrent. For some or the other reason she had been suggestive in her behavior since their first date. He had never slept with a woman, and while he was not indifferent to sex, he wanted to be in love and feel loved first. She was different: it was like she wanted to see how soon she could get him into bed, and it seemed to be not fast enough for her. Was it love, was it desire, or was it just a game for her? If he was honest with himself, he could not say that he truly loved her, but he hoped for love that would grow. Right now it was an attraction that was physical in the first place, and she was the driving force. She was playing with his emotions, intent on taking things a step further. Did she love him? He asked her once, and she laughed her sexy little laugh and told him that she loved to have fun with him. Was she attracted to him and showed it in her flirtatious manner, or what was her motivation? Her behavior puzzled him. He heard her call: "Simon, be a good little boy and call a cab. It's going to get later tonight." The tone of her voice and her remark sounded condescending and irked him. He knew that his short, trim stature and his features made him look younger than his twenty- nine years, but nobody had ever downgraded him to a "little boy". "I'm still a bit taller than you, and I'm not your little boy! But just to humor you I'll call a cab, teacher," he bristled. She laughed her sexy little laugh and found him hilariously funny.

They arrived at the house of one of her friends. In the large, dimly lit room groups of people were talking. Music blared from the stereo. Some couples were slow dancing. She seemed to be well known. Somebody whistled and shouted: "Oh, here comes bella Stella. Hey, who is that good looking new man?" He decided to answer quickly, stopping her from making a comment. "My name is Simon. Leaves me with the question: who was the old man?" An uproarious chorus of laughter from a few men was the answer.

One of them approached him with a glass in his hand. "That depends entirely during which month in which year, my friend! A year ago I was the flavor of the month!" He shook hands with him and gave him a sly wink. "Welcome! Nice to meet you, Simon. I'm Jim, your host. Here, have a drink."

Simon took the drink and joined the group. Any effort of having a conversation was almost drowned out by the music. The host passed more refreshments around. Quickly Simon emptied the glass and accepted the next drink. He noticed that Stella was sidling up to him, wanting to dance. It was not much of a dance, but rather a close embrace to a blues. The room was very warm with the many people socializing and dancing. She moved closer to him, he felt her cheek on his, her hips were sensually grinding against him, and her breasts were tantalizingly close. The host called the guests and invited everybody for snacks and drinks in the kitchen. They went, helped themselves to some nibbles and had a concoction that tasted like a heady, fruity beverage. Thirstily he gulped down a large glass full, and immediately somebody refilled it for him again. This tasted good and was refreshing! But he also noticed that the drinks served at this party were packing a hefty punch, quite different from the occasional glass of wine he was used to have on special occasions, and he noticed that Stella was watching him with a small sardonic smile. Together they sat down in the corner of a couch, and they embraced in the semi dark room. Time became something immaterial, but next she looked at him intently and suggested that they should go back to her place. They called a cab, and he went with her.

At her place they sat on the sofa together, and next she brought two glasses of orange juice with an ample shot of vodka for them. The orange juice without the vodka would have been enough, but he was thirsty and downed the drink anyways. In hindsight he noticed that he had overdone it this evening. The world was floating by in a lazy haze, it was getting later, but nothing really mattered. He put his arm around her, and with a provocatively grinding move she slid on his lap. "We could be changing locations", she breathed and ran her fingers through his hair. They went to her bedroom, and by now any inhibition had been erased. Hurriedly and excitedly he unbuttoned her dress. Her knowing hands unbuckled his belt, moved over his body, and her clever fingers teased and stimulated him to the point of no resistance. He knew that by now he was anything but sober, yet somehow he managed to remember the advice of his friend and took out one of the foil packages he had taken along. She giggled: "Oh, French letters! Gosh, you are so funny! You seem to think of everything, even when you are tipsy!" With playful, little teasing bites she kissed him, and he plunged into her with all the strength of his abstinence. It was over soon, like a blinding light and a shadow afterwards. She looked at him with the eyes of a winner. "Geez, you were a hard nut to crack! It took ages, but you finally came around! After a few drinks you are a wild man!" She laughed with her silvery, little laugh that seemed to tease him and even mock him. Lazily she stretched on the pillows and eyed him speculatively. "Say, are you new at this? That was kind of cute: super keen and totally green! Not bad for starters, and you'll learn fast." He was silent. The remark stung. He thought that she was attracted to him, but she had merely evaluated his performance, and with it came the sobering realization for him that this did not have anything to do with love. Alluringly she stretched out beside him, and with expert, enticing movements her hands went over him, her hair brushing his face, her mouth wanting more, her breasts touching his chest, and in a maddening, intoxicated frenzy that drove him relentlessly he took her again. She was out of breath and pleaded for him to finish. Her next remarks made him feel even more degraded. "Man, you are like an unexplored renewable resource. Are you a virgin or what?" He looked at her, and she saw embarrassment and anger in his face. "Not any more, that's fair to say." His statement sent her into spasms of laughter: "My lucky day, Simon, lover boy! I think I have to find myself some more virgins. A romp with a virgin is so much more fun!" He grimaced. She had toyed with his emotions and just made a joke at his expense. It sounded like she was getting her satisfaction from making new conquests. His initial gut feeling was correct. He had been a target all along, now he had been her prey, and her hunting instinct had finally been satisfied.

Even though he was impaired, he was not so drunk that he did not realize what was happening. She had teased him and toyed with him. Finally she got him where she wanted him to be, and he was merely a sex object to her collection but really nothing else. The words she said to him over time and today came back to him and stung like vicious barbs: coward... fag... a hard nut to crack... super keen and totally green ... not bad for a start... renewable resource...a romp with a virgin... He felt used, disgusted with her, and even more disgusted with himself. Here he was, drunk like a skunk and experimenting with sex like the guy who tried smoking his first cigarette! And his inexperience was a source of amusement for her.

She slid out of bed and put on the stereo. The tinkling music of Floyd Cramer's popular dreamy piano piece "Last Date" played in the background. Normally he thought that it was a nice relaxing piece of music, but today its title had a different connotation. It was like a reminder, ironically fitting and exactly how he felt about the evening. This was his last date with her! In hindsight he should have listened to this music a few months earlier! He grabbed his shirt. It still had a faint scent of her perfume and traces of her lipstick on its collar. What had been exciting a few hours ago was now repulsive to him. Quickly he got up and looked at his watch. It was after three in the morning. The world seemed to be in a blur around him, and his head was heavy, but now he just wanted to get away from this place. Next he reached for his pants and continued to get dressed. Quizzically she looked at him. "Hey, are you serious? You want to leave?" He nodded a yes. She laughed at him. "Party pooper! I thought that you came for a fun sleepover! No pajamas needed and champagne for breakfast!" He looked at her and shook his head. "No thanks, no champagne! I had too much to drink already. Give me some time to get back to being myself."

Love Built And Trust Destroyed

She shrugged her shoulders and gave him a quick, indifferent kiss when he left. He went to the phone in the apartment lobby and called for a taxi. At his place he stripped off his clothes and fell into bed. He hoped that he would feel normal again after sleeping off his drunken stupor.

The jangling of the telephone sounded like a concert of concrete drills in his aching head. He groaned, grabbed the receiver, and he heard the voice of his friend Michael: "Simon, I hate to bother you, but I have to take Rose to the doctor's office. She has been throwing up all day, and she is getting worse. Could you perhaps look after Christopher for a couple of hours?" Michael and Rose told Simon that they were expecting another baby, and Rose seemed to have more problems than with her first pregnancy. Simon looked at his watch. It was close to eleven in the morning. He had slept long enough, but his head was still feeling like it had been used as a ball in a soccer match. He agreed and stumbled out of bed. Quickly he grabbed an aspirin, took a cool shower and made himself a strong coffee. Christopher was fun to look after, and he wanted to help his friends. Michael brought Christopher to Simon's place. It was a bright day in December. Christopher enjoyed himself with the toys that Simon kept for him in a corner of his living room, and after lunch he read him a story and got him ready for his nap. Christopher rubbed his eyes. He put the little boy into his bed and gave him his favorite blanket. His cheerful presence and happy chatter were like an antidote to his brooding thoughts and his heavy head. Last night was the biggest mistake of the past year, actually the dumbest thing he had ever done: getting sloshed first and next getting into the sweaty tangle of sex with a woman who did not even love him. He had looked for love, had been under the rosy illusion that he was finding it, only to discover that yesterday's experience was not an elating fulfillment of love, but rather a sense of emptiness after a body function called sex. That was not what he wanted. And what a waste of time were those last six months! He thought that she was interested in him, attracted to him, and that she liked him, maybe loved him. Was he ever wrong! Usually he thought things through, but certainly not lately. He had been a total idiot!

Soon after a knock at the door startled him. This was too early for Michael and Rose to be back. Stella was at the door. Her face was one big smile. "I had to come by your place for a change; I have never checked it out! Gosh, that was fun with you last night!" He was not sure about the fun, gave her a quick, perfunctionary peck on her cheek, and offered her a coffee. She sat down and moved closer to him. Next she admired his place and walked around. When she opened the bedroom door she saw the sleeping child, scowled, and recoiled.

"What is that? What is the kid doing here?" He mentioned that he was watching his godson. His parents would be back soon.

She made a face. This was obviously not fitting in with her plans. She had envisaged some time alone with him. "Don't tell me that you have fun babysitting! Kids are a pain in the neck! My girlfriend has a kid, and she seems to consist of sticky fingers and a dirty bum." He gave her a straight look. "I always liked children. Hopefully I'll have some of my own one day." She grimaced. "Ugh! Not me, unless I have a fulltime nanny, and I can get them into boarding school next. I just don't like kids." He had to think that a cat would be a better mother than this woman. They did not hear that the bedroom door was quietly pushed open and that Christopher softly padded into the living area, dragging his blanket behind. He let himself fall onto the chaise, curled up beside Simon, shot a distrustful look at Stella and hid his face in Simon's lap.

Michael and Rose were back. Simon introduced Stella to them. Michael noted that Simon's face was unenthusiastic, even depressed. Stella, however, looked at Michael with her radiant smile. "How wonderful to meet you! I heard that you have been friends for a long time. I hope to see more of you." She barely gave Rose a look. Michael acknowledged the greeting and looked unimpressed. Simon watched her reaction. She seemed to crave attention from anything male, single or married, and he was not

Love Built And Trust Destroyed

that important any more. She was off to other pursuits. All her attention had shifted to Michael, and it seemed not to be to her liking that he was totally immune to her charms.

They were preparing to leave, and Rose reminded Christopher to say good-bye: "What do you say before we leave, Chris?" Exuberantly the little boy jumped into Simon's arms: "Bye! Love you, uncle Simon! Thank you for lunch!" With a reproachful glance he eyed Stella, turned away and declared loudly and clearly: "I don't say good-bye to her. She is not nice! She said she does not like kids!" He huffed, put his hands in his pockets and muttered: "And I don't like her!" Michael raised his eyebrows and rolled his eyes: "We'd better get out of here, before we have to listen to more profound words of wisdom!" Michael and Rose left with their little boy.

Out of curiosity Simon asked what Stella's plans were for this evening. She mumbled something about meeting an old friend, but then she was not quite sure... It occurred to him that she was very accomplished at being vague. Why did he not see that before? With a seductive glance at him she attempted to avoid further questions and purred: "We could check out your bedroom now since that kid is gone." For a moment Simon felt a flicker of excitement, but it was like a light that was switched on quickly and immediately off again. It had become only too obvious to him how she was operating: he was redundant when she had somebody else to play with. Right now his services in bed were requested, and otherwise she was on the lookout for new conquests. He recognized how she manipulated him and toyed with him. Not again! The memory of the evening before left him with a bitter taste. He raised his eyebrows. "No, not really. I just got out of the bedroom a few hours ago, and I know what it looks like." Her eyes were cold, when she answered: "Whatever! Suit yourself!" It was obvious that she was angry. Things were definitely not going her way. She grabbed her winter coat and left without a word.

The next Friday evening the Christmas party at his office was taking place. He did not plan on calling her, but she was on the phone again during the week. She sounded upbeat and cheery, and asked whether he would go to another party with her. The call was not something that tempted him. A repeat of the past experience was the last thing he wanted. He mentioned his commitment to be at his office party. Contrary to his expectation her response was very enthusiastic. She was very eager to come, as she found it always so interesting to meet new people! He was not thrilled, and only out of politeness he told her that she could drop in for a while if she really wanted to. He was determined to call it quits with her after that.

She arrived by taxi at the party venue, dressed to impress, in high spirits, and she gave him a close hug. "It is so nice of you to invite me." He felt the awkward necessity to be polite, but he had no plans to be nice on her terms. She floated around the room and talked to everybody. Simon's father observed her from a distance. He had met her before, and he was not too impressed with her. Her interests seemed to be confined to parties, movies and not much else. Watching her mannerism today did not leave a very positive impression with him either. The way she moved about reminded him of a cat on her prowl. She was holding another drink in her hand. Potent liquid refreshments appeared to figure prominently in her social life. She seemed to be something like a social butterfly. So much for the lauds and praises his sister-in-law had sung about this young lady! He was not about to meddle with Simon's private life, but he had the gut feeling that his son was in for a disappointment. On the other hand it was obvious that Simon did not seem to be too smitten with her.

Simon noticed that she appeared inebriated, and it was getting later. He was in an interesting discussion with several of his colleagues, when Stella approached him. "Would you take me home?" Her voice had a husky, tempting note. Michael was standing nearby and observed the reaction of his friend. He looked reluctant, even uncomfortable, and Michael had an idea and stepped closer. "Simon, I have my car here, and I have to take Rose home. She is getting tired. Just stay. I can drive Stella home too. It's not a big distance." He went out and drove Rose to their home. Stella sat beside him. After he brought his wife home he noticed that Stella's eyes were on him, probing and flirtatious. "It is so very thoughtful of you that you are taking me home, and it is great getting to know to you. Simon told me what a wonderful person you are." He nodded and drove on. She was not that drunk, but she was trying to rope him in with her charms. A short look in her direction showed him that this woman was up to her usual tricks, which Simon had told him about. Despite the cold winter day her coat was open to show off her low cut dress, and her skirt was pushed high, to expose her shapely legs and thighs. She could not have been more explicit. Her hand was on his arm in a playful and suggestive fashion. "It's just around the corner from here. You are a great chauffeur!" He parked the car and waited for her to leave. She did not move, but looked at him, seduction in her eyes and in her voice. "Michael, you are absolutely charming and great company. The night is still young. Let's go upstairs for a nightcap." Michael started the engine. She saw icy contempt in his eyes. Turning on the charm was not working here. His voice was ominously quiet. "Maybe you'd better pull down that skirt and button up your coat before you get out of the car. It is kind of chilly out there! And here are some other things you should know: firstly I don't have nightcaps when I drive. Secondly, I believe that you are friends with Simon, and I don't get cozy with my friend's girlfriend. Lastly, I'm married and not interested in nocturnal escapades with you. Quit messing around! Good night!" Her previously coquet smile was gone. She knew that he was looking through her, and she felt defeated. The seductive expression in her eyes was replaced by one of cold hatred. "Bastard", she hissed at him and left.

Michael gunned the car in direction of the party venue and muttered an expletive under his breath. This woman was bad news! He had to let Simon know about it. When he came back to the office party, people were leaving, and he beckoned his friend to come over. "Simon, we need to talk." They sat down in a quiet corner, and Michael relayed his experience with Stella to his friend.

Simon's face was grim. He already knew that his relationship with Stella did not have any future, but he was taken aback, when he heard Michael's story. He looked shocked and embarrassed. "This is just awful! Michael, I'm so sorry that you had to put up with that!" His friend looked at him with understanding and compassion in his eyes. "Simon, don't even apologize for that tramp. Holy smokes, what a bitch! I believe that this Stella-experience has not been great." Simon's face was somber. "What is worse, I have been a total fool; I should have listened to you when you first cautioned me." Michael patted him comfortingly on the shoulder: "Don't take it too hard. There are so many nice girls. You just got a rotten apple on the first try. Better luck next time, pal. She is not worth crying over." Vehemently Simon shook his head: " Right now I've had it with dating, and I don't even feel like a next time. It would take a very special person to make me change my mind."

He decided to call her the next morning, before she had a chance of calling him again. He was through with her and did not feel like being diplomatic or polite. The phone rang for a long time. Finally he heard a male voice answering "Hello". He asked whether Stella was there. The male voice called: "Stella, sweetie, get out of bed! There is some Simon-guy on the phone for you." Simon did not even want to talk to her. His reply was short: "I don't need to talk to her. Just tell her good bye from that Simon-guy, and have fun with your sweetie!" He hung up the receiver with a crash, almost angry that the phone was not broken. It felt like something in him had broken instead; trust was one thing. Tears of anger stung in his eyes, anger at himself, anger at her, but he decided that today he was beyond shedding tears. Any tear would be a waste on this woman!

The holiday season with his family and Michael's family was a breather and a time that restored his equilibrium to some extent, at least superficially. They opened the Laumann's Christmas parcel at Michael's house. It arrived just a day before Hanukkah. Ruth Hoffer unpacked the box of baking that Louise Laumann faithfully sent them each year for the holidays. She laughed and shook her head: "Well, that is different this year! Look at these! Michael, this must be your sister at work. She is the artist in the family!" She emptied a box of gingerbread cookies, and they saw an array of decorated creations that were almost too pretty to eat. It looked like the baker wanted to make sure that everybody got his share without any guesswork. Their names were piped with sugar icing on decorated gingerbread hearts and stars; there were gingerbread Menorahs as well as Christmas trees. Michael spotted some gingerbread figures and burst out laughing. Even without the names in sugar icing it was very obvious, that the cookies bore a likeness to their recipients. Here was a gingerbread-Michael, tall and strong with straight, spiky hair. Rose laughed: she had found her cookie, the gingerbread woman with a perky ponytail, and Christopher excitedly grabbed his little gingerbread boy. The Hoffer family had not been forgotten. Here was the gingerbread version of Paul, standing tall with a fishing rod; there was the gingerbread edition of Ruth with her shoulder length hair, and Simon, shorter and slim with wavy hair. Louise wrote in her letter that she baked the Christmas cake as always but had no say with the Christmas cookies this year. Martine had taken over, and she usually was the one who came up with something different.

Michael grinned: "This is so typically Martine! She always has ideas that nobody else is coming up with." Rose made some mulled cider. They all sat down to enjoy some of the treats. Simon put his gingerbread image and a heart and a star aside. The cookies were too nicely decorated and fun to look at, and he wanted to save them to decorate the tiny Christmas tree that was on his living room table. It was a cheerful afternoon, and anything was welcome to him to create a distance from the past few months. They were a chapter he found hard to put behind himself. It was still like a festering sore for him. He mentioned to his parents that he had stopped seeing Stella. There was no need for embarrassing explanations. They seemed to understand him even without asking any questions. Disappointment was written in his face. His mother tried to console him. "Too bad that we got wrapped in by the warm recommendations of my sister. You did not need that, but it's not the end of the world."

The New Year started with a load of work, and one morning Michael arrived at work looking unwell. In the course of the morning he went to Simon, who took one look at him and told him to go to the hospital. His stomach hurt that he was doubled over with pain. He felt terrible about letting his friend cope with additional work. Later that day Simon received a call from the hospital. Michael had to stay. He needed surgery. It was his appendix that was causing the problem. It seemed that the year 1962 was off to a troubled start. Three days after Michael had been admitted to hospital Simon got news from Rose. She was experiencing difficulties with her pregnancy and had to go to hospital, and there was Christopher. Rose who was usually so calm and equal tempered sounded worried. Simon went and picked up the little boy, and an ambulance arrived to take Rose to the hospital. Simon's parents were spontaneous in their decision to take care of Christopher. He liked to visit at their place and adored "Oma Ruthie" and "Opa Paul". They jumped in as substitute grandparents, and both of them did not mind it. It was a relief for the parents that their little boy was looked after by their friends, where they knew him to be in good, loving hands.

Simon saw his friends in the hospital. Michael had his surgery, found it difficult to sleep on the hard hospital bed and disliked the hospital food with a passion. He asked Simon to bring some of his work along, sat in bed doing rough drafts and calculations, and he complained about wasting his time being cooped up in the hospital. He was counting the days and wanted to go home, but the doctor wanted him to stay for a few more days. Rose was disappointed, as she had hoped that her problems would settle down, but her pregnancy was lost. She faced a small surgery and was apprehensive: "What a mess! And this is only the beginning of the year!" She missed Michael, missed Christopher, and another thought worried her: "I haven't even written to Michael's parents and told them that their parcel arrived. And now I'm stuck here!" Simon calmed her concerns. "Don't even worry! I still have their address, and I'll write to them today. They should know what is going on." He told her that his parents were spoiling Christopher, and that he would bring him for a visit to the hospital. He loved writing letters, but one thought crossed his mind: "Just thinking about writing a note to your folks…there is a bit of a problem. German is not my strength, and my written German is really a bad joke." Rose was confident. "Just write in English. Michael's sister Martine has learnt English in school, she has been in England, and she is really good at it. A while ago she had a pen friend in Ireland. She can translate for her parents, and she loves to write letters." Simon promised that he would send a note. After work he wrote a letter to Michael's family in Germany. He started to write in German. It felt foreign, awkward, and it did not look quite right either. They probably would laugh themselves silly over his blunders, but at least it was an honest attempt. After a few sentences he gave up. He had to think that Rose was right. It was better to write in English to get all the news across. He added a few photos that showed the group celebrating the holidays. This was a bit like throwing a bottle mail into the ocean, except airmail was reliable, and he knew that they would get his note for sure. It was another question however, whether he would get an answer back.

He leaned back and reflected: how many years had passed since he had seen Michael's folks? He still remembered Martin, the tall, quiet man with his acrid remarks and biting humor. Under this rough, unemotional surface was a kind man. Michael was almost a carbon copy of him, his loyal friend who critically looked at everything and did not stand for any nonsense, but despite a biting sense of humor he could show his feelings, and he had a heart of gold. He thought about Louise, the small woman, who was so devoted to her loved ones. She was the caring, warm soul of the family, so quiet and gentle-spoken. And there was Michael's sister, actually his half-sister. Michael mentioned that she was like a different horse in the stable, different in looks and temperament from him and his parents. She did not have the quiet demeanor of Louise but a contagiously bubbly personality and an outgoing disposition. Michael described her as a small ball of fire when she was a little kid, and yet she had taken over Louise caring and warmth. Even though there was no connection by blood, she had always been daddy's girl and was as outspoken and honest as he was, but his sarcasm and biting humor were foreign to her and could bring her to tears. She had seen her father's illness, and she was passionate about wanting to become a nurse ever since she was nine years old. He had seen family pictures at Michael's place. The parents had not changed much over the years, and it was no surprise that his half-sister looked altogether different. She had Louise's short stature, facial shape and nose, but the dark green eyes, the round, soft mouth, and the dark auburn hair were different from her mother's looks. The infectious smile was different from Louise's quiet facial expression. She was a pretty girl who looked more grown up and mature than her sixteen years. But all the differences did not matter. It showed on the photographs that there was a happy and warm connection between father, mother and daughter. They always had been a nice family, when Michael was a young boy, and nothing had changed. They looked like a nice family together now. He enjoyed writing his note, and it would be a bonus to get an answer, but he was probably too optimistic. Never mind; at least he had helped his friends being at ease during their hospital stay by notifying Michael's family far away.

February had to be the grayest and least colorful month of the year with gloomy gray skies, gray clouds, gray roads, drab brownish-gray yards, and depressingly dull gray, dirty remnants of snow everywhere. Simon walked home from the bus stop. Usually it was nice to take a walk home and create a distance from the workday, but not today! He put up the collar of his coat to

Love Built And Trust Destroyed

ward off the cold, damp weather. The display in the small corner store was the only bright color spot in the neighborhood. Bouquets of flowers were standing in the window in large tubs, red roses, pink roses, and other colorful bouquets. Heart shaped balloons, and arrays of colorful cards were on display, but this did not do anything to lift his spirits. It was Valentine's Day, which added a sour note for him. It was just something that kept the florists and other storeowners happy. He had hoped for love last year, and he had experienced a crash landing. Cautiously he stepped on the pavement. Freezing rain had started to coat the sidewalks. It was easy to have a crash landing on the road today, and he was sick and tired of any kind of mishaps. He had to wonder how many Valentine's cards were written that were just hollow statements about a thing called "love". What kind of love? What was real, and what was just something fake with a schmaltzy text and decorated with hearts and flowers? Gosh, he had all the makings today of turning into an ill-tempered cynic. *Stop it, Simon!* But this was easier said than done. He entered his building and looked for mail, expecting the usual assortment of flyers or other useless papers fit for the trashcan. To his surprise he saw an airmail envelope, noting that it came from Michael's family in Germany.

He entered his apartment, kicked off his boots, and made himself a cup of tea that would warm him up after walking through the messy weather. Some music could also help to lift the mood of a bleak February day. He grabbed a recording and put it on the stereo. The first movement of Vivaldi's "Spring" sounded brightly through the room, and the dancing, joyful tune of the violin defied winter, the icy rain and the dismal, joyless day outside. It could not stay like that forever! His glance went over the table to the glass pitcher with water that held three branches from the forsythia bush in front of his building. Three weeks ago he had cut a few small branches. They would burst into bright blossoms within a few weeks, and for fun he had hung the decorated gingerbread-Simon and the heart and a star with his name on the branch. Christmas was long over, of course, and his little Christmas tree was gone, but those funny gingerbread creations were like color spots that still made him smile now. The first small yellow blossoms were just starting to unfurl on one of the branches. Yes, there was life after winter, and also it was impossible to feel down and ill tempered listening to beautiful music like this recording! Next he started to read the letter. A lively picture unfolded as he read. This was like being invited to look at a scene from another continent; it was a warm and cheerful letter, descriptive, and humorous. Michael's sister had penned it down in a clear, tidy handwriting, and she and her parents had signed it. He was changing his mind about this grey February day. He could live without the fuss about Valentine's Day and cheesy cards. This letter was like an infusion of color into the day; it was bright, beautiful, and warm. This was genuine, full of life, and it was the nicest thing that happened to him today. The music from the stereo sounded even more beautiful, uplifting and life affirming now. He would remember this piece! After supper he decided to go back to the corner store, and never mind the freezing rain! He wanted to get a thank you card, as this letter had made his day.

Seven

Simon And Martine

A Bridge With Letters - 1961 to 1963

Letter writing had become a habit for Rose and Michael. Rose was the faster typist, and she enjoyed writing, and Louise and Martin eagerly anticipated the letters. They admired the pictures that had been included with the letter. Here was Christopher, the now three-year-old grandson trying to blow out the candles of his birthday cake. Louise wistfully looked at the picture of the little boy. He looked a bit like Michael had looked when he was small, except the eyes were Rose's eyes. One day she hoped that she could hold him and tell him how much she loved him. It hurt that her little grandson lived so far away across the ocean, but as she looked at the picture of his parents, it filled her with happiness that Michael and Rose had created their lives together and a new life as well. Martine had joined her parents. She sat on the armrest of her father's armchair. Dad read the letter to them. Curiously she looked at the photos. There was a picture of a family picnic at a place called Toronto Island. It looked pretty there, she thought. It showed a middle-aged couple and a young man joining Michael's family on the photograph. Mr. Laumann remembered: of course, here were Michael's good friends, the Hoffer's. They had done so much for Michael, when he had started his new life in Canada.

Martine wrinkled her forehead. She was familiar with photos of Michael and Rose, but she knew so little about the persons on the other picture. Of course her mother had mentioned that Michael had friends. There was the story of Peter, Michael's neighborhood buddy and the heartbreaking story of his death after the war. Also there was Simon who had gone to Canada as a young boy. Thoughtfully she studied the photograph and pointed her finger at the group of strangers. "So, is this the Hoffer family?" Mr. Laumann nodded. "Yes, this has been a long friendship. Here is Michael's friend Simon." His eyes looked far back, as he continued: "Michael helped the family to leave Germany. He arranged for it without our knowledge. They escaped in a cargo truck from Nazi Germany. And Mr. Menzinger's brother Leo was very much part of helping them. He was a truck driver at that time and drove them to the harbor city of Genoa in Italy. They were stowed away in a cargo hold in the truck." They sat in the living room together, and Martine heard the story of the Hoffer's, their trip to the North American continent, their care packages during hard times, their kindness, and the death of their daughter Sarah who had been Michael's sweetheart. Martine listened spellbound. Her glance went back to the photos, and she looked like she was in deep thought. "Life is so strange! This is like a book, and it goes back so many years. I wonder how the story will go on. I hope that it will be happier and not as sad as it has been. You told me about the war. It is hard for me to even imagine a time like this! But I still remember the war ruins here in the neighborhood. Everybody has been through a lot!" There was silence, and the eyes of Louise and Martin met those of their daughter. Louise agreed: "Yes, we have been through a lot. You know some of it, Martine, but there is more to the story. It is not a story that we can tell easily, and it is not a story we could have told you when you were a little girl. You will understand it now, even though it is still very upsetting and disturbing." Martine agreed: "Just tell me; it's better for me to know than not to know." Expectantly she looked at her parents and saw tension in their faces. Her father quietly held her mother's hand. He started: "It goes back to the beginning of your life, Martine. It started differently from what we ever expected. Your mother got pregnant, but I was not the biological father. The man who is your biological father was a French soldier. He forced himself on your mother." Martine's eyes filled with tears. "This is awful! Oh Mama, I feel terrible for you! And it must have been horrible for you, dad." Her father put his arm around her. "It is over, Martine. We don't want to upset you, darling. We love you, and we owe it to you to tell you about this. We should not hide it from you. This too is part of your life." Louise looked at her daughter seriously. "This is now way in the past. We were not the only ones who went through a day like that. You know our friend Marie Menzinger; the same happened to her on the same day. The day was terrible for all of us, yes, Martine. But terror cannot last forever. Horrible things can happen, but we cannot allow them to destroy or to cripple us. Your birth showed us that even out of the worst events in life miracles could emerge. You were born, and for your father and for me it was a day that changed our lives. I will never forget the expression on your father's face, when he first saw you. He cried. He loved you from the moment you were born, and you have been a precious living gift to me." Martine thoughtfully looked at her parents. "I always thought that I was so different from you, but now it all makes sense. And even though I'm different you have always loved me." Martin gave her a hug. "And you always loved me. Your first word was "ba-ba". But next you said "Mama" too, and you always followed her around like a little shadow. It made her so happy!" Her parents held her quietly, and Martine became calmer. She sat beside her parents and embraced them. "All of this does not change anything in my life. You are my dad, you are my mom, and I'm your daughter; I love you so much. You are right! This is hard for you to talk about, and it is not easy for me to hear, but I need to know about my past. I can only thank you now, and I'll thank you on every birthday for having me and being my parents."

The conversation left Martine with many questions. She felt the pain of her mother and father, looking back at a day of terror. She knew that they had a hard time telling her more, and yet she had the feeling that she needed to know about her past. It was like a painting with a blank spot on the canvas, and it meant going back to the beginning of her life.

She thought about Marie Menzinger, her familiar "Auntie Marie" who had gone through the same terrifying experience. She was her mother's good friend who came to help her mother with housecleaning, and Martine often went to the farm to pick up fruit or produce that they did not get from their own garden. Marie Menzinger also did some sewing for her mother or altered Martine's dresses. She quietly decided that she would go and talk to her soon. One of her nurse's uniforms had to be shortened, and it was time to pick it up. She decided to walk to the Menzinger's farm. As always, Marie's hands were busy, this time with needle and thread. She gave Martine a cordial smile: "Here comes my sunshine! You are always there with your big, happy smile, girl!" She looked for Martine's uniform and held it out for her. "There, it's all ready for you. And look at you! You look so grown up! You could pass for eighteen or more." Martine made a face: "Grown up? Five foot one is nothing to brag about! I'm even shorter than my mom!" She always wanted to be taller, but she knew that it was wishful thinking, and only high heels could help. Marie laughed: "You are lucky! You need less fabric for your clothes, and great things come in small packages! There is nothing wrong with you, girl! How old are you now anyways?" She shook her head, when Martine told her that she was going on sixteen. "It's hard to believe; time seems to fly by so fast. I still see you as the girl that loved to make mud pies, catch beetles and fall into manure piles, driving your mother crazy." Martine gave Marie a thoughtful look: "Not everything has changed! I'm still driving my mother crazy at times. I went to England on a student exchange, and she was worried sick. She always worries about me. But I think I know now why she is this way. It's about things during the war."

Simon And Martine

Marie noticed the sudden, serious expression in Martine's eyes. "You seem to be preoccupied today. I haven't seen you like that before", she observed. Martine looked into Marie's face. She saw a calm face, eyes that looked like they had seen joy and grief, and there was a sense of wisdom, peace and warmth around this simple farmer's woman whose lot had been little schooling and a lifetime of hard work in the house and on the field. Martine decided to tell her about the conversation with her parents. She knew about the hardship they had lived through, and it was obvious that this topic was not an easy one. She had heard the beginning, but she needed to know more. What happened in those tumultuous days of the war that was coming to its end? Marie put aside her sewing, and there was understanding in her face. She remarked: "I know that at one point you need answers, and I'm not surprised that you did not hear details from your parents. There is your mother; I know that it's hard for her to talk. She is always so quiet, so proper. She was raised to not even talk about intimate, female things, let alone about that evening and its events! And your father...well, he is a man! Talking about things like that to his daughter will make him uncomfortable." She put her sewing aside and got two glasses of fresh pressed apple cider for herself and Martine. "Let's sit down for a while. I'll tell you the story. You are not a little girl any more but almost a young woman."

And Marie told Martine about the last days in April 1945, about the attacks on people in this town, about the rapes and the injuries by the marauding soldiers. She described the evening, when she met Martin and Louise at the hospital, Martin with injuries after the assault by a soldier, and Louise as distraught and upset as she was after being raped. She told Martine the story she knew from her friend Louise. Three soldiers had prowled around the orchard, where Martine's parents were closing up the chicken coop. The prowlers had stolen two birds, killed them and roasted them over a fire. One of them had caught and attacked her mother; the second one beat up Martin, and a fellow called Jerome forced himself on her mother. It all happened on one evening at the end of

April. In contrast to the sinister happening it had been a beautiful, clear spring evening. Quietly she held Martine's hands. "I know that it's hard to listen to this, girl. But now you know. And I went through the same experience, except there were two soldiers who raped me in the house. Josef was in the barn. He did not hear the commotion in the house and found me later after they had left. At least he was not beaten up like your poor dad, but it took me a while to feel like myself again. I got sick with a venereal disease and I felt like garbage, like an untouchable person, stripped of my dignity as a woman, and I was feeling depressed. And yet I knew that I was loved. Josef was there for me, no matter how bad I felt. And somehow your mother and I helped each other too. We both had the same horrible experience, and we talked together a lot. Yes, we had been violated, but we were not worthless. We were hurt, but in time we would heal. We both sat together and thought about all the good things and the blessings in our lives, and there were so many! We were not cursed, but we were blessed. It was also the belief that good overcomes evil, and that love is stronger than hate that helped us to stand tall and proud. And then your mother had you. Your parents wanted to have more children, but this was not what they had imagined to happen. Nevertheless you were a living gift for your parents. I saw their faces, when they brought you home from the hospital; I never saw them so happy before."

Martine's eyes were somber. "But after being hurt like that it's hard to trust men. My Mama always says so. And to think about sex as being part of love…I don't know what to make of that. Mama says that it's something like the wife's duty and some chore after work. It actually sounds gross and disgusting!" Marie realized that she had to use simple words to tell this almost grown up girl some facts about love and intimacy that her mother could not convey to her. She knew that her friend Louise was mortified to talk about anything female or intimate. She noticed apprehension in Martine's face, and it was up to her to help her to overcome this feeling. "No, Martine, this is different! Sex together with love is neither a chore nor a duty. It's unfortunate that your mother sees it this way. But I believe this goes back to her upbringing, and the rape traumatized her terribly. There is nothing gross or disgusting about physical love and sex. Get these thoughts out of your head! Our bodies are a gift to us, something to treasure and to enjoy. What you heard about was entirely different: this was war; this was violence! Rape was all about owning, despising and abusing an enemy. It was used like a vicious weapon, and it is a crime. Sex as part of love is a beautiful gift between two people who love each other; it is something very special. Love is not about possessing or using somebody and is never violent. Love is about trusting, giving and receiving. You will know it when a man sees you as the most precious gift in his life. He will not possess you, but he will cherish you, and you will know it that you want to be together with this man. He is not a taker, but he is giving himself to you too, and it is worth it waiting for this man. And believe me, your aunt Marie: it is nothing to fear but everything to look forward to. You will grow up some more. You may come across some fellows that are not worth a second look, but one day you will simply know that you are loved and that you want to love with your heart and with your body too. And it will be beautiful." Martine wrinkled her forehead: "Oh, that sounds a lot different than what I thought! My Mama made it sound like the extra thing in a day that she does not like too much. But that is her opinion. What you said makes more sense." Marie sighed: "Oh, your poor mother!" Martine looked thoughtful: "Yes, I guess it goes back to her past! Both of you have survived so much, but for her it seems to be worse. It could be about my dad too. I have never heard him say 'I love you' to her, and he never gives her a kiss or a hug. I love her a lot; but - you know- I cannot do everything the same way as she does it and think the same way she thinks. I am different. Do I make sense?" Marie reassured the girl: "You'll just be yourself, Martine. There is nothing wrong about you being different from your mom. Thankfully you have not seen war and violence. The times now are different, peoples' attitudes have changed since the time when your mom grew up, and you'll grow up and be happy as a woman." The anxious expression in Martine's face was giving way to one of calm and understanding. Marie hoped that her explanation would make a difference for the girl. Quietly they sat together and finished the cider. Finally Martine prepared to leave and gave Marie a hug: "Thank you, auntie Marie. Thank you for telling me about the past and filling in the blanks. And thank you for telling me things my Mama could not tell me." The smile on her face was back. Marie smiled back at her and gave her an affectionate squeeze. "Yes Martine, it's good that we talked. I think it was necessary!"

Martine said good-bye and walked home. She felt more at peace with her past and confident about her future. Marie's words gave her a new sense of what it would be like to be a woman. She had put the truth into simple words, which gave her the assurance that she could be happy instead of feeling apprehensive. It felt good to be almost grown up, and she was grateful to Marie.

Christmas of 1961 was approaching, and Martine and her mom were busy with Christmas baking. Louise had started the tradition of making a Christmas parcel for Michael and Rose several years back, and she and her husband had never forgotten the help of the Hoffer's in the tough times after the war. For Christmas they also included homemade gifts for them in the big parcel. Louise stepped back from the kitchen table. She had finished baking Christmas cakes, and now she watched her daughter.

Martine was taking over the work of making gingerbread cookies this year, but Louise noted with amusement that Martine put her own ideas to work. She had used some of the cookie cutters, but now she was deftly cutting out gingerbread figures with a knife. Louise was curious, as she looked on: "What exactly are you doing here, Martine?" The girl had a cheerful twinkle in her eyes. "Just something different. It's like making Christmas cards out of gingerbread! Everybody will get custom-made cookies this year. What do you think?" She pointed to the figures. Louise shook her head and picked up one of the baked figures. She recognized Martin and herself fashioned in gingerbread dough. She laughed; this was not the first time that Martine surprised her with her ideas: "Seriously, you blow my mind! What will you come up with next?" Martine pointed to an array of gingerbread people that left nothing to guess about the identity of the recipients, and carefully she put on decorations of sugar icing and names as finishing touches on her creations, as she remarked: "Oh, next I'm doing Michael, Rose, Christopher and the Hoffer's! I looked into the photo album to get some details. They'll recognize themselves and will have some fun." Carefully Louise and Martine packed a large cardboard box with the baked items that smelled wonderfully of Christmas, a fragrance of cinnamon, cloves, orange peel, and lemon. Even though it was only early November, they were busy with their Christmas project. It would take six weeks for a parcel to make it to Toronto.

January 1962 sent swirling snowflakes over Southern Germany. Martine came back from the hospital, where she was a student nurse. Footprints by the garden gate told her that the mailman must have delivered some mail. She found the usual assortment of unwanted advertisements. One envelope caught her eye. The stamps showed that it was a letter from Toronto, but the sender's address was different. The clear, almost artistic handwriting was different from Michael's large, edgy letters or Rose's small, light script. She shook her head: she had not seen that before, but the letter was clearly addressed to the Laumann family. Martine went into the house. She felt tired after her ten-hour shift. One of her fellow students called in sick and she had to run a bit faster to keep up with the work. She kicked off her boots and gave her mother a hug. "Hey, I'm home! And I have a letter from Canada.

But I have no clue who is writing to us this time!" Cheerfully she waved the envelope in her hand. Louise sat down with her daughter, and Martin put his newspaper aside and joined them. They were happy to get mail from far away. Except this letter was quite different. It began in labored, faulty German:

"Dear Laumann family,

I wrote my last letter in German over ten years ago. I can still speak the language if I try hard, but it probably sounds funny. In the meantime my written German is not even funny, but terrible. Please forgive me that I continue this letter in English, but I trust that Martine will be a good translator. Rose told me, that she could help."

Martin passed the letter on to his daughter. "Now you have a new job description: nurse and translator! What would we do without you, and what the heck is going on there?" The letter continued in English, and Martine read and translated the news to her parents. Michael was in hospital and needed to have his appendix taken out. He was doing well, but he still had to spend some time in hospital following the surgery. Rose had suffered a miscarriage. She was in hospital too, just on a different ward. The family had received the parcel for Christmas and had been very happy to receive the homemade gifts. The Hoffer's were sending a big thank you as well. They had laughed about the gingerbread people. The delicious treats were almost too nice to eat, but except for a few they had already been eaten at Hanukkah! They all celebrated together, first Hanukkah, the Jewish feast, and Christmas was next. They rang in the New Year, celebrated Michael's birthday, but soon afterwards the medical troubles started. Since Christopher's parents were in the hospital he was taken care of by the Hoffer's.
Simon Hoffer, Michael's friend, had written the letter to the family to keep them informed. Martine looked up from her

reading. Translating English letters was not so bad after all! A few Christmas and Hanukkah photos showed a cheerful group of people enjoying the holidays. She recognized Michael, Rose, and Christopher. They looked like they were having fun, and the Hoffer family looked like such nice people. No wonder that they had been friends for so long! Louise Laumann looked at her daughter and voiced her concerns: "Well, that's a bad start into the year! I guess I hand over the job to you to write an answer. I'm a non-starter with English." She had never learned the language in school, just picked up a few basics when she went over Michael's and Martine's English homework, and she had never traveled out of the country. Martine agreed. This should be fun, a lot more fun than studying some English schoolbooks! It would be nice to keep on practicing a foreign language. It was one of her good subjects at school, and she learned a lot more when she spent a few months in England. She was lucky that she could practice speaking English with two Korean student nurses at work. It was great to have a secret language if they did not want to be overheard! Here was a chance to write a letter. Hopefully she would not make a total hash of it! She sat down and gnawed on her pen. Here was already the first stumbling block: how should she address the writer of this letter? He was a friend of her brother, but she did not know him. Judging from the Christmas picture he looked like a nice guy. Should she start with "Dear Mr. Hoffer" or "Dear Simon"? She took a quick look at the letter. No, he did not look like a stiff, formal, or stuffy individual, and he had finished his letter with an easy informality:

> *"All the best to all of you, and I hope that you can read my scribble. It would be nice to hear from you,*
>
> *Yours Simon."*

Martine settled into the couch corner and started her own letter.

"Dear Simon,

Thank you so much for your long letter. This is Martine, and yes, I can write in English. Don't worry; your handwriting was very easy to read. You should see some of the doctors' handwriting I have to figure out at my work! Now that is scribble! I hope that you will survive reading this letter. It may be full of spelling mistakes, which could leave you with a solid headache. Get out the aspirin, just in case!"

She wrote about her parents' concern for Michael and Rose, their gratitude to the Hoffer's for taking care of Christopher. Next she described how they had celebrated the holidays. She described the winter landscape in front of the living room and that they did not have a white Christmas, but they got enough snow for a dozen white Christmases in January. Next she described her work. She had to work on both Christmas Eve and Christmas Day, but at least she had the evenings off to celebrate with her parents. The student nurses had joined together and sung Christmas carols in the hallways of the hospital during their breaks. She hoped that her brother and sister-in-law would get back home soon. She felt sorry for them, as she knew from her work that hospitals were hardly known as places with cozy beds and wonderful food. When she was done, she looked at her writing with some satisfaction. This was not too hard! She did not even need a dictionary this time. It helped that she had a pen pal from Ireland for the past two years and she was also practicing by writing notes to Rose and Michael. She finished:

"A happy and healthy 1962 to you, and greetings to Michael, Rose, and Christopher. Tell them to stay away from hospitals. I'm only there because it is my work place!"

She had her dad and mom sign their names and thought briefly about the proper ending. What was the right finish here? No, she could not finish with "Love, Martine". This was a guy, and she did not want to give him ideas! What about "yours truly"? That sounded way too stuffy! She decided to add her own touch:

"All the best from the east to the west, Yours Martine (untrained secretary). I hope that I don't get fired!"

Michael and Rose's note arrived a few weeks later. They described the rocky start into the New Year, but in the meantime everybody had recovered again. They described the heavy snowfalls that blanketed Toronto, bringing traffic to a standstill. They wrote a belated thank you for the Christmas gifts. Rose had added a note to Martine. She mentioned that Simon had just received her letter. He had been surprised and happy to get an answer, and he said that it was the nicest thing that happened to him on this day. She closed by adding:

"Simon showed us your letter, and we all laughed about it. Such a fun note! Your English is just fine, and we all agreed that you would make a great secretary. So you are not fired! He said that he wanted to write back to you, and he hopes that you don't mind. Just in case your parents get worried about some guy from Toronto writing letters to you, tell them that we know him as a wonderful person and the best friend anybody could wish for. So you may have a pen pal again- this time from Canada."

Martine looked at this piece of news with surprise: a pen pal from Canada and a guy. Her last pen pal had been a girl from Ireland. But Colleen, her pen pal, stopped writing, as she was too busy with college. So here was a friend of Michael and Rose! Well, why not? But for starters she would write to Rose and ask her a few questions about this Simon Hoffer. She did not mind a new pen pal, but what was he like? She had seen some of the photos, and he looked like a nice person, but she wanted to know more before she ventured into writing letters to some guy. Sure, he was a friend of her brother, but did he also have Michael's caustic humor and direct, acrid remarks that she found at times hard to stomach, or would he hopefully be a bit different? She cringed at the thought of writing to some playboy-type who was out on a girl chasing expedition by airmail. She did not need a jerk like that! He was older than her, but then her brother was older than her, and the age difference was not a communication barrier or something that bothered her. She decided that a note to Rose was necessary, something like a girl-to-girl talk.

Work became busier for Martine. She had to sit exams, and the practical work added long hours to each day. Nevertheless she made time to write her note to her brother and sister-in-law. She received a letter from Rose directly addressed to her. Rose had written a very clear, observant note in which she answered her questions. She understood Martine's concerns and briefly described Simon. He was Michael's best friend, but the two were about as different from each other as day and night. Simon was a nice fellow, over two years younger than Michael, about five feet and seven inches tall, entirely different from Michael's towering six foot and two inch height. He had dark, wavy hair, different from Michael's medium blond, straight hair. Michael was gregarious and boisterous, could be abrupt to those who antagonized him, but underneath he was generous and good-natured. Simon was different: he was quiet, a thinker rather than a talker, and everybody knew him as an equal tempered and friendly individual who never had a bad thing to say about anybody. Under a quiet surface was a warm and loving person. Both of them had the same qualities of being meticulous and honest, and their friendship had been long lasting. Both loved their work and talked about it together, always bouncing around ideas. Simon loved his work as an architect, was artistic, and enjoyed painting and music as his hobbies. Michael was a hands-on guy: he loved fixing things around the house, tinkered around with the car, and did woodwork. Rose mentioned that Simon had met a girl at the recommendation of his aunt, gone out with her for a few months, and this had been a huge disappointment for him. Michael told him that she was a tramp and bad news and to get over it. The experience left him somewhat hurt and very guarded about girls, and he kept to himself. He was not somebody who was a playboy-type at all but was rather on the reserved side, and he did not have any of Michael's biting humor either. Rose described him as a gentle, kind, and trusting individual. She also mentioned that he was a helpful, loyal friend who loved children and a doting godfather to little Christopher. He liked writing, had many interests, and she could see that Martine would enjoy exchanging letters with him.

Martine felt reassured. Rose's description had answered all her questions. She would write letters to a person like him without any misgivings. This could actually be fun, like a bridge across the ocean or a window into another part of the world! She wrote a quick note of thanks to Rose and concluded it by drawing a happy face on the paper and adding:

"Thank you, Rose! It's going to be great to have a new pen pal!"

They had just received another report from the family in Toronto, when Martine's father brought yet another airmail envelope from the mail box. "Next thing we'll run out of writing paper," he grumbled, but it sounded like a good-natured grumble. He furrowed his forehead. "Oh, pardon me! This one is not even for me." He handed it to Martine who was sitting in her favorite couch corner studying her course material. Quizzically she eyed the envelope and opened it. She looked at a card with a printed "Thank You" message and a letter. Why a thank you card? She had to wonder about that, but then she read on and understood. It was a card from Michael's friend Simon. He was thanking her for writing back and describing the life of her family. He described that he as well as Michael were busy with the design of an apartment project. Nevertheless he had made time to go to a concert at O'Keefe Centre, which was a new concert hall in Toronto. He loved going to concerts or theatre plays. He mentioned that winter seemed to be coming to an end. The family loved being outdoors and was looking forward to that time. At the end of the letter she read some questions.

"Michael has told me a lot about your family. It is interesting to know that you are studying nursing, and I'm glad for you that you enjoy it. Which area of nursing do you like best, and what are your hobbies otherwise? I hope that I have not bored you with my letter, and I wanted to let you know, that it has been fun to read yours. No Aspirin needed, by the way! You would make a great secretary. I know from Rose that you enjoy writing letters, and it would be very enjoyable for me to hear from you again,
Yours Simon.
Best regards to your mom and dad as well."

Martine felt the eyes of her father resting on her, and she smiled cheerfully. "Yes, here is another letter! It's from Simon. Just a thank you note for my efforts writing back." She shared the letter with her parents. Her mom looked at her questioningly. "Well, but that doesn't seem to be the end of the conversation?" Martine grinned at her mother. "No, I don't think so either! Easter is coming up, and so I'll write an Easter card! And maybe I wish him and his family a happy Passover at the same time. They seem to celebrate both feasts. Good idea in my opinion! It's double the fun!" Martin groaned and rolled his eyes: "Good grief, Martine! Couldn't you pick somebody else as a pen friend than a man who is almost as old as your brother? You wrote to this Irish girl in the past, but why bother writing to this fellow? Is this a dirty old guy who is getting his jollies from writing mushy, schmaltzy letters to a blushing girl who is having a teenage crush?" Incredulously Martine looked at her father, and next she burst out in tears: "Dad, this sounds really mean! I made it a point to ask Rose, whether he is a nice person or not. You can read what she told me about him, and he is Michael's best friend too!" Quietly sobbing she went to her room.

Her parents stayed behind. For a while they were silent. Next Louise looked at her husband and sighed: "Usually I'm the one who worries, but this time you overdid it, Martin. Now she is really upset". Martin scratched his head: "I just meant to tease her a bit, and she got it the wrong way." He grumbled something unintelligible, went to her room and knocked at the door. "Martine, I think I have to talk to you. I am sorry…" Louise heard her sob: "Okay dad, but don't say things about a dirty old guy, mushy letters, or about me having a crush. It is not true, and it is not nice!" After a while Martine and her father came back into the living room. Louise saw that Martine grabbed a writing pad and a pen. Martin sat back in his armchair and remarked: "Just go ahead and write the card for Easter and that letter. I don't enjoy writing letters, but you seem to like it." Louise looked at her and smiled. "Well, so you are the writer! Rose enjoys your notes too!

You always surprise us with your ideas. What are you going to do next?" Martine had dried her tears, grinned her cheerful grin and replied: "Nothing much! Writing letters to practice English is fun! No worries, I'm just writing letters; I'm not taking off to Canada like Micky! Next I have to hunker down, study, and I have to make it through college alive". With this she continued her letter, and her course material was sitting in a pile on the table in front of her.

It was a foggy November day in 1963. The workload had grown over the last two years, and Michael was still at the office. He quickly called Rose to tell her that he would be later. Simon was sitting at the desk opposite, which was covered with an assortment of blueprints. Even though their workload had increased, Simon had dismissed the idea of hiring additional staff till now. He arrived early and stayed late, and he stated that he did not mind working extra hours. It was a heavy schedule, but he liked his work and after his personal disappointment it was his profession that gave him satisfaction and helped him to forget some of the hurt. Michael observed his friend thoughtfully. Simon had always been the thinker, the one who worked more than the rest, but he saw a shadow of weariness in Simon's face. He was never any different than his quiet, friendly self, but he was more withdrawn, which was different than in the past. Ever since this disappointing relationship with Stella he was quieter and looked more vulnerable. Michael put the papers in a pile on his desk. He was preparing to leave. His friend was still brooding over a project. Michael tapped him on his shoulder. "Maybe it's time for you too to call it a day?" Simon looked up. "It does not matter. I go home, I grab a bite, and I go to sleep. There is not much interesting on TV, and there is no concert at O'Keefe Center. So I may as well stay."

Michael sat down again. He had to talk to Simon. He started to worry about his friend. With his usual direct honesty he told him what he observed. He explained to him why he was concerned about him. He tried to impress on him to make time for himself, to go out, and meet friends. Simon smiled. It was a painful smile. "You mean well, Michael, buddy. You are right, yes; but don't even suggest that I look for another girlfriend! Forget it! Getting hurt once is enough!" He looked determined. "I'll consider dating on the thirty-first of February, and I'll fall in love when hell freezes over!" Michael nodded. "Yes, I do understand you, and that's not what I mean. What you need most is some time off! You work like a machine till the engine starts to cough and sputter. When was your last holiday? There is life after work, and with jet travel our world has become smaller. Maybe a trip would be interesting." This statement got Simon's attention: "I guess you got a point. I have not taken a break for two years. I have to think about that." Michael was not quite finished. "So, will you let me know when you need a break, or would you want a reminder?" Simon rose from his desk. "You are a tough negotiator, man! I'll go home now. And I think that we'll need more staff for the workload before the year is out. You are right; it is getting kind of much. My dad said the same. Yes, I will probably need a reminder when it comes to taking time off. You know how I get all caught up in work. But thank you for looking out for me! You are somebody like a big brother." Michael's glance flew over the desk of his friend, and he spotted an airmail envelope among the pile of papers. He was not aware that there would be any overseas mail to the office, and his curiosity got the upper hand. "Hey, what is that? Overseas clients?" Simon quickly pocketed the envelope. "No, that is just a letter from your sister which I kept." Michael looked at his friend with an expression of surprise. "Oh! Anything the big brother should know about?" Simon wrinkled his forehead. "Uh…yes… maybe." A tiny, almost embarrassed smile crept over his face. "Nothing to worry about, big brother. I'm not playing games or messing around with your sister. We have become something like long distance friends since last year when you and Rose landed in the hospital. Rose asked me to write to your family, and Martine wrote back. That's how it started." Michael understood: "Ah, I see! No worries, Simon; she deserves a friend like you, and you deserve a friend like her. It's all good."

Saying more would have been intrusive. But he found it interesting that more than one and one half years later they were still corresponding with each other. Knowing his friend and having observed his facial expression he wondered whether there was more going on than what met the eye. Michael had the feeling that he had not heard the last of the story yet. Both left the building and walked into the foggy fall evening.

Simon went to his apartment thinking about the conversation he just had with his friend. Michael always had a way to see things the way they were, and he was outspoken, direct, but never hurtful. He should have listened to him before. It would have saved him the disappointment that was still hurting deep inside. Maybe, just maybe he should think about travelling at one point in time. Air travel had become much more popular, and he had never been back to Europe. Somehow he thought of the letters he had been writing to Martine and her letters to him that were turning into a bridge between the two continents. As he arrived home he checked the mailbox. It would be nice to find a note from Martine. Her letters were like small color spots that brightened even a grey, drab day like this one. He shrugged his shoulders. No mail today! She probably was too busy anyways as she had exams coming up soon. He walked up the two flights of stairs and entered his two-room flat. The cozy place was a source of creature comfort for him. He kicked off his shoes, got some leftover Chinese food from the fridge, and put a pot on the stove to have a late supper.

A knock at the door startled him, and he went to open. It was his neighbor, the older lady from across the hallway. She held an envelope in her hand: "Good evening, Simon! The mailman dropped a letter for you into my mail slot by mistake. I just heard you come up the stairs." He thanked her and took the envelope. It

Simon And Martine

was a letter from Martine. His face lit up. The fog of the fall evening seemed to lift as he read the letter, and the world appeared to be a brighter place. Next he sat down and started to write a reply. As he was engrossed in writing, he forgot about his dinner, and the smell of burnt food made him hurry to the kitchen. Normally he would have been a bit annoyed about the mishap in the kitchen, but not today. He tossed the scorched meal into the trashcan and went back to the living area. Dinner could wait. He felt the connection that was reaching across miles of land and ocean. Over time it had become a very close connection, and it felt safe, warm, and comforting. She was such a nice girl, and in the beginning her cheerful letters were like an antidote to feeling down. They infused color into his days, and he admired her descriptive, insightful notes. Next she became a friend, and the age difference did not make any difference. They had so many common interests and understood each other in a way that amazed them both. They were thousands of miles apart, and yet there was a closeness of thoughts and similarity of feelings that bridged distances. Over time their long distance friendship had deepened. After the relationship with Stella he vowed to himself to be on guard with females, but he found himself falling in love with this girl. He observed that it was not a one-sided attraction. It came out in small, cautious remarks in her letters that she liked him. She seemed to be shy, and she was careful to not come across as gushy. He had to smile about their similarity: he did not dare to tell her how much he liked her, as he did not want to come on too strong. Besides, hadn't he just told Michael that he was through with girl friends? And how was that again with hell freezing over first before he would fall in love? He had to shake his head and grin about himself. Hell freezing over was a gradual process, and life was full of surprises.

He wrote about fall, Halloween, and the crowd of children that had come to the door at his parents' house. Also, he described Christopher's Halloween. The boy had been dressed up as a ghost and was very excited. He rummaged in a stack of photographs. Here was a picture of Christopher in his Halloween costume! There was another picture of the entire family and a photo of his parents. He hesitated shortly, but he decided to add a photo of himself. The Laumann's in Germany did not take a lot of photos, and Martine had not sent any recently. But he had seen some pictures at Michael's place that were going back some time. He thought briefly before adding: "This time I'm sending a few pictures, so you'll see the friends of your brother's family too. Our friendship goes back a long time. I would love to have a recent picture of your family, and I hope that I don't come across as too demanding." He mailed the letter the next day. There was a trace of doubt in his mind whether it had been the right thing to do. How would she feel about getting a picture from him? Was he too pushy? He would have liked to have a picture of her, but that could be taken as being intrusive, and he did not ask for one. Instead he rather asked for a picture of the family. He did not want to hurt anybody, and he himself was careful not to get hurt either. Too late now, he thought. The letter was in the mailbox.

A drab, drizzly late fall day was casting its early darkness over the suburban area. Martin Laumann came home from work, got his evening paper, and emptied the mailbox in front of the house. His eyes lit up, when he saw a letter from Rose and Michael. He found another airmail envelope that was addressed to Martine, and he unlocked the door.

Louise saw him come and took the small stack of mail. She raised her eyebrows when she saw the letter addressed to their daughter. Thoughtfully she looked at her husband. "What do you think about this letter writing to Michael's friend in Toronto? This has been going on and on, and he is writing even more often now! This is a fellow who is almost as old as her brother, quite an age difference for a pen pal!" Her husband gave her a reassuring look. "Louise, don't worry; just let her be. So she has a pen pal or maybe a long-distance friend. Friendship between people can jump age differences in unexpected ways. Remember, her best friend has always been Rose, who is also older than her." Louise agreed: "Well, she is going to be eighteen next month, but at times she floors me with her thoughts and strikes me as having an old soul. I guess it comes from having an older brother and older parents. But what is it about this Simon? She is awfully quiet about him." Martin sighed: "We have to accept that she has her own circle of friends and, as we know from Michael and Rose, he is a decent fellow. As far as I'm concerned she is not a child any more that has to share each and every letter with us."

Martine found the letter on the table later. Her face broke into a wide smile. Simon's letters were something she was looking forward to. They could have a dialogue about anything, whether it was about their lives, funny happenings at work or days that had not been going too well. It was surprising to both of them to discover the many things they had in common. They both loved exploring museums and art exhibits and loved going to concerts. It was fun for both of them to listen to pop tunes on the radio. Both were avid readers. In summer they both loved hiking and the outdoors. Both loved painting. She dabbled with pastels and aquarelle after having learned it at art classes a few years back; he liked painting with acrylics and had learned from his artist mother. She described life in Germany to him. He told her about Canadian customs and holidays, and they discussed the similarities of Hanukkah and Christmas and other holidays and their celebrations. Sometimes they regretted that they could not do things together, and he had mentioned that he wanted to take a trip and see her. He had become a very close, special friend to her despite the distance that was between them. She had not expected to receive news from Canada anytime soon as she knew about Simon's busy work schedule. It surprised her that even though he was busy, he made time to write more frequently than before.

Her parents and she were sitting together in the living room, and she opened the envelope. A few photos fell out, and she looked at them with interest. They looked like non-staged and unpretentious shots of a nice family group. One photo was a close up shot of Simon. She felt that her heart was stumbling, when she looked at his picture. Simon looked a lot younger than her brother, a handsome, dark-haired young man who had some of his mother's features with a warm, gentle smile, almost a bit shy. It was a recent photo, and it made the picture she had been getting through his letters more precise. She showed the pictures to her parents and mentioned Simon's wish to have a picture of their family. Louise Laumann got out the photo album with the most recent photos and handed it to her daughter. Martine selected two pictures from fall. They had gone hiking in the Black Forest. For a brief moment she paused. He had sent one photo of himself. Resolutely she also picked one photo of herself to send along with her next letter. She felt that her parents were taking note, and she saw a teasing glint in her father's eyes. He would probably joke again about her "invisible friend" and tease her because she was no longer reading his letters to her parents. But she did not expect his next frank comment: "Hey, Martine, you got yourself a long-distance, visible boyfriend! Good looking too! If he is still as nice as I remember him, he may be a keeper!" This was enough to get her thoroughly flustered. She turned beet-red: "Dad! He is just a pen pal!" Martin grinned amusedly at his daughter. "Oh sure! He is also breaking all previous records in writing letters, calling you his "dearest Martine", and he is probably sending umpteen paper hugs and kisses by airmail. And I see you grin like a Cheshire cat, whenever you are getting mail from him! You even like the guy enough to knit Christmas gifts for him. Just a pen pal, you say? Do you think that your old dad is stupid?" Embarrassedly Martine hid her face in her hands: "Oh dad! I don't know what to call him! Okay, you win! He has become more than just a pen pal. Simon is a great friend." Martin chuckled and patted her on the shoulder: "Sorry, I just couldn't resist teasing you. You are cute when you are embarrassed!"

Martine saw her dad's observant eyes on her. This was not just a teasing remark from him. He did not seem to believe her story and knew more than what she was prepared to tell him. She was thankful that he did not make another comment. Later she pocketed the letter and put the photograph into her purse. She looked at it again and felt butterflies in her stomach. She loved his smile, his eyes, his mouth, and he looked like a genuine and open person. The picture matched the letters she had been receiving from him. It would be nice to meet him one day. The thought made her feel excited.

Her dad's comments had an unsettling quality. She realized that he knew her so well, often better than she knew herself. Of course he looked through her lame statement, that Simon was just a pen pal. She had admitted that he was a great friend, but in reality he meant more to her. She could never tell this to her parents, but she had to admit it to herself: their friendship had intensified and had become love. Falling in love was not something that happened suddenly, but it was a growth of feelings over time. First she tried to deny it. How could he see anything more in her than a young pen pal? He was older than her. But she realized that denial did not work. This was a mutual attraction, which did not go away. His letters were much more affectionate than just notes from one good friend to another, and he was writing a lot more frequently than before. He was gentle but persistent, and his notes were loving but never overbearing. It was an emotional bond that felt close, warm and secure. More than once he wrote that he wished that there would not be this large distance separating them and they could talk together and he could give her a hug. And in this letter he had mentioned that he was thinking of a Europe trip in the near future and hoped to see her. She sat down in her room to answer his letter. It would be so much easier to talk to him, but this was not possible. Today she found it tricky to write. Usually she spoke her mind spontaneously, and this applied to her letters too. Critically she looked at the started page.

"My dearest Simon,

I was so happy to get your letter today. It made my day as always. I felt like sailing away on cloud nine! I really love your picture, and I have it in my purse, so I can look at it often. You are such a special friend, and I like you so much! It makes me happy when I think of you. I didn't know that a wonderful person like you existed…"

Abruptly she stopped. Hold everything! What was she doing? This was way over the top! She ripped up the page into little pieces. If she wrote like this he would probably think that she was a silly goose who had a stupid juvenile crush on him! She heaved a deep sigh of frustration, as she started her letter over again.

Writing letters in English was not the problem at all. It was hard to tell him that she liked him, without coming on too strong! She told him, that his letter had been the highlight of her day after she came home from work. She wrote to him that she was happy to get the pictures, and she told him that she liked his photo. It was a good shot of him, and it was nice to look at the picture of a friend. Her father had already dubbed him the "invisible friend". So he was very visible now! In her letter she also mentioned that she felt lucky to have him as a friend with whom she could share so many thoughts. Friends like him were very special, and she too was hoping that they would meet in person one day. Hanukkah and Christmas were coming up, and she knitted a scarf for him and made a tuque in an intricate Fair Isle pattern. Hopefully he would enjoy it, and this would help him to stay toasty warm on the cold winter days ahead. She mentioned that her parents' Christmas parcel was on the way, and she had made Christmas cookies for them. She was thinking of him and the entire family and wished him and his parents a happy Hanukkah and an equally happy Christmas.

She read her letter one more time. Yes, this was more like it! The next day she brought the package with her letter to the post office. It was probably the quickest reply he ever got and an early Hanukkah and Christmas gift along with it. She wondered what he would think.

A wintry sky hung over Toronto. It was close to the holidays. Michael and Simon walked out of the office. They discussed their plans for the upcoming holidays. Hanukkah was coming close as well. They decided to continue the tradition of celebrating Hanukkah first at the Hoffer's place. For Christmas they would all meet at the Laumann's. There were a few holiday parties that they had been invited to. Simon groaned as he thought of office Christmas parties. The one Christmas party, where Stella had made her last appearance came up in his memory. It was still like a thorn in his flesh. "Really, I have no appetite to go to all of those evenings. Everybody is holding on to a glass and a plate of nibbles, and it is just boring party talk. I hate to waste my time. Could you do me a huge favor? On behalf of Hoffer and Co. I'll go to half of those parties, and you do the other half?"

Michael was not enthusiastic either: "You are a bit of a hermit crab, but in this respect I agree. I dislike these functions too. Let's split those non-events between the two of us and waste only a minimum of time. I have a good excuse, as Rose is pregnant." They walked in silence. Michael mentioned that he had just received a Christmas parcel from his parents. "What about you?" he asked his friend. "Anything for you from Santa Claus from Germany?" Simon had a smile in his eyes. Michael looked at his friend with surprise. He had not seen him smile in the longest time and gave him a friendly nudge. "Hey, somebody actually looks happy today. That's a rarity!" Simon looked back at him. "Yes, Santa Claus sent something per airmail! Two days ago I had a surprise package in the mail from Martine. I was curious and opened it. There were some pictures of her and the family, and she has sent me a Christmas gift; she has knitted a scarf and a tuque for me. And her letters are like a gift already, so alive that it is like a look across continents. It's actually fun to have so many conversations by mail about anything that is interesting in life!" He did not mention to his friend how thrilled he was to get her picture and that he had framed it already. His heart took a leap, when he found it in the package! Casually he continued: "A few weeks ago I sent her a pair of soft leather moccasins from a Native Indian craft store for Christmas, and for her birthday I found an amethyst pendant. I hope that she'll like it." He did not tell his friend that he selected a heart-shaped pendant on a gold chain. He wanted her to have a special gift from him, and he wished that he could see her reaction, when she opened the package! Michael agreed. "Great idea, an amethyst from Thunder Bay! She loves anything about art and culture, and that's something beautiful from Canada! Nice of you to think of her!"

He was hesitant to say more or ask any questions. Simon was his best friend and a very private individual. It was good for him to have another friend, even if this was just a long distance friendship. Martine was younger than him, but this girl had an old soul and had surprised him and Rose with her insightful letters she had written to them. Michael had to think that friendship across the miles was harmless and uncomplicated enough for his sister. Martine was busy with college and practical work. He knew from his parents that she was a sociable, outgoing girl with a bunch of girl friends, but she was cautious about boys. In one of her letters she mentioned that at her workplace she noticed that a lot of guys were notorious skirt chasers, and she did not feel like wasting her time with jerks like that. No need to worry! Simon was not one of those types anyways, he was still struggling after a disappointment, and he was a few thousand miles away. Let them write letters! This was harmless stuff! He had to acknowledge that this letter-writing business and long distance friendship seemed to do his friend some good. He appeared happier than in the past. As always Simon was quiet, but his face lit up whenever he talked about Martine, and his affection to her came out in his remarks about her. Simon was still "Silent Simon", but at times his face could be like an open book.

The last day of the year 1963 was a time to celebrate. A cheerful group had gathered in Michael's and Rose's home. They all sat down for an early dinner together, Michael's family and Simon as well as his parents. They looked back at a healthy and happy year for all of them, and they looked forward to 1964. It was like two celebrations wrapped into one: New Year's Eve and Michael's birthday on New Year's Day, which they would toast to at midnight. They looked forward to an eventful year ahead since Michael and Rose were expecting a brother or sister for Christopher. Michael looked at the clock, rose from the dinner table, and went to the telephone. Rose cast him a questioning glance. "Who are you calling now?" Michael's answer surprised her: "This is one of my crazier ideas! It's not quite midnight in Germany, but it will be in a while. I'll try the overseas operator to get a connection to my folks just to surprise them!" Rose cautioned: "They probably think that somebody is sick or dying here when they get the call. Better tell them right away that nothing is wrong." They all knew that overseas calls were a way of communicating in very special circumstances, and these calls also took a while to go through. And this was New Years Eve, which could make waiting times even longer! Rose understood. There was a wait involved, but obviously Michael had made up his mind. He hung up, and waited for the operator to call back with the connection.

In the meantime a lively conversation was developing. What was in store for the upcoming year, and what plans did they have? Michael planned some home improvements right after New Year's. He wanted to renovate the basement, dividing off another bedroom and adding another bathroom. He had planned this for a while, and now the family was growing. Simon was planning to get himself a used car after Christmas and to buy a house. He had looked around and contacted property owners who planned on selling. His mother could see that he wanted a vehicle. He was frugal and had postponed the purchase for some time. But she gave him a questioning glance when he mentioned the plans of buying a house. She wondered about the wisdom of such a commitment, and Simon explained that sometime later in the coming year he intended to invest the money he had saved. His father nodded in agreement with Simon's idea. His son had a head for business and finances. Thoughtfully he observed him. Simon always had been a long-term planner. It was hard to read him, but it was unlikely that he would want to have a house as a single man. And there was the long distance friendship with Michael's sister Martine that had been going on for almost two years. Her name came up often, but it was hard to extract any news from Simon. He hemmed and hawed, and as usual he was masterfully unspecific. Probably there was more going on than what he was prepared to talk about. He decided to ask another question: did he have any other plans for the New Year or maybe a long deserved vacation or a trip?

But before they could venture into a further discussion the phone started to ring. Michael grumbled about the long wait. "Well, it's about time! Over thirty minutes of a wait for a phone call." He picked up the phone, heard the long distance operator and next his father's voice. "Laumann." He had to think that his was typically dad, never wasting any word! Exuberantly Michael boomed: "Dad! All is great here! Have a happy 1964! We are just catching you before midnight." Martin's father heaved a sigh of relief: "So glad that nothing is wrong! Overseas calls are not something we get every day!" A quick exchange of news followed. Michael's mother came to the phone, and he heard how happy and excited she was to hear his voice. Rose took the receiver and wished her in-laws a happy New Year, and the phone went back to Michael. "What about the kid? Is she home?" He still called Martine 'kid', even though she had turned eighteen two days ago. He heard Martine's happy laugh in the phone line. "Yes, the kid is home, old man! Happy birthday to you, and happy 1964 to everybody!" Michael wished her a belated happy birthday. He heard her news: she had lots of work, and exams were looming. She had celebrated her birthday with some of her girlfriends. They went cross-country skiing together and had birthday dinner together at home. Later they listened and danced to the latest hits, till the neighbor from the flat above came down and told them to keep it quiet. Michael had a twinkle in his eyes. "Hey, listen sis, maybe you want to finally say hello to a good friend of yours. Guess who?"

He beckoned Simon to take the telephone. "Come here, pal; say something!" This was unexpected, and for a moment Simon felt like he was tongue-tied, but this feeling disappeared when he heard Martine's voice. She sounded happy and excited. "Hi Simon, it's so nice to hear your voice. I can really imagine how you are celebrating. It would be fun to be there!" She thanked him for his Christmas and birthday presents, and she described how they had celebrated Christmas. It struck him, that she chatted away, and there was no language barrier at all. He told her about the holiday celebrations and thanked her for her Christmas presents. "I love both. It really touched me that you made the tuque and the scarf yourself. You have so much work already and so little time!" Michael observed his friend. Simon was simply beaming as he talked to Martine. "I miss you too! I wish I could have given you the gifts in person and given you a kiss under the mistletoe." He heard her laugh. "Those moccasins are so cozy! And most of all I love the amethyst heart and the beautiful chain. This was a surprise that bowled me over! You are spoiling me so much! It is very special to me, because it reminds me of you every day." She paused. "About that kiss under the mistletoe-can you save that for me?" She hesitated and added with an almost embarrassed note in her voice: "Not the mistletoe, I mean."

His face looked like he was dreaming of something that he was longing for. She could not know it, but Simon's facial expression was not lost on Michael or on Simon's father. "I love the idea, Martine; sure, I'll save it for you. Rain checks are always good!

Are you serious or are you just kidding?" He heard her take a deep breath before she answered: "It took me a lot of guts to say this. As a matter of fact, I'm not kidding. Yes, I'll take a rain check on the kiss. Forget the mistletoe! Maybe we'll meet in 1964?" He smiled as he answered. "You are funny! I like it! It sounds like a great idea! Sometimes I wonder whether you can read my mind. For now there is a letter in the mail for you." Once again Michael had to wonder about Simon and his friendship with his sister. Rain checks, mind reading, and great ideas... what did they have to yarn about now? The expression on Simon's face puzzled him. His friend, the serious thinker, looked like a man who had dreams. Michael had to stop himself making a comment. Letting his curiosity get the upper hand was not an option. This was like a developing story. All he, Michael, had to do was keep his mouth shut and his eyes open. Paul Hoffer chose to remain quiet too, as he knew the taciturn nature of his son. Getting Simon to talk about private matters was like going fishing or treasure hunting. Time would tell, and whatever was going on, one thing was certain: he would not have to deal with another train wreck like the Stella-experience from two years ago!

A letter was rustling in Martine's purse. Simon had written, and she had not even expected a note. Their letters must have crossed. She opened the letter during her break in the staff room. It was quiet, and nobody else was there. She saw a Valentine's Card, and she remembered from previous English classes that Valentine's Day was a day, which was celebrated in North America, but it was not something that was customary in Germany. Today it was a letter, which was longer.

"My dearest Martine,

We have exchanged many letters, and I have written about many events that have made life interesting over the last two years. I feel like I know you so well despite the fact that we have not even met at this point. Having a friend and a soul mate like you is a chance like one in a million. Our friendship has become something I treasure and a very special part of my life. It has made my otherwise very quiet life vibrant and colorful. Every letter from you is like a beautiful gift, and I'm grateful to you for infusing even dull February days like this one with a deep sense of happiness. While I feel that I know so much about you, I believe that you do not know everything about me to have a clear and honest picture of me. What you are going to read may be troubling to you. I'm taking a risk that you may never want to write back to me after this, but it is a risk I must take. I owe it to you, because I love you, and love can only be built on honesty and trust."

Martine put the letter down for a moment, wondering what was troubling him so much that he found it hard to share. But she read on. The letter spoke of his experience with Stella, the young lady he had met at the urging of his aunt. Martine knew from Rose that he had a disappointment quite a while back, which upset him very much. She knew from her sister-in-law that he had buried himself in his work ever since to a point that Michael worried about him. Now Simon was telling her about this time, and she shook her head in disbelief. She could see that this experience had left him hurt. This female was a person that she and her friends would call a slut. Obviously Simon's aunt had no idea what kind of person this woman really was, when she introduced Simon to her. Coming from a good family was not any guarantee either. He had simply trusted that he would be going out with a nice young lady, but this woman had played games, lied, and had toyed with his feelings and with his inexperience. Martine huffed a sigh of disgust. Some people could be predators and victimizers, women as well as men, and he had encountered such a person. She had heard of similar stories from some of her girl friends, and they felt the same way like Simon felt: hurt, used, dirty and unlovable.

They blamed themselves, and their capacity to trust had received a blow. All of them went through a time of depression, and it took them time to recover. She heard some details that were scary, and she had tried to console two of her best friends after a bad experience. As a result she was cautious about some of the male staff at the hospital that made their rounds and acted like they were irresistible. She had seen enough and did not want to be the next girl on the ward who experienced heartbreak. And here was Simon still hurting two years later!

Determinedly she grabbed a writing pad and her pen. She would write a letter back, the sooner the better. He had to know that his letter did not make any difference in her feelings for him. To the contrary: she was grateful that he had shared his past with her. This event was more than two years back, but obviously it still bothered him. It was more important that he forgave himself instead of blaming himself. He had to get over his hurt and had to heal. It seemed that they both experienced pain in different ways.

She had to think about her father. His illness was flaring up again, and the future was uncertain. In her letter she mentioned that father's illness had taken a turn for the worse. It cast a dark shadow over every day, and yet, life had to go on. Her father reminded her how important it was to not dwell on the bad, but on the good that every day had in store. It was difficult, but it was a truth that applied to Simon's previous disappointment, and it applied to her trying time as well. It occurred to her that she was now seeing another dimension of him, warm, caring, honest, and decent, but he had been hurt and was disappointed. And yet he had the courage to love again. Her eyes looked over the one sentence in the letter "…because I love you." Oh Simon! She had to think of him so often, but so far she did not have the courage to tell him, how much he and his friendship meant to her. This was not just a crush, rather a mutual, steady affection that had been growing over the last two years. It was a long distance relationship, but at one point they would meet. She wrote to him that he had to allow himself to heal; otherwise his life would be in the shadow of loneliness and depression. At the end she paused. He had told her that he loved her, and the sentence had touched her deeply. She hesitated. What would she write to him? She knew that her own feelings for him had grown from affection to love. She had seen heartbreak in the circle of her friends, where some of them had been falling in love and out of love, which had made her cautious. He had written about trust and honesty as a foundation of love, and he had the courage to reveal his feelings to her, even though he was hurt in the past, and he also could not know how she would react to his letter.

After reading his letter she found the courage to write about her own feelings to him with the knowledge that he would understand her. She wrote down her thoughts, no longer afraid to speak her mind, and she felt a sense of joy, when she wrote the last few words to conclude her letter: "I love you to the moon and back". It felt liberating to write down her thoughts without the need to hide! Today her lunch break was longer than usual, and she used the time to write her answer. Quickly she downed a bowl of soup that had turned cold and grabbed a cup of coffee. There was no time for anything else, but this was not important. It was more important to her that her letter was in the mail. This time it felt like she had sent her heart to him, but she also knew that it would not be broken.

Simon saw the familiar envelope in his mailbox. His palms felt clammy. He was apprehensive. It was just over three weeks ago that he had sent his Valentine's card and letter. What was her reaction to his note? Hastily he opened the letter, started reading, and as he continued, his anxiety subsided. She told him that she wanted him to have an answer soon. It had been written in a fast handwriting. She had used her break, did not have much time, and yet this letter was full of thoughtfulness and care. She told him that he did not deserve the treatment he had received in the past. Her contempt was aimed at the person that had inflicted hurt on him, and she emphasized how important it was for him to forgive himself for the past and move on to the present. Six wasted months and one bad evening were only a fraction of his life, and he had to let go of this time. He read about her concern that he would isolate himself from people. She also mentioned that wounds could heal, as long as he was willing to let go of the hurt that would otherwise sap the joy out of living.

It filled him with sadness to read that her father was so ill. How could he comfort her? Thousands of miles were between them. His eyes stopped at the end of the letter. She thanked him for his honesty and closed with a passage that provoked a feeling of deep happiness in him:

"I'm grateful to you for telling me all about your past, and I love you for your courage and your honesty. I felt like you have given me a hug when you told me that you love me. I have sensed it, but up to now I have not had the courage to tell you how much you mean to me. There were times when I started writing a letter, wanting to tell you that I love you, but I was scared to send it. What would you think of me? Would you understand that this is not some juvenile crush? So, after having been a coward for too long, I need to be honest with you too. I love you the way you are, and you have become my dearest and much loved friend. Every time when I look at the amethyst heart from you, I know that my heart belongs to you. In the past I was afraid to fall in love, but it has happened. I never thought that I would get to know to a wonderful friend like you. You are so close, and at times it hurts that you are so far away. It is my biggest wish for you that you feel loved and happy, and I hope that you'll get this letter soon. Why can't they send the mail by rocket? A big hug to you, my dearest Simon, I love you to the moon and back.

Yours, Martine."

Simon And Martine

He sat quietly, reading the passage again. "My heart belongs to you...I love you to the moon and back"... The way she had written about her feelings to him touched him so much that his eyes were filling. It must have taken courage for her to wear her heart on her sleeve. He knew that his feelings for her were not one-sided, but warmly and sincerely reciprocated. She was younger than him, but she seemed to be wise beyond her years, a wonderful and caring friend who loved him the way he was. Also he felt that a burden was being lifted from his mind.

Her letter had been like a comforting hug to him, an impulse for him to allow himself to heal. He heaved a deep sigh. On the one hand it was a sigh of relief, on the other hand it was a sigh of preparing himself for a task. It was a process of removing an old burden, and it was a task of letting go. Nobody could do this for him, and it was up to him. He had to change his negative thoughts that were so easily creeping into his life. Increasing his workload to feel worthy had not helped him to feel better. He had prayed for forgiveness, but this had not been all that was needed. He had forgotten to forgive himself and let go. Today would be the start. Life was about changes, but he also knew that it was a process that would take some time. He sat down and wrote his answer, telling her how much her letter had meant to him and how much she meant to him. He told her how he felt for her in her sorrow about her father's illness, and he wished he could give her a comforting hug. But he was so far way. A thought surfaced in him, and he decided to share it with her:

> *"Your letter has been an impulse for change. As a result I believe that this year will be a year of changes in my life. I have been thinking more about travelling after I have not taken a break for two years. Your brother has suggested it to me before, and I realize that I have been postponing the idea for too long. I'm not sure when I will travel, but I have decided that it will be later this year. It is my greatest wish to finally meet you. Right now I feel how much it hurts that you*

and I are so many miles apart, and I can't be there for you to hold you and to comfort you. I also feel how painfully limited I am with letters to tell you how much I love you. My dearest Martine, I think of you so often, and I love you so very much- make it to the moon and back or to the furthest stars away. I loved how you said it in your letter! You are always in my thoughts and even more in my heart.

With love, Simon."

He sat back and thought. Yes, he was thinking of her often, and he had told her that she was in his heart, but he had not told her yet that he wanted her in his life forever. He would tell it to her in person. With this thought he got up, put the letter into an envelope and went out to mail it.

It was a bright Saturday morning. The last remnants of snow had melted in a mild March sun, and the air smelled like winter was over. He walked down the road to the post office, and afterwards he decided to take the bus to Yonge Street and to walk down the shopping area there. This was a stroll he had not taken for a while. He also wanted to get a gift for the new baby of Rose and Michael. They were so happy when little Tim arrived two days ago! On his walk the display in a jewelers store caught his attention. He had bought the amethyst pendant for Martine here a few months back. She had been thrilled and had written in her letter that she was wearing it every day. Resolutely he entered and looked for a diamond ring for her. It should remind him to finally make the trip later this year. He realized that this was a daring leap of faith, but deep down he also knew that this time he was not the fool he had been two years ago.

Rose and Michael arrived home from the hospital, holding the tiny human bundle in their arms. Five year-old Christopher looked at the baby. He was feeling like a big boy now, and protectively he stood beside his baby brother. "I can watch Timmy", he announced proudly. With a thoughtful glance he stated: "But I don't think that I can play with him. He is way too small!" The parents laughed. "You are such a good helper, Chris!" They sat down, and Rose was in deep thought. Under all the happiness of welcoming a new baby Michael spotted some sadness. This was not like Rose at all. He looked at her. "Something must be on your mind. Are you all right?" She smiled reassuringly. "I'm fine; don't worry about me. I'm just thinking. So we have two children, and the years have gone by-almost nine years, would you believe it?" Michael understood. He leaned back on the couch and grinned. "As a matter of fact, this is a big year. Here we are with a new baby and Christopher, and my folks have not seen their grandkids. And you probably want to see at least your stepmom? Next comes Martine's graduation from nursing school. So I have been tossing some thoughts around." A shadow went over his face. "Also there is my dad. He seems to be more tired and is getting weaker. It's a bittersweet journey with happiness and sadness so close together. We have already discussed this before." Rose gave him a thoughtful smile: "Yes all of that was on my mind all of a sudden. Here we are with a new life, and across the ocean your dad's life seems to be fading away."

Michael put the sleeping baby into his crib, and they kissed Christopher good night. They sat together and pooled their ideas. Both decided that flying later in spring would be best. It was important to have time with Michael's dad. They could expect nice weather, and little Tim would be easy to take along on the trip. They could be there for Martine's graduation. Rose was adding another idea. "You always tell me that Simon has turned into a workaholic and a hermit crab. We are going to the town where he has spent his first eight years. Do you think that he would like to join?" Michael laughed: "You know, this sounds like a fantastic plan. He has to get out; he should travel." For a moment he had to think. "You know, we have to virtually drag this guy away from his desk. I'll talk to his dad to figure out whether the two of us can be away at the same time. It should work, as we have trained two new employees."

A few weeks later Michael knocked at the door of Paul Hoffer's office. Simon was in a meeting with a client. They would be able to talk without being overheard. Simon's father had time for a chat: "Come in, come in! What's up today? Any design problems?" Michael chuckled. "It depends how you see it. All our commercial designs are running smoothly. But there is one design, which Rose and I have come up with. Let me be more precise: it is a plan we have regarding a vacation for Simon." He explained that he had talked to his friend, watched him work more, withdrawing more, seemingly just living for his work, and how his well-meant advice had been fruitless so far. Hoffer senior agreed: "I have been watching him too, and I'm worried. I have mentioned it to him to take a break." He wiped his glasses and sighed. "But what else can I do? Lately he seems to be a bit less withdrawn and looks happier. You probably have more of a wire to him than I do. You are his best friend." Michael agreed. He had a plan, but he was not sure whether it would work. He started: "You may remember that about nine years ago you handed me a ticket and told me to go back to see my folks, traipse down memory lane, take a break, and realize that it was time to live? You never wanted to get paid back for it, but Rose and I thought that it was time for us now to look out for Simon and give him an airline ticket. He should go back, traipse down memory lane, take a break, and start enjoying life." He told Simon's father about his plan to travel and see his parents. He mentioned that it would be fun for Simon to join the family on this trip. He could return to his old hometown, see all the changes, and there were many scenic areas to explore in the area. Next he explained that he planned to organize a birthday party for Simon on the following Sunday and spring the surprise on him. Would it work with the vacation schedule? Paul Hoffer laughed uproariously and clapped Michael on the shoulder. "My friend, don't even worry about any vacation arrangement!

Consider it done. This is a wonderful plan! We'll come to the party, and frankly, I can't wait to see his face." He laughed again: "And of course I don't know anything about this, right?" Michael turned to get back to his desk: "Neither do I"; he replied, "let's keep it quiet!"

He continued his work and noticed after a while that Simon was back at his work place. It was almost time to stop working for the day, and he did not seem to have any work related papers in front of him. He was reading some mail. Michael noted with surprise that Simon had a smile on his face. Serious Simon! Dad Hoffer had been right. Lately he had been a bit more talkative and outgoing. But he adamantly refused to socialize more. Michael took the opportunity to get started on his plan. "Hey, you are back and smiling! Was it a good meeting?" Simon stepped over to his friend's desk. "Yes, it was a successful meeting." He paused and showed Michael an airmail envelope. "The reason that you saw me smile is this." Michael eyed him questioningly. "So you had a letter from Martine? Gosh, you guys must be spending a fortune on airmail!" Simon's eyes were quietly happy. "It is a small fortune well spent! Any letter from her is a beautiful highlight of the day. She is a great friend and a wonderful person." Michael leaned back and scrutinized his friend. "Well, it is good that you got her as a pen pal. Must be fun! We enjoy her letters too, you know. My mom and dad write to me as well, but it is almost like she is taking over. Yes, she is a great girl." He paused and then went on: "Hmmm… it is a while since I have seen my family. Sometime I should fly across the pond to see my folks again." Unobtrusively he observed his friend's reaction. Simon looked like he was in deep thought. "Travelling is something interesting! Sometimes I think it would be great to go back to my roots." There was excitement in his face but also caution, as he continued: "But I don't quite know when. I want to take a trip, but so far I have been procrastinating that it is becoming ridiculous. I know that I'm overripe for a vacation, and next I have to give myself a kick in the butt!" Michael felt a wicked sense of satisfaction. Simon would not even have to give himself that kick. He would get it next weekend!

He was ready to take the next step in his scheme. "Oh, by the way, Rose and I just talked about next weekend. How about a backyard barbecue next Sunday afternoon? It sounds like we are getting a stretch of those early warm spring days! Wouldn't you like to come over? We haven't done that in a while!" Simon agreed: "You know, I'd like that; thanks for the invitation! Anything I can bring?" Michael shook his head: "Just yourself and a strong stomach."

On his way home Simon was thinking about the conversation he had with his friend. Michael and his funny remarks! Bring yourself and a strong stomach! Otherwise his friend had thrown a good idea at him. Travelling sounded tempting. It would be like an adventure to see the old country again. In a way he felt vulnerable and insecure. His language skills were not up to snuff. He had left Germany so long ago, and the country had undergone tremendous changes. This was like jumping on a merry-go-around in motion. But he also noticed a sense of curiosity. He could travel, explore, and go back to the old haunts. Last but not least it pulled him to meet the person who described life in the other country so vividly to him in her letters that he could imagine it so accurately. More than that, she had become the special person in his life who had given him the courage to see the goodness in people again, and he had fallen in love with her. He had to think of Martine and his plan to see her.

He arrived at home. A small package was in his mail slot. It was from Martine. Hurriedly he opened it. He saw a birthday card, a book with pictures from Martine's hometown, a silk tie in a dark burgundy –his favorite color- and a pair of cozy knitted cashmere socks, perfect for loafing around at home. He sat down to read her note. It was a beautiful early birthday gift, and this was the highlight of his day. His glance went to her picture that he had put on his dresser. He looked at it so often, the picture of this young woman with her open face, the eyes that were speaking to him, and her contagious smile. It was almost like he knew her so well already, but the last step was seeing her and telling her in person what he could not convey in his letters. The diamond ring he had bought for her was in the box, which he kept in his bedside table. He did not need it as a reminder as now his mind was made up. He would speak to his father about holidays, and he wanted to wait for his birthday to bring up the topic. One month off or even a little longer for travel some time this year would make the perfect birthday gift, and this was his only wish.

Everybody from the Hoffer office was gathered in the backyard of Michael's and Rose's house. It was a perfect April afternoon, and lively chatter and laughter filled the air. Michael stepped out of the house and motioned to the group to be quiet. The most important guest had just arrived. Rose greeted Simon at the door and she invited him to go out to the back patio. He stood rooted in his steps, when he was greeted by boisterous shouts of "Surprise!" He stared speechlessly at all the colleagues that had come. Everybody broke into loudly singing "Happy Birthday." He was thoroughly surprised. "You are knocking the wind out of me! But my birthday is only on Tuesday", he protested, but it was only a weak protest. Michael grinned. "Yes, it's an early party! Nobody has time on workdays like on a Tuesday to celebrate big parties!" Simon went around and shook hands with everybody. It was a happy afternoon with lots of talking and laughter. In the middle of the celebration one of his colleagues called for silence. "We could not let the day go by without giving you a gift from the entire gang at Hoffer's." He carried a large box, which was wrapped up with colorful paper. He sat down to unwrap the gift, a suitcase for airline travel. Michael tapped him on the shoulder. "I should give you Rose's and my gift too. It is needed to make the trip a bit more complete. Happy birthday, pal! Please don't throw it out with the wrapping paper." Simon opened the envelope and sat still like a statue, when he discovered the flight ticket and itinerary. He wanted to make a comment, but it was impossible for him. He stood up and gave his friends a big bear- hug. His father stood up. "It is all written down on your birthday card, Simon. We hope that after two years of being a workaholic you will like the idea of an extended paid vacation! Take time to live! Enjoy summer off, maybe early fall too. We are not talking about time limits today!" He and his wife gave their son a big hug. This was almost too much to grasp. It was like they all had read his thoughts and forged ahead, while he had still been hesitating and thinking. Everybody had been in on the surprise, while he did not have any idea! Finally he found his voice. It was quiet and almost breaking with emotion. "I wanted to thank you all-everyone of you. It is just beyond description how you have made my day."

After the celebration he went home. He felt how the entire group had given him a day with gifts of their love, caring, and friendship. He felt loved, almost felt like in a dream, and he let himself fall onto the chaise in his living room. He had closed himself off from the people that cared for him, and he had buried his bitterness and disappointment under a load of work. Michael talked to him, and he did not listen. Martine's letters helped him to start healing. Now his father mentioned that he should start taking time to live and to take an extended break, and Michael and Rose had overwhelmed him with their generosity of giving him a flight ticket. For a moment he did not know whether he should laugh or cry. Finally he cried like he had not cried in a long time. He had not been able to shed any tears, not even when his belief in love and trust had been shattered over two years ago. Now it was like a cleansing and liberating feeling of letting go of that last burden, which he had bottled up for so long. At the same time it was an uplifting feeling of indescribable joy. His heart was overflowing, and he had to talk to somebody. His friends had seen his reaction, and they knew how he felt. He wished he could talk to Martine, but long distance calls across continents were complicated, involved operator-assisted waits on line, and besides it was in the middle of the night in Europe. Frustrating! Would they ever invent something better in the way of communication? Months ago he had felt the cautious wish to travel and meet her; now he felt the keen sense of pain about the distance that separated them, and meeting her could not come soon enough. She had become a friend he loved dearly, and he had to write to her now. He wanted to tell her about the upcoming trip, his longing for her, and his fondest wish to finally see her face to face, wanting to hear her voice, and in this letter he poured out his feelings for her in a way he had not dared to express them before. There was no doubt and no fear of rejection, as he knew that she loved him, and she would understand him.

The mailman dropped two airmail letters into the Laumann's mailbox and walked away. Louise came in from her garden work to check the mail. She shook her head. This was getting a little bit too much! She quietly had to wonder about Martine. Every month she got at least two letters from this Simon Hoffer, her brother's friend, and lately there had been a lot more. Since quite some time Martine had not read her letters to her parents. Her dad had teased her a few times in the past about her letter-writing boyfriend in Toronto, and Martine had blushed and smiled, but she did not say much more. Louise had to agree with her husband: Martine was a young woman now and came across as more serious and mature than some of the giggly nineteen-year olds from nursing school that were her friends. She was a young adult and had her own circle of friends. All the same she was concerned about her daughter and the long distance friendship between her and Michael's friend. What if he was one of those men who were out to take advantage of a girl? Martine was young and did not know the world. She found life complicated with a growing up daughter, even though Martine had never been rebellious or difficult.

She would speak to Martin later. He had a different outlook on life than her. She sighed. Maybe it was the realization that she had to let go of her baby. After graduation Martine would probably have to find work in another town. She had to get used to the fact that it would be just she and her husband, and the children had flown the coop. Louise also felt a sense of anguish.

Martin had been ill for so long, and lately his health had been slipping precariously. After his doctor's appointment today she knew from Martine that his illness had taken a turn for the worse, and nobody knew how long he would live. Her heart was heavy as she thought of the future. She went inside and opened the letter of Rose and Michael. Her eyes went over the lines, and she was thunderstruck by the news. "Martin, come quick," she called out. Her husband had been resting and got up to join her. Both of them read the news. The family from Toronto, Rose, Michael and the two grandchildren were planning to arrive for a visit at the end of May. They wanted to come for Martine's graduation. They also mentioned that Michael's friend would be joining them to see his old hometown, and also informed their parents that they made arrangements for their accommodation, as they did not want to impose. Martin's pale face broke into a big smile. He had always wanted to see his two grandsons!

Louise pointed to the letter that was addressed to Martine. "It is getting a little much with these letters, and for her birthday he gave her the heart pendant, which she wears day and night! So, now he is going to arrive here. It worries me." Martin saw the concerned expression in Louise's face. He knew that his wife was protective of their daughter. She looked at him thoughtfully. "She has lots of girl friends, but she has never had a boyfriend, and Simon is a man who is quite a few years older than her. She does not tell us much, but I know that she likes him a lot. I don't want her to get hurt." In a way he could understand her, but he also knew that his wife was easily worried. A few weeks earlier Martin had teased his daughter about paper kisses and hugs in an envelope referring to the letters that went back and forth. She had teased her dad back with an impish twinkle in her eyes and told him that things would very likely not just be paper any more once they would meet at one point or another. When she saw the expression of concern on his face, she gave him a hug and told him to wait with further worrying till they would actually meet. He had shared this conversation with his wife, but both did not know then how imminent this meeting was. Martin tried to reassure his wife: "We know from Michael that Simon is his best friend and a good and decent person. Martine would have never become friends with a questionable individual. She is quite picky with all her friends. And Louise, you have to stop thinking that every man is up to no good. Simon is not a savage, Martine has never been a boy-crazy teenager, and I tell you, I don't feel like worrying in the time I have left. You will have to worry without me." Louise's face still looked worried: "But she is still very young for a serious relationship, Martin," she lamented. Martin looked back at her with a deliberately serious expression that dissolved into a teasing grin: "Oh yes, Louise, I hear you! What about you? You were not quite eighteen when I fell in love with you. I believe that this has now been a fairly serious relationship for the past forty years. If I remember correctly, your mother threw a fit, and your father threw me out of the house. Is history repeating itself?" His answer had such a disarming quality that all she could do was laugh. Martin and his fitting comments!

Martine came home later in the evening. It had been a trying day. In the morning she went with her father to the doctor's office. The lab test results were showing a further decline in Martin's condition. The doctor had mentioned that Martin might need another hospital stay and a blood transfusion. He had been relatively stable living with leukemia for nine years, but the disease had returned with a vengeance. Martine knew enough about the illness to realize that the condition was now even more serious. She suppressed her tears, and tried to sound optimistic for the sake of her mother. With a heavy heart she went to work at noon.

The workplace was out of control and a perfect recipe for insanity: two colleagues were off, she almost could not keep up with the work, and the head nurse was even more irritable and bitchy than usual. Next the young assistant doctor who had given her the eye before made a pass at her. He was a good-looking guy and acted like he was God's gift to anything that wore a skirt, but the way he looked at her gave her the creeps. She told him very clearly that she was not interested to be the focus of his attention and that her behind was not a subject for the anatomical studies of his greedy hands. When he did not leave her alone, she called for the head nurse, slapped him soundly on his hands and heatedly called him some colorful names, much to the merriment of some of her colleagues close by. The head nurse admonished her sternly that her behavior of name-calling was unprofessional. She was outraged! She reminded the nurse, that the unprofessional individual was the assistant. He could do no wrong, she was fair game, and she was not taking that! After her work she stormed out of the ward, and she complained at the office of the hospital administrator. He was supportive and mentioned to her that she was not the first one to complain. He would look into the matter and try to switch her to a different ward. This was a bit of a relief: she did not need the head nurse's attitude and especially not assistants like this individual. Also on May 28 would be her graduation. Another few weeks after that her contract was ending, and she would take off a week or two. But after a day like today already those twenty-nine days till her graduation felt like a towering mountain! It was the entire day that got to her: worries, sadness, work stress, a slimy assistant, and a bitchy nurse. This was more than enough! What she needed most was some peace and quiet to calm down after a chaotic day. All she wanted was a warm bath, her bed to curl up in, and sleep!

When she walked into the kitchen, she spotted a letter from Simon on the table. She had to think of him so often. Her heart beat faster, and her eyes flew over the lines. Simon's words were warm and loving. He had told her before in his letters how much she meant to him, a friend he loved very much, but this passionate love letter went to her heart, and its words made her almost feel dizzy. He was telling her about his feelings for her, about his ardent wish to see her, and how he was feeling the pain of the long distance between them. He also wanted to let her know that he loved his birthday present, and how much he appreciated that she had spent time to make it herself. Next he described his

Simon And Martine

surprise birthday party, and Martine noticed that it must have been an emotional event for him to be surrounded by so many loving friends. She let out a gasp, when she read the next passage, where he described the surprise gift that Michael and Rose had given to him. He announced that Michael and his family as well as he planned to visit them. He could barely wait. The trip could not come soon enough for him, and he was counting the days.

The letter fluttered down on the table, and she buried her face in her hands. A barrage of thoughts rushed through her mind. They would meet, and she had hoped for this for some time. She knew that he loved her, and she had fallen in love with him, even though they had never met. They had become soul mates, had so much in common, and knew each other so well despite the distance that separated them. For a short moment anxiety almost paralyzed her. Was she just chasing a dream, and what would reality be like? What if he had created an ideal picture of her in his mind, and she had created an image of him that was vastly different from reality? She had never been in love, and all of a sudden the person she had come to love so much would be standing face to face with her. At the same time she realized that she was very likely not the only one who had a case of nerves. Simon would have similar feelings, and he was probably feeling as excited as she was. Most likely he was on the same emotional rollercoaster ride of apprehension, excitement, love, happiness, and other feelings. On top of all he was facing a long trip into a country he had left so long ago and the prospect of trying to understand a language he barely remembered. Both of them were in this together, she on this side of the Atlantic and he on the other side. All the reasoning and rationalizing did not help her right now, and the tears came uninvited. Today had been simply too much to deal with! She could not just sit here losing it and bawl like a three year-old. What if her mom or dad would see her like that, sitting here in a puddle of tears? Get a grip, Martine!

Quickly she wiped her eyes. What a day! His arrival was on May 24, and today was April 29, only twenty-five days away. He had mentioned earlier that he planned a trip later this year, but this was faster than she imagined. In twenty-five days they would meet! This day felt like a wild ride: first the ominous news about her dad's health, next a bad day at work that had tested her to the limit, and now the opposite: a letter from Simon in which he told her how much he loved her, the news that he would be arriving soon, and also the knowledge that Michael, Rose and their children were coming for a visit. It felt almost unreal! She still sat at the table, entirely overwhelmed by a tumble of feelings of love, complete surprise, and happy excitement, when her mother came into the kitchen. Louise took one look her daughter. "Martine, what on earth is going on? Are you all right?" Martine looked up and pointed to the letter. "Just in a state of total shock. I read the letter from Simon. I can't believe it! Michael and his tribe and Simon are coming for a visit." Surprise and excitement were written in her face. Louise's voice was excited: "We had the same news from Michael today." She handed the letter to her daughter and happily gave her a hug. "I'm so excited and so happy! So is your dad." Quizzically she looked at Martine. "What do you think about the fact that Simon will come too? You must be looking forward to meeting him!" Martine's face showed that she was in deep thought, thinking of her friend who was half a world away, a friend who had become the soul mate she loved. Louise knew her daughter. She knew that the exchange of letters with Simon was going much deeper than just friendship between two pen pals. It was written in her face, even though she tried to sound very factual and controlled: "You know, Mama, this will sound strange to you. After writing letters back and forth for so long and talking about so many details that fill our lives, it feels like I know Simon already for a long time. I have seen pictures; I know what he thinks. He is a great friend and a wonderful person. Seeing him face-to-face, hearing his voice and talking to him will be like completing the picture that I have of him. Yes, I'm excited!" She swallowed hard, and her voice turned shaky with emotion. "Michael mentioned that this is his friend's first holiday in two years. Simon wrote to me that he is looking forward so much to meeting us. I really look forward to finally meeting him." Louise's smile was thoughtful as she stated: "Never mind meeting us! He has written lots of letters to you. The one person he really wants to meet is you." Martine lost her carefully kept composure and burst out in tears. "Oh Mama! Today I'm losing it! My exams are done, and they did not even rattle me, but today is like a roller coaster ride! First there was the news about dad, next I had a rotten day at work, and I was really down in the dumps. Now I'm home, and Simon wrote a letter to me that swept me off my feet and made me fly sky-high. And there is the news that they are all coming to visit! This is unreal! I always hoped for this, and now I'm so excited, and I'm counting the days! You probably think that I'm crazy! I don't even know how I can fall asleep! I'm happy, I have butterflies in my stomach; right now I feel like a nervous wreck!" "And you are in love, darling; I know", Louise added and quietly put her arm around her daughter's shoulders. Martine realized that it was of no use to deny the simple observation of her mother. She wiped away her tears, nodded and saw understanding, but also an undercurrent of worry in Louise's eyes.

She knew that sleep would not come easy, and in the stillness of the late night she sat down to write a letter. Rose, her dear sister-in-law and her lifelong friend was a great confidante. But this was not the only letter she was writing. Her heart was overflowing, and she wrote to Simon. It was a letter that would bring tears to his eyes and dispel any anxiety about meeting her: it was a glowing, heartfelt confession of her love to him, of her longing for him, of her excitement and happiness about finally seeing him face to face. Soberly she realized that letters could never be enough to convey all her feelings to him, but in this letter she did not hold anything back, and knowing this she could finally fall asleep.

Eight

Love, Forgiveness, Death And New Beginnings

Bridges That Continue - 1964

Rose looked at the suitcases that had to be packed and heaved a sigh. The list she had made was helpful, but all the same it was complicated: they were planning for an extended trip, and there were so many details to think of. At least Christopher was at a friend's place to play and was not around to "help" with the packing! He wanted to pack everything from his teddy bear to his scooter! She had hoped for a quiet time to get things organized, but Tim, her usually peaceful baby, decided to have a cranky afternoon. Today she could not win! She stopped selecting the clothing for the trip, put the suitcases aside and picked him up. Of course he was quiet now! Maybe it would help to walk around with him till he fell asleep.

She stepped out of the house to the mailbox and collected some envelopes and the paper. One letter came from Germany. She recognized Martine's handwriting, and this time it was addressed to her, not to Michael and her. She wondered what was going on. Usually Martine would write to both of them, but if she needed somebody to confide in, the note would be addressed to Rose. She went back to the house to read the letter. It was not a long letter, but she noticed that Martine needed a listening ear. In this letter she wrote that she had received the letter from Simon and read Rose's letter about the upcoming trip. The letter made Rose smile, and yet she felt for Martine who was happy, anxious, and nervous at the same time, and much too excited to sleep.

"My dear big sister Rose,

It's one in the morning, but I can't sleep, and I need to write. What a day! Today I'm just beside myself. This was like a rollercoaster ride that left me breathless in my seat. First I went to the doc with dad. The lab results are not good. I tried to sound upbeat, so poor mom would not worry so much, but it put a cloud over the entire day. Yes, it is sad. We are taking one day at a time. It is already a miracle that he is still with us. I'm so happy that you will come soon. This seems to be like a race against time. Thank God my exams were finished last week. I aced them all! Next I had an absolutely lousy day at work today, and when I finally came home I got the news of your upcoming trip. I'm thrilled to bits! We are all so happy! This is wonderful news especially after a rotten day like this one. First it felt like something knocked me over, and now I'm too wound up to sleep. In the same mail I had a letter from Simon too. It was a letter that made me incredibly happy. This was like the last drop that made the bucket run over. I just sat and cried. I'm not sad at all. To the contrary, I'm so happy that it is hard to express. Rose, I love Simon so much!"

Rose was thoroughly surprised as she read this sentence. It was news to her that Martine had fallen in love with Michael's friend, and she continued reading:

"He is the most wonderful person in my life, and I'm like walking through a dream after reading his letter. I knew that he loved me, but this letter I'll keep forever! I never told you that I am in love; so you know it now. I can tell it to him,

and I can tell you, but I cannot really let it all hang out at home. Dad already teases me half to death about my long distance boyfriend. You know how good he is at that. And Mama worries about me, even though I tell her not to worry. She is worried that I get all these letters from Canada, tells me that Simon is older than I, that I'm too young, and then she worries some more. And I find that an age difference is not an obstacle with a wonderful person who is so close to my heart. I haven't said much to her, but today it was she who told me that she knows that I'm in love. Yep, busted! Mothers with their sixth sense! So I let it all hang out in this letter, and I want to write to Simon too. Better not say anything to Michael. He is as good as dad at making fun of me. 'Ha-ha, the kid is in love! Too funny!' I can almost hear him! I tell you, even good news can be something shocking when they are shockingly wonderful! I can't wait to see you guys after so many years, and I'm looking forward so much to meeting Simon. That is an understatement! More than very much! I am practically counting the days, hours, and minutes! He has become a soul mate who I love with all my heart, and it hurts that he is so far away. Just thinking about finally meeting him makes me fly high like a kite."

Rose read the next lines. She never knew that Martine and Simon were more than pen pals. But this letter gave it away. Martine could barely wait till she would meet her friend, and her wish to finally meet him was coming true. And now she hoped that they would have a wonderful time together. Rose could relate to her young friend and the tumultuous feelings she had written about. Her dear friend and sister-in-law Martine sounded like she was head over heels in love! Michael had never mentioned anything to her, except that she and Simon were making the postal service rich with their frequent letters to each other. He joked about it and found it very funny! He obviously had no clue of what was really going on! Rose shook her head; up to now she had no idea! And of course, Simon, quiet as he was, had never said a word either. Silent waters seemed to run deep! But now the truth was out in this letter. She would keep it to herself and not share it with Michael!

The sound of the doorbell startled her. Quickly she put away the letter and hid it in the bookshelf. Michael said that he had to run some errands after work. This would not be her husband. She put Tim back into his crib and went to answer the door. Simon was standing outside. He looked like he was nervous and feeling uneasy; this was different from his usual quiet self. Rose could understand him. Probably he was anxious and excited about the trip, which was coming up fast in a few days. But after reading Martine's note she realized that there could be more. Rose eyed him quizzically: " Simon, what is up? You look like you are totally stressed-out! I feel for you! Here I'm trying to pack, and it is a real pain!" Simon looked into Rose's calm eyes that seemed to see so clearly through everything in life. A slightly embarrassed smile went over his face. "Sorry that I just invade here without calling before. I seriously need some help. I think that you can help me more than Michael can. You are always so practical." He needed some advice about their upcoming trip. It was so long since he had seen the other country. Rose patiently sat down and wrote down a list of useful notes. She did not think that he would experience severe language problems. Lots of people were familiar with English. She explained that people were a bit more formal over there. He might want to pack his clothes accordingly. He asked about maps. Rose told him to wait till his arrival. Travel cheques would be useful. His electric shaver would not work there, as the current was different. He knew about the weather.

After Rose's advice about travel he appeared to be still preoccupied. Rose sensed that Simon did not talk about all his concerns, and she decided to get to the bottom of his worries. "Well, so much for the travel list; but I believe this is not all that is on your mind?" Obviously her statement surprised him, and after a pause he took a deep breath and heaved a sigh. "You must have a sixth sense. Yes, there is more." She waited, and when he remained silent, she decided to tell him about her thoughts: "I know - or shall I say that I think that I know? - This is not just about the travel details. It is about Martine too, isn't it?" Now he looked even more surprised, silent for another moment. "Are you a clairvoyant? How come you know? It is true; I think of her so much. First she was a pen pal and a long distance friend, and I have fallen in love with her. It feels like she has become a part of me. I cannot wait to meet her. Rose, but now I'm also apprehensive and on edge. I'm a few years older than her after all. She may not like what she sees. What if…" Rose shook her head: "Simon, you are nervous; I understand. But you must stop being so negative. Yes, I mean it! I need to share something with you; but please, keep it to yourself." She stood up, went to the shelf and reached for Martine's letter. "I'm not a clairvoyant, but I just got this in the mail. Before that I had no idea! This letter tells it all. Normally I don't pass on mail that is addressed to me, but seeing you in the state you are in I have to let you read it. Sit and relax for a bit. How about a cup of tea?" He nodded thankfully. Rose came back with two steaming mugs and sat down. She remained silent. He needed some time to absorb the news, and she was grateful for a break as well. Quietly he read the letter. He seemed to be at a loss for words. His face was working, and he had trouble to stay composed. He was getting calmer, and his eyes shone with joy. "Thank you, Rose, for the tea and for listening. It seems you are Martine's and my confidante. I hope that she will forgive you for letting me read her note and will not be upset with me for being a snoop." She nodded in agreement. "I believe that Martine will understand you. She feels just as excited as you, and she loves you, Simon. Are you feeling a bit better now?" She had never seen such a happy smile on his face. "A difference like night and day! Sorry for being a nuisance here and acting like a bundle of nerves." He looked at the watch. It was time to go home. He realized that he too had to get organized for the trip.

Rose was surprised about her conversation with Simon. It was rare that he opened up about private matters, but obviously he was at the end of his tether and needed a listening ear. Following their conversation she was not surprised when the phone rang after a while, and she heard that he was on the line. "Thank you again for your travel tips, and thank you for letting me read the note you got from Martine. It helped me to stop being a nervous wreck." She heard him pause and trying to stay calm: "I just got home, and I had a letter from her as well. It simply overwhelmed me. It is hard to describe how I feel." He could detect a smile in her voice: "Happy, I hope?" She could understand him when she heard his answer: "Yes, oh God, so happy, Rose! I'll be even happier once I'll meet her at the airport."

He hung up the phone and got out the new suitcase. The last few weeks were like a blur, and the trip was so close now that he was starting to count the hours! A thought hit him. It was not even five in the afternoon. It would be six hours later across the Atlantic. He knew which shifts Martine was working this week: noon to ten in the evening. She should be home by now.

For a few moments he agonized over a decision, before he decided to call her. Maybe it was crazy, but so be it! He called the overseas operator. This was not a Sunday or a holiday, so he had a chance of a shorter wait for the call to go through. The ringing phone and the call from the operator made him jump. His throat was dry, when he picked up the receiver. After two rings the phone was picked up. It was not Martine's father or mother. He heard her voice: "Martine Laumann." He was excited: "Martine! It is me, Simon." He heard her gasp with surprise: "Simon! You? Is something wrong? Are you okay?" Usually phone calls from overseas were something that were reserved for urgent matters or emergencies. His voice became steady: "Yes, yes, I'm fine. Don't worry! No problems! But I simply had to call you. I got your letter today. It made me so happy, Martine! I love you so much! It hurts that you are so far away. The trip is almost here! No more letters; we can talk! I'll see you in three days." He heard excitement in her voice: "I can't write it all in letters! I'm so excited! You know, I have been counting the days. Call me a nut! Now I'm counting the hours. This is like looking forward to Christmas, a birthday, Easter and everything else together! I can't wait!" He answered: "Maybe it's weird that I call you so late, but I need to tell it to you in person, not just in a letter: I love you. Can't tell you how much!" He heard her laugh: "Fine, so we are both weirdoes! Simon, I love you so much. Letters are not enough. I'm so happy that you called. It will be wonderful to finally see you! Good Lord, but this phone call is going to cost you a small fortune!" She heard happiness in his voice:" It is worth it just hearing your voice. I'm glad that the trip is coming up. Otherwise my phone bill gets sky high, I go crazy, or both." She laughed: "You know what? That makes two of us. I'm just about to go crazy too. Sixty-five more hours!" He agreed: "Yes, you figured that one out! Oh God, every one of them is a small eternity. I'd better let you go to sleep. Do you want anything from Canada, anything special?" He was touched by her answer: "Just you, Simon. Travel safe! There is nothing more special than you coming and visiting. I have dreamed about that for a long time." She heard his reply: "I'll have something for you anyways! Good night! You are so sweet!" He heard her answer: "Have a good night too! If you were here, I'd give you a kiss good night!" "What if I want more than one?" He heard her laugh softly: "Oh! I'd love it! See you soon! Love you lots!" Martine heard him say: "I love you! Can't wait to see you. I'll dream of you."

There was a click in the line, and her father came into the kitchen to get a drink of water. He eyed her with a questioning glance. "You and your chatty girl friends! The phone never gets a rest in this place." He stopped short and observed the facial expression of his daughter. "You look like you had some terribly exciting stuff to chat about, late as it is!" She could not lie to her father. He could tease her, he could make an abrasive joke, but today it did not matter to her. "This was not one of my girl friends, dad; it was Simon who called. He'll be here in sixty-five hours, and we are both beyond excited." To her surprise there was no teasing glint in his eyes but a small smile of understanding: "Yes, darling,

I know; not only excited but in love too. Be happy; I won't tease you about that. I understand you and him. Sleep well now." He gave his daughter a hug and left the kitchen. Martine listened into the quietness of the room. Her beloved friend was so far away, but his voice was still in her ears. She closed her eyes, trying to imagine how it would be meeting him. It was getting late, and tiredness caught up with her. Sleep was good! The hours till his arrival would get less.

The large DC-8 jetliner had quietly lifted off Toronto airport, soaring into the clear evening sky on a day in late May. Michael and his family settled down for the long trip across the ocean. After the flurry of excitement of planning the trip, packing suitcases and finally arriving at the airport, it was a sense of relaxation for the adults to sit back, almost lulled to sleep by the steady hum of the jet engines. Christopher was too excited to settle down. He wanted to look out of the window. For a while he watched the clouds and wondered why they were below them and not above them. Simon held him on his lap and patiently explained to him that the big plane went so high that it left the clouds behind way below. This satisfied the little boy. He found it even more fascinating, when the landscape below became visible. It was a clear evening, the clouds were gone and the icebergs of Greenland become visible like an icy wonderland. Again Christopher had to wonder about the ice he saw. He thought that it was spring and all the ice had melted. Michael took over and told his son what icebergs were. Rose and the baby had fallen asleep. The cabin lights were turned low, and the passengers were napping. Michael started to doze off. The last thing he heard was Simon reading a book with Chris. The little boy was fascinated with "Green Eggs And Ham". He had to think that Simon was a saint! Here he was reading the same story for the second or third time. It was too bad that he did not have his own family. He would make such a great dad. It was good for him to have at least Christopher as his godson.

Daylight was dawning after the shortened night, and Rose woke up. Baby Tim was squirming and needed to be looked after. Michael was stirring and squinting. Both of them looked over to the neighboring seat where Simon was reclining. He was sound asleep. Christopher was asleep too, nestled against his chest. "Green Eggs And Ham" had fallen down on the floor. They were glad that they had a chance to catch some sleep. Michael smiled, as he pointed to the two tired travellers in the other seat. "Thank goodness, we are all getting some rest. Just look at these two! What a picture." He continued: "I hope that we all will have a great time. It will be such a switch, not just the time switch of six hours." He voiced his concern that his friend and he should do some sightseeing together to keep him entertained. Rose nodded absentmindedly, and Michael noticed a smiling, thoughtful expression on the face of his wife. He wondered: "What are you thinking and smiling about? You look like the cat that ate the canary!" She surprised him with her answer: "I make you a bet that our friend will be mostly invisible for us during this trip. You don't have to worry about him. He won't be bored." Michael cast her a questioning glance. "Oh, go on! Do you really think that he'll take off on his own?" Rose determinedly shook her head. "No, that is not what I mean! He and Martine..." When she saw the expression of doubt on her husband's face, she continued: "Michael, you don't seem to have any idea, but face it: these two are in love. Take it from me!" He grinned: "Aw, come on! They are just pen pals! If I wouldn't know you better, I'd say that you read too many Harlequin romances!" She laughed: "Wait and see. Life is like a good book. Turn the next page, and we'll read it together!"

The jet was circling over the hilly landscape of southern Germany. All travellers were woken up by the announcement of the flight attendant to prepare for landing. Silent tension and restlessness hung in the air. A slight thump of the machine signaled that they had landed smoothly on the runway. The landscape and buildings flew by, and the plane taxied towards the main building.

Christina Schilling

They walked down the stairs onto the tarmac and entered the airport building. Michael's chest tensed up. He thought about his father. Would he be there? Lately he had been very unwell and tired. His thoughts went to his mother, the quiet, patient and steady woman who had not changed much over the years. What about his sister? Last time she was a spunky nine-year old with a mind of her own, and she cried when he and Rose left. Now she would be a young woman. So many changes! He walked up the stairs. The family walked behind, Christopher on his own, and Rose with the baby.

Simon followed. A few days back he felt like his stomach was in a knot at the prospect of travelling. He was about to travel to a place that was not well known to him. He would finally meet the girl he had become so close with despite not having met her in person. Now the knot had miraculously untwisted, and after the sleep his head was clear. He felt happy anticipation of the new, as he went through the sliding doors to the meeting area. It felt like a step into a different chapter, something that was yet unknown. His look followed Michael's glance. His friend was looking for his family. For a short moment he felt a sting: he had no family here. Next his glance stopped at a group of three in the crowd of people in the waiting area. He recognized Michael's dad. With deep sadness he noticed that Martin Laumann looked like an older Michael, but so tired, so pale. And here was Louise, Michael's mom, still the woman he remembered from such a long time ago, aged of course, but still a good looking woman who carried her years with vitality and grace. For a moment he stopped abruptly, when he saw Martine. He stood transfixed as he gazed at her. She waved happily to the arriving travellers, and he saw her eyes that were filled with a warm smile and happy excitement. When her glance locked with his, he felt an instant and profound connection that hit him and shook him to his core. There was an expression of intense astonished happiness in her face, and he saw her mouth form his name. It was impossible for him to take his eyes off her, and her eyes hung on him. She was everything he had seen in her pictures and read in her letters, the girl he had been thinking about so much. His steps got faster; he almost overlooked the last two steps of the stairs, and he approached the family. Michael and Rose hugged the parents. He approached Martine, and quickly she stepped towards him and held out her hands to him. The look in his eyes made her stomach flutter. Passionately he enfolded her in his arms, and she felt like she was embracing the beloved friend she had known for so long and had been waiting for till now. She had tried to imagine how it would be to meet him, but this was different from anything she had imagined. It felt like an invisible force made her want to stay in his arms, but this was neither overwhelming nor intimidating. Both could not let go of each other and looked at each other like they could never stop. "At long last, Martine", he whispered." He was too overcome with emotion to say more but his eyes never left her face, which was glowing with happiness. "O my God! I can't believe it that you are here, Simon!" She struggled for words as much as he did, and they stood like in a dream, just feeling the closeness of their embrace and looking at each other again, oblivious to the others around them. The other family members looked on and observed their interaction with amused curiosity. Michael touched her shoulder. "What about me, kid? Do I finally get a hug too?" He saw her blush deeply. Simon was still holding her in his arms and looked at his friend. "Not so fast, big brother! First I have to let her go, and I'm not ready yet." The two men looked at each other in silent understanding. Martine gave her brother a big hug. Michael observed his friend. This was not the quiet, reserved Simon he knew, and he started to wonder whether Rose had been right with her statement during the flight about him and Martine. Happily she went to Rose, who gave her an exuberant hug, and she hugged her excited nephew Christopher, and took baby Tim into her arms. All of them went to the Laumann's place. Simon stood close to Martine when they entered the hallway of the house. She saw that his eyes were on her and she felt silent tension that was between them. "Martine," he stepped closer and whispered into her ear." It is like a dream that

I finally can see you and talk to you. Letters cannot do it all, and phone calls are not enough either." She studied his face and saw excitement and happiness that matched her own feelings. "I was always hoping that we would meet. Now it feels like something from the movies that we finally see each other face to face. Only this is better than any movie; this is real! It just blows me away! Did you want to say something else, Simon?" She had seen him hesitate. He swallowed nervously. "Yes, something is still on my mind. I see that you are wearing the amethyst I gave you. It's about the phone call on New Year's Eve, when I told you that I would have liked to give you your gifts in person." His eyes searched her face, and he held her hands. "You asked me to save you the kiss under the mistletoe." He saw a warm, tender smile on her face: "Sure, I remember that call! So, is the rain check still good?" He pulled her into his arms. "Oh Martine!" He saw her face, her mouth, and he felt her melt into his embrace, when he kissed her. It took all of his self-control to release her from his arms again, and he saw her love for him in her face. He had never seen an expression of love like this in the eyes of a girl, never felt loved like this before, and it was a feeling of elation and happiness. She moved close to him, quickly looking around. Nobody was watching them. "Simon, I …" Her voice was just a whisper. "I want to kiss you good night now. I have to go to work soon!" Furtively she kissed him back. He embraced her again, and they held hands, finding it difficult to let go of each other.

The evening was like a big homecoming, with all the reminiscing and talking. They were planning the next day already, when Martine looked at the clock. "I would much rather stay home, but now I really have to run! I'm working the late shift, but I'll be back for breakfast! Wake me up!" It was Rose who watched Martine and Simon exchange a long glance. The family continued their time together. Martin Laumann looked at all of them. "I'm grateful that you all could come. This includes you, Simon. Welcome after all these years! It is like we have known you forever." He turned to his son's family. "The years are just falling away. It seems like we just continue on from the time we met last, which was nine years ago." They talked about their plans. There was so much they wanted to do. The men wanted to go to the Menzinger's farm for a visit. They were still busy running their small farm, and Hans, their son, had modernized the operation. Leo, the hard-core bachelor and vagabond, had moved into a small town close by, was married and had a large family of his own. They hoped to see him too. Rose wanted to visit her stepmom. But the travellers were tired and needed some sleep first. They walked the few blocks to the small guesthouse where they planned to stay.

Martine wrestled her way through a ten-hour shift. It was a difficult night. A patient with end stage lung disease had been admitted. Her colleagues and her looked at the health history. He had never been ill, but his lifelong habit of smoking was finally taking its toll. "Too many Gauloises", he said with a raspy voice, and the pungent smell of these cigarettes was surrounding him like a cloud. There was a tone of regret in his voice. It was too late now. Everybody of the staff knew that he did not have long to live, and it was always trying to look after a patient with a terminal condition. The only thing they could do was making his last days more comfortable. It was a sad situation. The man had no family, no relatives, and only very few friends who lived far away in France. Here was somebody whose health was failing, but there was also an almost palpable emotional burden. Seeing all of this was mentally exhausting for Martine and her colleagues. She started the patient's chart and sucked in her breath: he was not even sixty years old, and he looked like a person in his late seventies! He was born in Orleans, France. She printed the name on the chart: Jerome Leduc. His first name evoked a feeling of unease in her. She had heard the story from her mother's friend Marie some years back: nineteen years ago French soldiers had shouted the name "Jerome" to the person who emerged from the evening shadows and assaulted her mother. She sighed. Sometimes it felt like her capability of caring was being tested like now. Why did she have to look after a person with a name, which had a sting and was like a dark spot in the memory of her family? But this was a patient who was at the end of his life. It was not his fault that he had a first name that was associated with a terrifying event in her family's history. Never mind the name! He needed compassionate care and peace. Diligently she made sure that he received the medications that had been ordered for him, and she propped him up with an extra pillow to ease his breathing. Gratefully he looked at her: "Thank you, ma petite". She gave him a quick smile and left the room. She did not mind her new nickname "ma petite". She could live with the fact that she was short. It was a lot better than always being teasingly called " Martini" like by some of her colleagues. This sounded like she was a chronic drunk, and she found the name really annoying! It was too bad there was so little she could do for the patient, and she felt pity for him. She had to think of her father. He too was very ill, but every new day was like a gift for him. He looked at life with deep gratitude, and he always told her that there was so much to celebrate in every day he still had left. It was painful to see the suffering of this patient. He was not only at the end of his life, but loneliness, a sense of hopelessness and depression made his lot even worse. What a poor, unfortunate soul! Finally she took the first tram at five in the morning to make her way home. Thankfully this was her last night shift! A few hours of sleep would help. The family wanted to meet for breakfast at home later in the morning. Silently she let herself into the flat, went to bed and sank into a bottomless sleep.

She woke up from the excited voice of her small nephew Chris. He wanted to see his auntie Martine. The door to her room flew open, and he bounced on her bed and gave her a big, smacking kiss. He was eager for her to come and sit with him at the breakfast table. She was surprised that it was already mid-morning, and she quickly got ready to join the family that had gathered for a leisurely late breakfast. Immediately she was caught up in the happy excitement. They wanted to know about her schedule. She looked tired, but had a big smile on her face. "I'm free like a bird today! No more night shifts!" Exuberantly she flapped her arms like wings. "And tomorrow will be an early morning shift!" She felt Simon's gaze on her; its intensity made her hands unsteady, and she spilled her morning coffee. Of course Michael had to tease her. "Oh you klutz! Still spilling your drink exactly the way I remember you! Good things never change." She made a face, grinned at her brother and stuck out her tongue at him. "Sure, good things never change! You are teasing me exactly the way I remember you, big guy!" Simon made an effort to defend her. "Hey Michael, be nice now! She has worked all night! Wouldn't you be tired?" Martine observed Simon's face. He was reading her, and she blushed. Of course he knew that tiredness was not a factor in the coffee spill. She cast him a quick smile, and he looked back at her with a little conspiring smile in the corners of his mouth. She felt his hand searching for her hand and his knee touching hers under the table. There was the same mutual magnetic connection as before that pulled them together like a powerful current. She felt it first when he approached her at the airport, and this feeling had not gone away; it only intensified. Simon looked into the round. "Let's go and visit the farm folks this morning. I have an idea of what I want to do this afternoon. It would be great to walk through the city. I thought of going to a concert later. They have some great events here, more than in Toronto." He hesitated and looked at Martine. "Would you like to join me? I mean, only if it's not too much. You must be tired." She noticed that the entire group was watching them, and it felt like her face was on fire. He saw that she was looking forward to his suggestion. "Trust me, I won't be too tired! Go and visit now. I'll catch a few hours of sleep."

Together with the children Rose walked to the house where she used to live. She felt a mix of emotions: she was happy to see her stepmother again. But there was also a sense of unease and apprehension about possibly meeting her father. Contrary to her Christopher was excited and happy. Tim was sound asleep in his baby carrier. Everything looked the same as before at the place of her father and her stepmother: the old metal railing, and the stairs that were worn from their use over the years. There was the timeworn, yellowed sign "Kerner" beside the doorbell. She felt nervous and unsure. It was Christopher who pressed the button. The buzzer sounded, and she walked up the flight of stairs. Everything felt curiously familiar and yet so far removed. Her stepmother stood at the door, her face one happy smile." Rose, it is wonderful that you are coming to visit!" She hugged her stepdaughter and grandson and gently stroked the soft cheek of the baby. They sat down together in the living room. Time seemingly had stood still here too. It was the same table, the same armchair that her dad liked to sit in, even the same wallpaper. Rose's stepmom mentioned that Rose's father did not know that she was visiting today. As it was his habit, he had gone out for a morning walk, and Rose's visit was a leap of faith. Both of them did not know how he would react to meeting his daughter nine years after his bitter words. Rose knew from her stepmom that her dad had mellowed. After she had left, he had quietly sat and cried. He told Olga that he had done everything wrong, and now it was too late. He was certain that any connection to Rose was gone. Whatever pain he had, he carried inside. He looked at pictures of the family far away with regret in his face. He never had been a great correspondent, and the few sentences he added to Olga's letters were awkwardly written. Rose realized over time that her father tried to communicate, but as in the past he had great difficulties expressing himself and showing his feelings. Olga sighed: "He has always been strong willed. He is good, but the good is buried under a lot of rubble. You know that he can be stubborn like an ox. The war has not killed him like your poor mom. But he has his wounds that are still healing. God knows whether they will ever heal! And he has scars that he'll carry to his grave. The

Love, Forgiveness, Death And New Beginnings

neighbors have forgiven him for his stiff-necked, fanatic attitude in the past. He has friends now, and this helped him. But it has been a long journey." The older woman held Rose's hand. "You have a lot of courage, Rose. I don't know what will happen now. He may be angry and bitter or he may be not. If it becomes unbearable to you, I'm not taking it personal should you decide to leave. We can always meet in town."

They heard the sound of a key turning in the lock. Rose's dad was coming back. He entered the living room. His eyes widened, his mouth opened, but he seemed to be unable to utter a word. Rose saw that his face was contorted with pain and anguish. She had never seen him like that. She stood up and held out her hands towards him. "I have come back, dad." He held on to her hands, and he was shaking uncontrollably. His eyes were overflowing. Rose expected either silence or an outburst, but this time her father found his voice. "Rose, if you find it in your heart, please forgive me. I don't even deserve it. I have done too much wrong. I wanted to say it for a long time and I could not. And I wish I could rewrite my life." Rose hugged her father in a hug that calmed him and comforted him. "It is over, dad. Leave things in the past! Yes, it is forgiven! Let it be over for both of us." He sat down heavily, and she sat down beside him, quietly holding his hand. He became calmer. Christopher climbed on his lap. The little boy was easily distressed, if he saw anybody who looked unhappy. "I don't want my grandpa to cry. I'll kiss him better." Rose's father looked at the family group. "I never believed in miracles, but I'm believing now." They remembered, looked back at the tapestry of life and all the shades of it. The hours flew by fast.

Rose's father had another wish. "I would like to see Michael, but only if he wants to come." Rose nodded and smiled. "I'm sure he wants to. He told me so."

Michael and Simon returned from their visit to the Menzinger's place. They were greeted with a warm welcome and spent a happy few hours there. They wanted to meet again with the whole family. Old Mr. Menzinger put it into words. "We all lived through a lot.

It is time for all of us to celebrate life." Michael made his way to Rose's father's place. The two men eyed each other. Rose's dad looked at Michael with caution. "I have been an old, stubborn ox! It took me a long time to realize my faults, and this is the second time today that I want to ask for forgiveness." Michael's look reassured Rose's father. "Yes, at one point you told me to go to hell. Remember?" He chuckled at the memory. "Look, the past is over. I have grown up, and you have grown older. Let's bury the hatchet! It is time to enjoy now and go forward. Life is too short to waste it on old grudges. Come over across the ocean and visit us some time; it is time to catch up!" The two men embraced. Rose joined them with the children. There was much to remember and so much more to look forward to.

Martine felt that she slept long enough. She hurried to get ready, looking forward to going out and exploring the city together with Simon. It was a beautiful day, perfect for walking around. The doorbell was ringing, and the family arrived. Simon waved to her, and she quickly stepped out of the door and met him outside. He saw her looking at him happily and expectantly, and he felt simply content walking together with her. He smiled at her. "It's a beautiful day, and I'm so happy that we can both enjoy it together now! This is much better than writing about it in letters." Hand in hand they walked to the tram stop together. He talked about his morning visit at the farm. Now they wanted to go and look at the landmarks in the city. The tram whizzed by the hospital, which was Martine's workplace. She heaved a sigh of relief: "Ah, it feels good! I'm done for the day. I still can't believe that you are here. Pinch me!" He laughed, gently pinched her cheek, and there was an impish smile on her face. "Yes, I believe it now; I'm so happy that you are real!"

He was tempted to give her a kiss, right here in the crowded tram, but he caught himself. Not now, not here with dozens of

Love, Forgiveness, Death And New Beginnings

curious eyes observing them! They walked for a long time: there was the school building, which had been rebuilt after the war, where Simon and Martine's brother had been students together for two years. Simon noted that a lot of new structures had sprung up. They walked to the concert hall across from the large park, and he bought tickets for the evening. She was looking forward to it. Concerts and theatre performances were special events that she enjoyed.

They sat down in a quiet corner of an outdoor café in the park. He wanted to know about her plans after graduation, and she told him that it was a matter of finding a position. But she was not worried. He wondered whether she wanted to stay in her hometown or not. "You must have friends." She took a deep breath: "Friendship seems to be possible across the miles." Thoughtfully she looked back at him. Cautiously he wondered: "No boyfriend?" She looked down, played with the ice cream that was melting in her glass, and shook her head. "No, I never had one. There is the saying that you have to kiss a few toads before you find a prince," she remarked. She looked back at him. "I guess I'm different. I don't feel like kissing toads. Some of my friends did it, and I was the shoulder they cried on. Lots of tears and no happy ending." He took her hands in his and looked at her with a glance that made her dizzy and feel weak in the pit of her stomach. Her heart felt like it skipped a beat or two. "Martine, I want nothing more than to be that prince. I hope that I have a chance." Her eyes turned wide. She moved closer to him, her eyes mirroring her happiness, her mouth whispering his name, and he wanted her with an overwhelming intensity, a feeling he never experienced before. He kissed her softly first, then with rising passion, when he heard her say: "You are the only one who has a chance. I love you so much, Simon." He felt an aching hunger for her, and she responded to his kisses with all the love for him that had grown in her. "I loved you before, and when I saw you arrive it was the most incredible feeling of loving you and feeling loved. This felt like the happiest day of my life!" Between kisses Simon caressed her face: "It was the same for me, like a dream come true. Martine, I waited for you, hoped for love like this, and I love you so much; I can't even express it in words." They did not need words, and they did not know how long they were sitting in their embrace.

They did not see the waiter who went by shaking his head as he removed the two glasses with the uneaten melted ice cream, leaving a bill behind. Later they sat together in the concert hall and enjoyed the presentation of the evening. An encore piece concluded the program, and the first bars of jubilant violin play floated through the hall. It was the well-known first movement of Vivaldi's "Spring". Simon was entirely absorbed by the music, but his eyes never left her. Martine knew the piece, and she felt Simon's hand reach for hers. Gently she touched his hands and leaned against his shoulder with a question in her eyes. What was it about the music that was touching him so much? After the concert they walked out, and he stood away from the exiting crowd, putting his arms around her. "This last piece really touched me. It has a special meaning for me." She thought about his statement: "For me it means life, and it reminds me of the beauty of a season. I listen to it sometimes, and every time it makes me feel happy! It fits that we were listening to it together at the end of such a wonderful spring day, our first day together!" He agreed:" For me it is something truly extraordinary. I listened to this music on the bleakest day in February two years ago. It was Valentines Day, and I had just walked home from the bus stop after work. It was a rotten day with freezing rain, and I put this piece on the stereo. I had just received your answer to my note that I had written to your family, which was such a nice surprise. I was not sure at all that I would get an answer! When I was reading your letter, the grey clouds of the day seemed to lift. It was like a curtain opened, and there was light after a time that felt dull and depressing. Life became colorful again. And this music piece sounded even brighter than before. Today we listened to it together. For me it is like a circle that has closed. Finally I can be with you." She felt the warmth of his arms and saw his eyes that were full of love for her. "This is such an incredible coincidence. It almost makes me cry." He pulled her closer into his embrace. "Don't cry, love. Let us be happy together. Life can be incredible." He felt her hold on to him and take a deep breath. "I'm so happy that you are here. It feels like a dream from which I don't want to wake up." She felt his loving, comforting embrace and heard him say: "I love you, Martine. We are together now. It is real, and this is not a dream that will end."

As he held her, he felt that he could never have enough. The last day had been an end of his journey to finally meeting her, but he knew that it was only the beginning of their journey together. They walked through the park, sat on a bench, embracing each other, talking about their lives, and savoring the feeling of finally being close together physically after becoming so close in their hearts over the miles. He found it difficult to see the evening come to an end. "The day is not long enough for me, but we have to go or we'll miss the last tram. And you need your sleep!" Martine agreed. It was late! What excuse would she have for her parents? They walked through the silent streets, and he went with her to the door and kissed her. "I wished it would be tomorrow already, so I can see you again, Martine." He could not tear himself away from her. With her newfound passion she held on to him, wanting to be close to him. "Don't go yet! Tomorrow is now. It is after midnight. Right now I don't even care that I have to be up at five." They were startled when Martine's father opened the door. "Time to call it a day, you night owls," he grumbled. Next his glance went from his daughter to Simon, and a tiny, humorous smile went over his face: "Oh well, maybe I should cut you some slack! Go ahead and kiss her good night some more. It's probably more fun than writing about it in letters." They did not need an additional invitation. Martin nodded to them and closed the door again. He went back to the living room where Louise gave him a questioning look. "What was all that talk about at the door?" He chuckled: "That was Simon and Martine. They just arrived and are still outside kissing each other good night. Don't ask me for how long. It looks like they have to make up for lost time. Just leave them alone!" She sighed and looked back at Martin. "These two! I've seen enough! Shall we start worrying now?" Martin put his arm around her and shook his head. "Louise, this is a hopeless case of love where worrying is a waste of time, and I also believe that our time is too precious!" Arm in arm they sat in the living room together.

The shrill sound of the alarm clock made Martine jump. This felt mercilessly early! No wonder! Four hours of sleep were not really enough. The last evening with Simon was a wonderful time, and it had followed her into her dreams. It was sobering to wake up and to not feel his embrace. She missed him already now. But she could not get caught up in daydreams. It was time to get ready and get through the day! Quietly she tiptoed to the bathroom to avoid any unnecessary noise. Her dad was not well, and he needed his sleep, and her mom would not be awake either. This was not even five o'clock, such an ungodly time. After a quick shower she hurried to get dressed. Never mind breakfast. She could have it later at work. A warm coffee or tea would be nice! As she opened the kitchen door, she was surprised to see her mother busy preparing a drink. Louise brought a cup of hot chocolate to the kitchen table.

They both sat down. Louise's eyes were resting on her. It was late last night, and she owed her mother an explanation. "It was after midnight, Mama. The evening just went way too fast, and it was wonderful! I know I kept you and dad up late, and I hope that you are not mad." Louise shook her head. "No, I'm not mad; not after what I heard from dad." Martine looked at her questioningly. Her mother took her hand. "Your dad and I know that the time of you and Simon sending paper hugs and kisses to each other by airmail is over. We understand that." She gave her daughter a cautious glance. "I'm your mother, and I still tend to be a mother-hen who worries about you. Your dad is different; he said that he does not feel like worrying. What do you say?" Martine gulped down her breakfast drink. Her mother was always concerned about her, wanted to protect her and wished the best for her. It was time for her to open up to her: "Oh Mama! I know you want my best. Simon and I have become very close through our letters. I love him and I trust him. He loves me very much, and he has written it to me many times, but now that we finally met it feels like we always wanted to be together. This is not a vacation fling or something that happened suddenly. We grew close and fell in love with each other over the last two years, and now...Mama, I loved him before; but now it is much more than I ever imagined. I wish my workday would be over already, so I can be with him again." There was a pause. The bubbling water kettle on the stove and the ticking of the kitchen clock were the only sounds. Louise's eyes seemed to look at a time that was way back in the past. "Martine, I was there too many years back where you are now. I met Martin, when I was eighteen, and I have been blessed with a faithful and steady life partner. I know, I remember, and I can understand you. Now I have to trust and let go, and that has always been the hard part for me." Martine gave her mother a hug. "Thank you for being there for me. I'm off to work now. Say hi to everybody." She smiled at Louise. "Tell Simon that I miss him and that I love him. I love you Mama, and I really don't want you to worry, please!" She darted out of the door.

Louise quietly busied herself with her housework. She had to get breakfast ready for the family. The early morning hours were quiet and a source of serenity for her. She thought of her daughter. Martin's observation yesterday was right. It was obvious that Martine loved Simon. She saw the expression of Martine's face. What about the young man? Was he in love with her as much as she with him or was he not that serious about it? She hoped that Martine would not experience heartbreak over her first love, but she also realized that she had to let go. It occurred to her that she always trusted Martin, but she was deeply distrustful towards men in general. And now Simon had arrived for a visit. It was irrational that she would now distrust Martine's friend and pass judgment over him. Martin and she had a long talk after Martine came home last night. He always saw things clearly, always had a way to set things straight in his sober, pragmatic fashion. She sighed. She wished her daughter happiness. Why was it so difficult to trust? Was it the shadow of the past that was still following her or was it her own experience? After a childhood and growing up years full of poisonous abuse she had escaped into marriage. She had hoped for love and found partnership. Martin was a good man and a steady pillar of support but he could not show emotions, tenderness or love. Life took a different course than hopes and dreams, and in moments like now it still hurt. After her own married life had been far removed from her hopes and dreams she had as a young girl, she fervently wished more love and more happiness for her daughter. Quietly she went out into the garden. Despite the work it was a quiet place of relaxation and refuge for her, and her mind became calmer. Martin was still asleep, and she could get all the watering and weeding done before her family appeared for breakfast.

She did not pay attention to time, till she heard fast footsteps by the garden gate. She noticed Simon who arrived earlier than the others and saw that he was somewhat hesitant to come in. She waved to him and invited him to enter. How could she communicate with him? He mentioned that his German was terrible; she knew only snippets of English, and Michael, Rose and Martine were not around to translate. She smiled and looked at him. Maybe he could understand her if she spoke slowly and kept things simple. "Did you have a good night? Would you like coffee now?" A quick smile of understanding went over his face. To her surprise he responded in a somewhat accented, halting German, but otherwise correctly: "Yes, a good night, thank you. A coffee is nice to help me wake up. I wanted to talk to you for a bit." Unobtrusively Louise observed him; she saw a gentle young man with warmth in his eyes, quiet and unassuming. He had been the same way as a young boy, quite different from Michael, and yet these two had been best friends for decades. Louise invited him into the house, and he sat down at the kitchen table. She expressed her surprise that he still could understand and speak a language he had not used much for over twenty years. He replied that some things were still in his memory, but he felt very rusty and needed practice. Thoughtfully he looked around: "It is funny! We are sitting at the same table almost twenty-five years later. Michael, Peter, and I sat here after nailing shingles on the tool shed in the last summer before I went away. We polished off a whole bowl of pudding, and you gave us heck for licking the bowl." A shadow of sadness was in his face. "I would have loved to see Peter, but this was not to be." Louise looked at him seriously. "Yes, living through wartimes has thrown terrible and unexpected things at us. Life is fragile. Surviving it all has been like a gift of second chances for all of us. You know a lot of stories from Michael, of course, and you know Martine's story too."

She was touched by his answer. "Yes, I heard her story from Michael, and I can only be in awe at fate and how life unfolds in the most unexpected ways. I admire you and your husband, and I can never thank you or Martin enough. Thank you for being her mother, for giving life to her, for raising such a wonderful daughter."

He asked about Martine's work. He knew that she had to work early, and he apologized that he was late bringing her home. Louise placed a cup of coffee in front of him and sat down herself. "I know from my husband that the day was not long enough for you and Martine, and I understand, Simon. After over two years of writing letters you want time to see each other in person. We are glad that you had a beautiful afternoon and evening." She saw quiet happiness in his eyes. "It was a wonderful time, and it was still too short for me and for Martine too." An expression of longing was in his face. "I miss Martine already now, and I can hardly wait for her to be back." It was the same passionate expression she had seen in Martine's face earlier that she saw in his eyes now, a love that was deep and sincere. "Yes, Simon, I know. I know that Martine also can barely wait till her work is done. We had a talk this morning. She asked me to tell you that she loves you and misses you. I understand you both." She paused for a moment. "What are your plans for today? More exploring in town?" He nodded eagerly. "Yes, there is so much to see. Michael and Rose wanted me to join them in the morning. But I want to pick up Martine from work. She is finished working around five, isn't she? You don't mind if I want to spend the time after work with her?" She smiled at him and shook her head: "No, I don't Simon, I know how you feel! Don't apologize, and enjoy your time together! You want to surprise her picking her up from work?" She observed his face. It gave away all his feelings. "Yes, that too. But most of all I find it hard to wait. I love her so much, and I waited so long." He knew that Louise understood him, but both remained silent, as the family was arriving, and this was a conversation that was meant to be just between him and Martine's mother.

Louise had to quietly admit to herself that her husband was a better observer than she was. This was not a one-sided affection of her daughter to Michael's friend. Simon and Martine were very much in love with each other, and nothing would change this, not even her worrying.

Despite her lack of sleep Martine found it easy to get through her work. The patient with the terminal lung condition needed more help. Jerome calmed down, when she came into the room. He still called her "ma petite", and her colleagues smiled. She was the one of the nurses he felt most comfortable with, and they often called her to look after his needs. His first name still instilled unease in her, but compassion won over.

Jerome was tired, weak, and laboring for breath. He needed oxygen. She spoke to the doctor on call, and later she went back to see how he was doing. His color was getting better, and he was more comfortable. He held on to Martine's hand with a small, timid smile. "I wanted to thank you for being there, ma petite. Often I feel that I don't deserve it." She touched his shoulder, trying to calm him and to reassure him. "This is my work as a nurse. Everybody deserves it to be comfortable, Papi Jerome." She had used the comforting French word for "grandpa". For a moment his face lit up, but like a cloud the shade of depression immediately returned. He sighed: "I have no children and no grandchildren, but call me 'Papi Jerome' anyways, ma petite; you are an angel." She turned to leave: I'll be back. I hope that you are resting easier now."

This was so much sadness! What terrible burdens were weighing him down? He was living out his last days, and he was not at peace. He was a man at the end of his life that was overshadowed by pain and emotional burdens. She looked at him intently. There was something oddly familiar about his looks. His hair had a dark auburn shade, and age had left it with a few grey streaks. Her auburn hair color was identical. It occurred to her that she had seen eyes before that looked like his; her own eyes had the same dark green color. This was a sudden, fleeting thought, which vanished from her mind as quickly as it had appeared.

She slipped out of her uniform and got into her street clothes. Finally it was five o'clock! She felt almost feverish thinking that Simon would be at her parents' place, and she wanted to see him soon. Also she wondered what the family had planned for the rest of the day, and quickly she went down the steps to the entrance. She stopped in her tracks, when she spotted Simon who was waiting for her at the entrance door, holding a bouquet of dark red roses. She had to stop herself from running to him and simply embracing him like a long lost friend. Out of the corner of her eyes she noticed the gossipy admitting clerk staring at her and at Simon. She would be the first one to spread the news that nurse Martine had been seen smooching with a man in the lobby, and tomorrow it would be all over the hospital ward if she followed her first impulse of running to him and embracing him. Simon saw the inquisitive stare too. He stepped towards Martine, handed the roses to her, and he moved closer, as he did not want to be overheard: "I love you so much, and I'm running out of words, Martine." He heard her whisper: "I love you so much, but I can't even give you a hug here with people staring at us. Let us get away from here, quick." Quickly they stepped out of the building, away from the watchful eyes of the doorman. Outside they fell into each other's arms. "Martine, I could not wait till you were home." Her smile was radiant. "You are wonderful! I never expected you to pick me up. I love you, and I missed you all day." She admired the roses: "You are spoiling me way too much!" She kissed him, and hungrily he took her mouth. Since they met he felt that his life had become complete. She had been the missing part. They were connected in an unbreakable emotional bond, which now was tangible, physical, and more intense than ever before. He felt it in her response to his kiss and saw it in her face that she felt the same way as he did. They strolled through town, stopped at a small café, and later they took the tram and went back towards her place. He told her that the family was visiting with Rose's father and stepmom.

It was a beautiful late afternoon, and they decided to go for a walk in the adjacent fields and the forest before going to her place. It was a quiet area overlooking the valley below, and they were in their own world, enjoying walking close together, their arms wrapped around each other. He took off his jacket and spread it out on the grass under a wild rose bush that was in full bloom. They sat down and looked into the canopy of blossoms and the evening sky above. She looked at him, and he saw happiness in her face and a sense of wonder, as she put her thoughts into words: "It feels like you have been part of me for years, even though we could not be close like today and yesterday. Now I just want to hold on to this day and all the others while you are here." He took her into his arms, saw her love and devotion to him in her glance, and his voice was raw with emotion. "Martine, I can't imagine to leave without you at the end of my trip." His face was serious,

Love, Forgiveness, Death And New Beginnings

when he continued: "I have the nerve to say this! I'm older than you. Do you want a fellow like me? I'm your first boyfriend, and this is our second day together. I hope that I have not upset or scared you. But I had to speak my mind."

She had never seen this look on his face, a look of love, vulnerability and hope. He had bared his soul. There was nothing possessive or demanding; it was the look of a man who wanted to give everything of himself to her, and she knew that all she wanted was to be with him. She nestled closer into his arms that had become so familiar to her in the short time since he had arrived. "Simon, I love you, and you are part of my life; without you there would be a void that hurts. A difference in age does not matter when two people are soul mates. I found that out over the last two years, as we grew together. So what, that you are my first boyfriend? Finding love like yours is like destiny. No, I'm not upset that you speak your mind on our second day together." He cradled her against his chest and heard her say: "I'm speaking my mind too. Being together with you, the man I love so much, is nothing scary. Being apart from you hurts a lot. I don't want to think about it." There was so much love and tenderness in his eyes. "I don't want us to be apart any more. You are the love of my life; I want to spend all my days with you, Martine. Will you come with me, and will you be my wife?" He saw her face, which was not the face of a girl that had just fallen in love, but the face of a young woman who was deeply in love and certain of her commitment. There was no sign of doubt or hesitation, only quiet confidence, trust and happiness. "I'll come along with you! Yes, I want to be your wife, I want to be with you, and that's forever; I'm certain of that." She saw that he was happy and in deep thought. "You are thinking of something else; what is it?" He looked at her thoughtfully. "My face seems to be like an open book for you! I'm dreaming about our future together." She looked into the distance. "It is going to be in Canada; so I'd better get my papers in order. I want to be wherever you are, even if it is at the end of the world." He saw that her face was serious, and he wondered: "You will miss your parents, and it is going to be a change. And there is your dad who is so ill. But I'll be there for you." She heaved a sigh. "This is now, the immediate future. It has been hard for Mama and for me. We have cried, we have seen him die a bit every day." She told him how Michael had written in his letters that he did not want his mother to be alone and wanted her to join his family. Her father' s life would not last much longer, and she was grateful for every day that they could still enjoy his presence. She continued: "The change of living in another country and on another continent does not scare me. I'll be fine. There is our life together. I can see it like an album of pictures. I look forward to it so much." Simon agreed: "Michael always sees things very clearly. I believe that he is right, and I hope that your mother will accept his suggestion. But I want her very much to be part of our lives too." He paused shortly and continued: "Tell me how you see our future together. What is your dream?" Her face became soft, as she replied: "There are so many pictures that I see in my mind. I see us together, you and I, and we will enjoy our lives together, busy days, not so busy weekends, being happy together; but I also see us together with our family. I see us with our first child, but I would like to have more than one. We are celebrating Hanukkah, Christmas and special days with your parents, Michael, Rose, their kids and Mama. We'll remember those who are not with us. There will be tears, but there will be laughter too. Our children will argue who will get to blow out the candles. They will have fun, drive us crazy, but we love them, no matter what." He smiled into her eyes. "I see us live in a house with a yard. We can think about that, when we are in Toronto. It will be nice for a family. I'll build a tree house for them. The kids will play with their cousins and neighbors' kids and make snow men in winter." She laughed: "Yes, and we will play with them! First they are little; I love kids. At one point they'll grow up. I'll probably work as a nurse. You and I will have time for each other. We will still talk about our dreams together in the future, and we will count our blessings." He was thinking of Martine's father and mother. "I admire your parents, and my own parents have been

Love, Forgiveness, Death And New Beginnings

an inspiration to me. They lived through difficult times together. We don't know our future, but together we can face it."

She had painted a picture of everything that he had envisaged for their future together. They lay together on the soft grass, and his embrace became more passionate, as he felt her softness, her skin, her breasts, and the curve of her hips. Loving her deeply had developed over time. She had become part of him, part of his thoughts and part of his life. Physically wanting her was like a primal urge that had escalated into an ardent desire ever since they met. After having suppressed and ignored his sexual desires for so long, his want for her had burst forward like a new spring. He dreamed about her, and he wondered whether she wanted him physically as much as he desired her. He knew that he was her first man and did not want to scare her, but he needed to know how she felt, and he continued: "I love your dream. I see the same pictures in my mind. You talked about children. It is my dream too to have a family. I want children with you, Martine. I want to make love to you, and I want you soon." They lay in each other's arms, and she looked at him lovingly. "Yes, I want it too, even though I have not experienced it. I have loved you with all my heart for a long time, and I dreamed about you, and I know that making love is going to be something wonderful with you." She felt his body against hers, felt his heat, and she craved his closeness with an urgency she had never experienced and heard him say: "Oh God, Martine! I want it to be beautiful for us. I have loved you for so long." He saw warmth and desire in her eyes, and as she clung to him, he could read her answer in her face, felt it how her body wanted his, and heard her murmur: "Simon, I want you too." They could not make love here, close to a forest path in the grass under a rosebush, but they lay entwined in their passionate embrace and felt the heat of their bodies and desire that was pulling them together. The world around them did not matter, as they lay sheltered by the bush, dreaming together, touching each other and feeling their bodies close together. After a while Simon released her from his embrace, sat up and dug in the pocket of his jacket. "Martine?"

She sat up and leaned her head against his shoulder. "What is it? You are thinking again. I can almost hear the gears grinding." He realized again how well she knew him. "I told you that I wanted to bring something along for you. I bought this in Toronto a while back after I received your letter telling me about forgiveness and letting go of hurt. You also told me that you loved me. I knew that I wanted you in my life, and I also knew that I would see you this year. Giving it to you had to wait till now." He handed her a small box and kissed her. She touched the soft, velvety surface and held her breath. "Oh Simon!" She stared at him and at the ring with the sparkling diamond. His hands caressed her as she lay in his arms. "I want you for life, and I'll wear it forever just as I love you forever, Simon." He put the ring on her finger, and it was a snug fit. Cautiously he wondered whether she should get it widened by a jeweler in town. She shook her head: "No, no, I want to wear it now; I love it!" She paused and wrinkled her forehead. "Well, I guess you are right! But that is for tomorrow. Today my parents will get the shock of their lives, when they see me with a ring." He laughed softly. "I don't think that they will be too upset." She let herself sink into the depth of his gaze; she stroked his face and his hair and felt swept away by his passionate kisses. Feeling his hands that were caressing her evoked feelings of want for him in her, which she had never felt before. She felt sublimely happy to be with him, her friend, her soul mate and her love, and he knew that he could not be without her. As he held her in his arms, he felt immense gratitude for their togetherness. He was thankful for a kind fate that brought them together and for their life together that lay ahead of them.

Darkness had fallen, and after a long time they got up and slowly walked back to the house. Martin heard them come into the flat. He had not been feeling well. Martine and Simon sat down beside his bed. There was still the old spark of teasing humor in his eyes, when he greeted them. "You are back early today! I can't even call you night owls." His observant eyes went over them, as he acknowledged in his usual direct way: "Love birds would be a more fitting name from what I can tell. You got beautiful roses there, by the way!" He looked at Simon. "I'm so very glad that you are here, and I can still meet you, Simon. I have always teased Martine about her invisible long-distance friend." Simon thoughtfully smiled at Martin. Even though there was still a language barrier, it was becoming easier for him to understand and to speak, and Martine did not always have to translate for him. "Martine is much more than a friend. I love her, and it is going to last for a lifetime." Martin nodded. "I'm not blind." His glance went back to Simon. "I have seen your faces, and I have noticed the little sparkle on her finger. And I know how much she loves you. Be happy, both of you! I'm happy that it is you, Simon. Life has been good to me. I have seen my daughter grow up." Martine gave her father a hug. "You did not go along with the others and visit today, dad. Are you all right?" They saw his tired smile. "Just trying to rest; it is one day at a time. I want to be at your graduation in two days. I'm so proud of you, Martine! Every celebration is precious, and I feel fortunate that I can still celebrate with you." His spirit held him up, but his health was failing. They knew how fragile his life had become; it was like a flickering flame that would not last long.

Michael and his friend decided to get on their way to town. There were some old school friends they wanted to look up, and the meetings were brief, but cordial. They strolled through the alleys, looked at the changes that had transformed the city, and at lunchtime they decided to go out for a bite to eat. Next they sat down at a table on the cobbled patio of an old tavern near the market place. Michael observed his friend. He had never seen him like that. He was cheerful and animated. Michael felt satisfied. It was gratifying for him to see that the trip was doing Simon some good; he was happy to see him come out of his shell. They placed their orders, and the waiter put the two glasses of wine they ordered on the table. Simon leaned back, a picture of relaxation. Michael had to voice his astonishment: "We haven't sat together like that in years! It seems like this vacation is the five hundred dollar cure for you, pal. Here we are just a few days into the trip, and you are a changed man already! What happened to the silent, serious Simon?" Simon took a sip of wine. "Oh, this guy is past tense!" Michael saw a humorous sparkle in his eyes, and his friend continued. "You may remember a conversation we had a long time back. You were reminding me about going out, socializing, and I was anything but thrilled. I told you then that hell had to freeze over first before I would fall in love with another woman. Well, in the meantime hell has frozen over solid, even though it's May!" For Michael this was a surprise that hit him unprepared. "What?" Impulsively he jumped up and bumped into the table. One of the wine glasses fell, and the splintering crash of glass caused a few guests to turn their heads and look disapprovingly at the scene. Simon grinned amusedly at his friend. "Easy, man, or they'll throw us out of this establishment, and you can kiss our lunch good-bye! But you are getting the idea already. There is usually a wine glass shattered at Jewish weddings." Michael let himself fall into his chair, and the laughter of both of them made a few more heads turn. Michael shook his head in surprise. "My goodness, Simon! I never knew that you had a wild side! This is fast and furious! What did Martine have to say?" Simon looked at his friend, his face now serious and solemn. "As a matter of fact, I gave her a ring yesterday, and she was so happy! By the way, it was not this fast; our love had time to grow over two years, Michael. We grew together, and we fell in love, even with the distance between us. You know me; I just kept quiet about it. You probably thought that we were nothing more than long distance friends. But now it is like destiny. I told her that she is the love of my life, and I want to spend my future with her, and she loves me and told me that she wants to be with me for life. It seems like we have been waiting for each other for all these years. I know that I won't leave this country and go home without her, and I figured that you should know."

Michael seemed to look back in time. It was a bit similar like it was years ago, when he left the country with Rose, except he did not know then whether they could be more than just friends. The future had been wide open. It was a time of a friendship that had to grow first, a friendship that they could not develop before. They needed time to rediscover their connection from the past and build a bridge from the past to the present. With Simon and Martine it was different. They had steadily grown together in their hearts over the miles and had an intensely close emotional, loving connection that grew like a steady flame. Their meeting now was the last fuel that made the flame burst into a blaze, which nobody would stop. He understood and nodded to his friend. "You better get started with the paper work. It will take a while, but it is not too bad. I'm really happy for both of you! But what a surprise!" The waiter brought a new glass of wine to replace the broken one and wondered what they were celebrating. The two friends raised their glasses. "To now and to the future!"

The next few days were like colorful jewels on the string of time. Martine's graduation was a happy event. The family went on a day trip together, visited friends, and every day was special and memorable. Simon did not find the time to write a letter to his parents. He quickly called after his arrival, and he picked up a stack of the newest photographs he had taken. All he had time for was a fast note to the effect that he was having a wonderful time and the remark that a picture could be worth a thousand words. Here was an assortment of photos that must be worth several thousand words! There were pictures of the Laumann family and him and photos of him with Martine, Martine and him hugging each other; these were photos that showed the happiness he was experiencing. His parents would get the message, and he sent the letter by express mail. That should get their attention!

It had become a special time for Simon and Martine, when he picked her up from work. Every hour was precious, and they wanted to spend their time together. She packed a picnic, and they went to explore the area close by. They walked and talked about their future. He was describing the house he wanted to buy in Toronto. She mentioned that she had saved money to buy some furniture. She took him to all the places he had seen when he was living in the area, and he was astonished at the many changes. He admired the historic structures; she pointed out the modern buildings. She took him to a good-bye party of the student nurses, and they found themselves dancing exuberantly to the music of the "Beatles", belting out their newest song "I Want To Hold Your Hand" to the wild applause of Martine's friends, till they were ready to collapse on a couch. They were caught up in an evening of lighthearted happiness, and he could not remember when he had so much fun! He told her about Toronto, and she felt like she was already walking through a city with him that became more familiar and interesting through his descriptions. He insisted on taking her out after work to some cozy restaurants, which they both enjoyed. On other evenings she told him that it was better to save their money, and they prepared supper together and sat on the bench under the trees in the garden of Martine's parents like an old couple. Often they went back to the grassy nest in the forest under the wild rose bush, dreaming together in their loving embrace that became more passionate with each day. Nobody of the family was surprised, when they arrived home late; they just made good-natured joking remarks about their absence. It was obvious to everybody from the start that they were in love.

One late afternoon after her work they strolled through the old town center. Simon mentioned that he wanted to do some shopping. The beginning of June felt like summer already, and they sat in the cool shade of an awning at a small restaurant. She was prepared to get up, but Simon was still sitting at the table. He had a paper serviette in front of him and was methodically writing a list. Martine looked over curiously. "What are you writing there?" He put his arm around her. "I think that I will need your help with this." When he saw her questioning glance, he bent over to kiss her. "I'm thinking about a guest list for our wedding, and I'm sure you want to add some names!" His smile deepened. "I hope that you say yes." She kissed him back. "Yes, Simon, I love the idea, and yes, I have some names for that list too! You manage to come up with surprises that knock me over!" He got up, and they walked along the shopping area. He turned to her: "Let us go in here! That is what I wanted to go shopping for today." They entered a small jeweler's store and found a set of golden wedding bands, which he bought. In a quiet courtyard they stood still, embracing each other. She teased him: "This is starting to be an expensive evening. You have to stop shopping or you'll be broke next. It's my turn to spend some money and buy a dress for the occasion." She went into a store close by, and after a short time she had made her decision and walked out in a white, summery lace dress that she planned to wear for special occasions, not just for her wedding day. They had talked about an informal garden party, and she did not want a formal gown. As they left the store, his arms were wrapped around her; his mouth was urgently on hers. "You won't be wearing this dress for long. I'll take it off you if you let me!" She looked at him with her impish smile: "Tell me if you need any help from me!" He burst out laughing, but turned more serious again: "Let us get married soon, Martine! The question is when?" He heard her happy laugh and felt her nestle closer into his arms. Her bold one-word answer surprised him and excited him even more. "Today?" He felt her mouth responding passionately to his kisses, and her eyes showed him that he was not alone to feel the mounting tension and desire between them like a wave that was sweeping them up. She saw hunger and want in his face, and with every fiber of her body she wanted to be with him and love him. His mouth was at her ear. "Yes, today rather than tomorrow. I want you now, or I'll go insane!" The expectation and an overpowering feeling of physical desire for him made her feel almost weak. She held on to him, and he saw her looking up to him, her mouth waiting for his. He heard her murmur: "Yes, today; now, Simon." Hearing her response and feeling her body against his heightened his arousal. He felt a flood of hot desire for her wash over him, and she heard his breathing become heavier. He stopped at a street vendor, bought a bouquet of colorful summer flowers and handed it to her with a kiss. She saw his eyes that seemed to embrace her: "You are wearing the dress already, and flowers should be a part of the celebration too." She looked at him and whispered: "It will be a wonderful evening for us."

They took the tram back, got out at the familiar stop, and arm in arm they walked swiftly along the quiet side road. "Where do we go?" Martine wondered. He stopped and kissed her. "Not to our little nest under the rose bush; come along to my place?" He heard her whisper a "yes", saw passion and want in her face, felt her body seeking his closeness, and felt her mouth opening to his. His kiss was raw and demanding, and she felt heat and excitement surge through her body. They turned the corner to the guesthouse where he was staying, and hastily he unlocked the door. His eyes spoke of his need for her. "Martine, I can't stop now." She came into his arms, gave him her mouth, her neck, and she slipped the dress off her shoulders. He felt her breath, and both felt the pounding of their hearts. Between his kisses she whispered: "I love you, Simon; I don't want to stop!" He saw the look of arousal and expectant eagerness in her face, helped her take off her dress which now lay discarded on the floor, and his hands gently touched her breasts and went over her body. She helped him unbutton his shirt, and lovingly she stroked his chest and felt the smooth skin of his back. Both were locked in a naked, sensual embrace of exploring and feeling each other. Daylight was waning, and a soft evening light filled the small room, letting them forget everything but the awareness of each other's bodies. His hands invited her to feel and touch him, and tenderly his hands touched her, loving her, cherishing her, and he felt her feverish response. She desired him as urgently as he wanted her. They sank onto the bed, and she moaned under his caresses and felt how her body fervently welcomed him. His kisses were not raw and explosive as before but slow and deep, and he loved her with an intensity and tenderness he did not know he possessed. He did not want it to end, and he felt her respond to the moves of his body. She was clinging to him, her arms around his neck, and her fingers in his hair. Both felt their union like a gift to each other in a soaring climax.

They caressed each other with the undemanding pleasure after making love. She saw deep happiness in his face. Her face was glowing. Lovingly she looked at him, fulfilled and relaxed. "I wish we could stay here all night without watching the clock." He sighed. "So do I, but I believe that we have to go to your place a bit sooner today." She stayed in his arms and remarked: "It is still early." He savored the feeling of their togetherness. "I don't want to go, but we cannot wake up your parents at midnight or later and announce to them that we want to get married. We'd better get into the details of making it official for the rest of the world. What do you think?" Tenderly he kissed her. "Are we coming back here tomorrow?"

She laughed softly and clasped her arms around his neck: "Yes, but twenty-four hours are such a long time!" His desire flared up more than before. "Oh God, Martine, I can't wait this long!" She saw unrestrained passion in his eyes, felt an almost painful yearning for him, and their lovemaking felt like they could never let go of each other.

The door was opened after they rang the doorbell. It sounded like a cheerful gathering of the family inside. Michael laughed, when they entered. "You are back a bit earlier today! Are you tired out or out of cash? And look at those flowers! What happened? You look…" Inquisitively he looked at them but stopped in mid-sentence, when Rose gently nudged him. She realized that they both were in their own world. Simon's answer was short and cryptic." A lot has happened!" His friend knew him well enough to suppress his next remark. Together they stood before Martine's parents. Simon looked at both of them. "We wanted to ask you for your blessings to get married." The group fell silent. The glances of both parents went from Simon to their daughter. They stood together, their arms wrapped around each other, a very visible union. Martin spoke first. "I saw it coming, you two. We want you to be happy together." Thoughtfully he looked at them. "I hope that I'll still be around at the wedding." Louise joined her husband. She had tears in her eyes. "You simply have to be there, Martin! I'm so happy for both of you. And we are so blessed to see the family grow." Everybody was excited.

The hubbub woke up Christopher who had fallen asleep in the room next door. Curiously he ambled into the living room, eyed the excited family and asked Simon and Martine: "Can I be a flower boy instead of a flower girl? When are you going to have a baby?" Rose rolled her eyes at her inquisitive son: "Christopher! You should be asleep!" Michael chuckled: "This kid! I'm sure that he'll get an answer later. Maybe tell us the wedding date next!" Martine's and Simon's look went to Dad Laumann. In all their happiness they felt a deep sadness. His health was failing. He knew it, and they all were sadly aware of it. Simon looked at Martine

Love, Forgiveness, Death And New Beginnings

and at the group. "If you ask me, the sooner the better. We have to deal with all the paper work. What about a date in July, as soon as reasonably possible?" He knew that Martine's father was ailing, and there was not much time. He looked at his watch. "My parents will be the next ones to be surprised. We have a six-hour time difference between Toronto and here. They will get a wake-up call in a while." He turned to Christopher: " Listen, we will need you as our special flower boy!" Christopher's eyes turned round: "Oh great! I'll be really good too!" After a pause he nudged his aunt: "So what about that baby? I am good at watching Timmy. I can watch your baby too!" Martine noticed that everybody was laughing and felt that all eyes were riveted on her, and she blushed. Simon took over and answered: "Chris, a baby takes nine months. You really have to be patient." Christopher made one last attempt to negotiate: "Aw! Can't you hurry up just a bit?" Rose propelled her talkative son back to the bedroom: "Christopher, go back to sleep. First you'll be the flower boy at the wedding. Good night!"

Across the ocean the phone shrilled insistently through the early morning stillness at the Hoffer residence. Simon's father groaned. This was not even six o'clock! He went to the telephone in the kitchen and picked up the receiver. He felt uneasy. Phone calls at odd times rarely meant good news. He received this one call at an odd time, when Sarah was killed in an accident. Even though it was many years back, he could not shake the feeling of apprehension whenever the phone rang at an unusual hour. A crackle in the line and the thready voice of a long distance operator made him listen closer. It was a call from overseas. The connection was not crystal clear but next he heard Simons' voice. "Dad, I'm sorry for the early morning call, but it is important! Can you get mom to listen in too?" He called for his wife. They both listened to news that they had not quite expected, and yet they were not entirely surprised about. Simon on the other side of the ocean heard the answer, the excitement and happiness that were obvious in their voices: "Yes, we'll make it happen. This is wonderful news, and we are so happy for you. We have been wondering before, and those pictures really gave it away! Of course we are coming to the wedding. Tell us the exact date, and we'll be there. We cannot stay long, but we believe that it is important for everybody of the family to be there. Sure, we'll celebrate here too later!" Paul Hoffer smiled at his wife. Earlier they had wondered about the long distance friendship of their son with Michael's sister. Just a day ago they received the stack of photos of Martine and Simon, and now they received this phone call that would send them on a whirlwind trip to Europe within a month's time. What a start of the day!

Martine was still working the last few weeks after her graduation. Some patients were quickly discharged, but the one patient who suffered of late stage lung disease was still on the ward. He had no visitors, and the nurses wondered whether there were not any relatives or family; but he did not seem to have anybody.

Often he asked for "ma petite Martine". Martine would look after him, and his face brightened up when she entered the room. All the nurses tried to make his lonely days more tolerable and took turns bringing him reading material or taking extra time talking or listening to him. He was a man who seemed down and depressed, approaching the end of a life that had not been good. Even though he was not even sixty years old, he was tired and worn out. He spoke German with a pronounced French accent. After some hesitation he mentioned that he had arrived in the tumultuous days of the time when French soldiers marched into Germany. He must have been a handsome man in his younger years with striking looks, but only his deep auburn colored hair and eyes that looked like a dark pine forest were still a reminder of his previous vibrant appearance. He had lived together with a woman who was his close companion for many years, but she passed away. Martine was looking after him during one of her shifts, when one of her older nurse colleagues came into the room.

Love, Forgiveness, Death And New Beginnings

Thoughtfully the eyes of the nurse rested on the patient and went from him to Martine.

They stood together in the staff room, and Martine's colleague was wondering whether Martine had any relatives in France or whether there were even any ties to the family of the patient. Puzzled she shook her head. No, there weren't any. She wondered why her colleague would be asking her this question. The answer came as a shock to her. "I always thought that there are striking similarities between this patient and you. You have the same hair color, and his eyes have the same shade as yours, both unusual. The shape of your mouth is identical to his. All of this has puzzled me from the beginning when he was admitted to our ward." Martine stared at her colleague. The words of her left her stunned, and her stomach lurched. She already woke up this morning feeling out of sorts, but now she felt weak and close to passing out; and she had never fainted in her life! Her colleague held on to her looking concerned: "Martine, sit down! You are white like a sheet. Are you getting sick?" She sank down on a chair and weakly shook her head.

She told the nurse about the way she had come into the world. She had known for a long time that Martin was the devoted dad who had raised her. But who had been her father? He had been the dark shadow at the end of the war on one horrifying evening that had violated her mother and inflicted injury and emotional distress on her dad. She knew that the tumultuous events of the war were not subjects that her parents could look back on easily. There had been too much horror, too much pain. They did not talk about much of this. She was grateful to her mom's friend, Marie Menzinger, who told her details her mother would not talk about. It was about the evening that had caused her mother and her father too much distress. It was not easy for Martine to hear the story of the two women, which Marie Menzinger told her, but she found that it was necessary for her to know about her life and the past. At the same time she realized that all of this had never changed the fact that her parents always loved her deeply as their child, her dad as much as her mom. This realization was a source of comfort and gratitude for her, and she realized that she would never know who her biological father was. This was an empty spot in the mosaic of her life. But for her it was comforting and more important to know that her dad and mom had loved her from the time she was born, her dad a steady pillar of protection and support and her mom a source of love and warmth.

Martine looked determined. She knew that this older colleague was an astute observer. She would not have mentioned to her an observation if it had been less obvious. In addition there was his name: Jerome. She could not wipe away all of these facts. Her voice was shaky but determined. "I have to find out more. It feels like I'm looking at an empty spot on a map." Her colleague encouraged her. "You have to talk to him, Martine. He is not going to live much longer. Better do it soon." She brought dinner to the patient and sat beside his bed, helping him. He gave her a thankful look. It took all the courage she could muster to ask him, when he had come to Germany, the time and the circumstances of his arrival. He finished his meal looking tired and depressed. She wiped his face, cleaning away traces of food. He sank into his pillow and started:

"It is not a story that I have told to anybody, and it is a burden that will never leave me as long as I live, and now I'm at the end of my life. I came into this country here, into a southern suburb of this city with a group of soldiers at the end of the war. It was an unsettled time, and I had no relatives in France. So it was like a new start, and I stayed." His breathing was labored. "I don't know whether you want to hear all of this, ma petite. This is not a nice story about the good old times. You may hate and despise me, when you hear it, but then I deserve it. It is something that has been weighing me down, something like a confession I need to make before I die. I'm grateful to you for listening, but only if you want." Martine quietly nodded, and he continued: "Yes, we had invaded, and we were in a wild mood for doing whatever felt good to us, and it really brought out the worst in us, a bunch of soldiers

Love, Forgiveness, Death And New Beginnings

on the loose. We pilfered, and we destroyed. We took what we wanted. Looking back we were worse than animals. In this time of spring, in April 1945, when there was new hope for life as the war ended, we destroyed hope and violated lives beyond belief." He halted. "I'll never get over what I have done. Two of my cronies and I had gone into an orchard and made a fire to keep warm. We were free to roam around, and we decided to live it up. First we got two birds from a chicken coop, killed them and roasted them over the fire. We had stolen some hooch earlier, and we had gotten drunk in the euphoria of victory over the enemy. Yes, we decided to have a feast! It was a beautiful spring evening, and it was getting dark, when we watched a man and a woman come into the orchard where we sat by a fire before. They wanted to look after their small flock of chickens. This evening I did the worst that I have ever done in my life. Stealing from people was harmless in comparison to what I did next. My two friends knew that I was greedy and wanted a woman bad, and they got a kick out of it! One of them jumped on her and caught her. I still remember this small woman, her face, and her eyes, that were filled with terror. The other one of my army friends beat up her husband and knocked him out. He was a tall, wide shouldered man, and yet he had no chance to defend her. So I forced myself on this woman and raped her right there. I did not think, I did not care, I was drunk, and I was like an animal in a rut. But afterwards the evening came to haunt me. I could never forget his screams or her cries, and I can never shake off the memories. They have been with me ever since, a burden of guilt. O God! What have I done? Sorry nurse! It just had to come out." His face betrayed his anguish as he looked at Martine before burying his face in his hands. He sounded like a haunted man: "The worst is that I can never atone or even ask for forgiveness for the suffering I have inflicted on these two people. So, this was my start in this country, and I regret every moment of it." He broke down and cried. Between sobs he said: "I deserve to rot in hell, and hell has been with me already for the past nineteen years. Thank you for listening." Martine found it difficult to keep her composure. Silently she stood up and held his hands: "No, I don't hate or despise you, Jerome." She got some tissues and wiped his face. "It is all right Jerome, and it is good that you could talk about this." Telling his story had exhausted him. His eyes closed, and he was drifting off into sleep. Quietly Martine pulled the blanket over his arms, and she looked at her patient. With a feeling of disbelief she saw his hands and the shape of his thumbs. Her hands were like a copy of his hands. The eyes that were like her eyes had been the first feature she noticed, and the high arching eyebrows were like hers. It was easy now to see the connection, so easy and yet so very painful. With a start she noticed the shape of his ears, also identical to hers. Her look went to the chart at his bed on which his name was written: Jerome Leduc. The name burnt in her eyes, worse than weeks before, when she had written it on the admission papers.

Swiftly she left the room and went back to the nursing station. Her older colleague saw her distraught face, told her to sit down and brought a cup of coffee for her. Usually she enjoyed the drink, but today the smell alone made her nauseous, and she made a dash for the washroom. Her colleague sat down with her and told her to go home, but she refused. Her shift was almost over, and she wanted to finish her written chart work. After a while she felt calmer. So, this was the man who had assaulted her mother, and she was the result of this assault! It was obvious from her looks. His description of the evening sounded identical to everything she had heard before, so cruelly accurate. This man was related to her, half of her genetic material. He was her biological father, but her true father was Martin, the father who had loved her unconditionally from the moment she had been born. Jerome was part of her biological origin, but there could not be any other connection. For her he was the last piece in a missing link, a bridge to the past, a piece in a mosaic of her life. Acutely she felt the horror her parents had experienced, yet in a way it was a relief for her that she could now look at the beginning of her life with a feeling of closure, knowing that the mosaic was finally complete.

Love, Forgiveness, Death And New Beginnings

The shadow in the orchard that had been the unknown part of her beginning now had a face, a tired, weary face that was marked by death. Even with the knowledge of him having committed an unspeakably evil act, she could not feel hatred. What he had done haunted him throughout his days. He had been like a condemned man who had been serving a life sentence shackled by a burden of guilt from which there was no escape, and guilt had sapped the joy out of his life. He had fathered a child in a self-centered, violent, and unconscionable act, but he never experienced the happiness of having a family and seeing a child grow up. His only companion had passed away, and now he was spending the end of his life in loneliness. In a way justice had been served: he lived a life under a heavy burden, and now he lived out his last days gasping for breath and yearning for peace, which he could not have. Only his death would finally release him from the emotional and physical torment that he had brought upon himself. At the same time she felt uneasy, realizing that she had to make a decision. Should she share this with her parents?

Simon picked her up at her work place. Her serious face told him that something at work had shocked her and was of great concern to her. They sat down on a bench in a park, and she told him about the encounter with the patient at the hospital. Simon held her hands, calmly and reassuringly. They decided that it was necessary to tell her parents about her experience. Simon was thinking aloud. "Some time ago you wrote to me in a letter that we could only heal once we let go of hurt. Your letter spoke of forgiveness. It is the last necessary step that makes us whole. It has helped me. It will be necessary for all of you who are affected. But I also know how difficult it is, especially in this case. Your parents should know about this. But ultimately it is their decision what they want to do."

They entered the house and joined Martine's parents in the living room. Martin picked up on the serious expression that was on both of their faces and wondered: "What is the serious news today? I hate to be blunt! Are you pregnant?" Her face showed a

277

trace of embarrassment and a tiny smile. "That is entirely possible, dad." Dad Laumann raised his eyebrows. "Oh my goodness! As direct and honest as always! Just as well that the wedding is only a few weeks away!" Martine heaved a sigh. "Yes, that's me, dad. We are both similar. But this is not the serious news; the serious news is about something different. I have reasons to believe that I'm caring for a man at the hospital ward who is my biological father." She told her parents about the events at her workplace. The news was unexpected and shocking, and they sat in stunned silence. The evidence was there. The description of the evening and the location had been accurate beyond any doubt. She also described this man, who was close to death, yet not at peace, a person who had done something grievously wrong. In a way he deserved it to be in his own hell of guilt and regret, and yet…Martine looked at her parents. They looked at each other. Martin Laumann spoke first. "Had I met him much earlier I would have had the capability to murder him. But now he is just a shadow of himself and a dying man without peace. In a way I feel pity for him. He needs peace and forgiveness and cannot get it." Louise took his hand. "Do you think that we should go?" She also looked at Martine and Simon, who nodded in agreement. Her husband had the same thought: "Yes, but only if you can do it. We have suffered, but we have been blessed with Martine. His days have been a curse for him. But we need to put that last chapter of a story behind us. It will help us. I need peace in the time I have left, and maybe he can find more peace too in his last days."

Martine's shift was close to finish. She went to the patient Jerome Leduc. He was awake, and as always his face brightened up a bit, when she arrived. "Everybody here has been so good to me. I can't thank you enough." Martine sat down beside him. Cautiously she mentioned to him his thoughts about asking for forgiveness that he mentioned before, and she saw sad resignation in his face. "If I would only know these people…but I don't." Martine spoke into the silence. "I know them. They are my mother and my father. Your description of the events of that evening

Love, Forgiveness, Death And New Beginnings

confirmed it beyond any doubt." He understood the implications of her statement and looked at her, seeing the similarities between him and her with a sudden and shocking clarity. He groaned:" Oh God, ma petite! This is too much. I don't know whether you will ever forgive me." Martine stroked the restless hands of the man. "Yes, Papi Jerome, yes, I do! If it helps you, my parents are here to see you; but it is you who has to decide." He agreed and swallowed the sob that was rising in his throat.

Martine and her parents stood at the bedside of the patient. He looked like a broken man, his life haunted by regret and emotional distress. His anxious eyes met the faces of Martine's parents. Martin and his wife put their hands on his hands. The patient's voice was tired and shaky. "I wanted this so much, to ask for your forgiveness. I am so very sorry that I have done such evil, and I can never atone." Tears ran down his cheeks. Quietly they held his hands. Louise Laumann spoke first. "Our daughter told us about you. I came to offer you peace. We have tried to find it, and this is the final step needed. I forgive you." Martin had his hand on the shoulder of the patient."I have forgiven you, Jerome. You have done evil, but even out of evil good can emerge. We have Martine, and she has been our blessing. We want you to be at peace knowing this." Martine held his hand. "I wanted to tell you, that I have forgiven you. Meeting you has been like the last piece in the puzzle of my life. Have a good night now, Papi Jerome. I'll be back tomorrow." They stayed quietly at the bedside and held his hands. He cried, and finally he looked up. "I thank you for coming. It is something that I never expected. If you find it in your hearts, say a prayer for me." He heard their calming words: "Yes, Jerome, we will. We want you to have peace. Sleep well now." Quietly they left the room and went back home. He stared at the small bouquet of summer flowers that they had left on his bedside table, a visible sign that this evening had not just been a surreal dream. They all knew that the incredible had happened, which made it possible for them to close a chapter of their lives. Jerome Leduc knew it too; it applied to his own life as well. It showed in his face that he had found peace, when he passed away in his sleep ten days later.

Simon went to pick up Martine from her work place. He was happy for her: this was her last day! But he also knew that it would be happiness with a drop of sadness for her. She was finished with her work contract at the hospital, but it also meant saying good-bye to her colleagues. He was not surprised to see a shadow of quiet sadness on Martine's face, when he picked her up at her work place. He had been waiting for her and took her into his arms. "It is a chapter that has closed, Martine, I know." Seriously she looked at him. "Yes, but it is not the only chapter that has closed today. Jerome passed away. He just went in his sleep early this morning. It is over; Papi Jerome has peace now." She fought tears. "It is irrational that I start crying. I'm glad that he had a peaceful end. But it feels like I'm losing my past! And it feels like a double blow today. Despite everything he still was a part of my existence, part of who I am. I can't wipe it away; it is a fact. But his death also reminded me of the fact that my dad who has always been there for me will not be with us much longer. Oh Simon, right now all of this hurts so much!" It was always taxing when a patient died, but his death was especially poignant for both of them. Simon held her quietly. "You need distance from work and time off. Where do you want to go, love, any place that you enjoy?" Tenderly she embraced him. "No, I just want to be with you. This is all I really need." He put his arms around her. "I'm here Martine, always. Just being with you is all I ever wanted. Soon we can always be together."

Quietly and in deep thought they took the tram and walked together to Simon's room. They lay in each other's arms, and their lovemaking was passionate and precious. They were grateful for life and for their love. She felt sheltered and calm in his embrace. He had to think about her remarks earlier that she called the patient "Papi Jerome", and he wondered about this. With a thoughtful smile she told him that she had called him by the familiar French word for "grandpa". It had started at the beginning of his hospital stay. She wanted him to feel better. He had always called her "ma petite", but at that point she could not even imagine that there was a blood connection between them. Now she looked at Simon with a glance that was serious yet happy. "It was simply an endearment then, but it makes much more sense now that I refer to him as Papi Jerome, Grandpa Jerome." Simon looked at her with a questioning glance. "Are you telling me...? Oh, Martine!" She nodded: "Yes, I suspected something already a while ago, and today in my break I quickly saw a doctor to have a test, and I got checked. We'll have a child, Simon." He was overwhelmed with joy. They both had dreamed about a family. It was almost too much to grasp how close love, life, and death was together on this day.

Preparations for the wedding had been a hectic few weeks. There was the knowledge about Martin Laumann's rapidly worsening condition, the main reason why the celebration had been planned very quickly. A wedding in Canada was out of the question, as Martin was too ill to travel. Everybody felt great sorrow about Martin's illness, but at the same time the family felt grateful that they would all be present to celebrate together. It was Simon's and Martine's biggest wish that everybody would be there. Martin went to the hospital briefly and a blood transfusion stabilized him somewhat. He was even weaker than before, but his fondest wish was to be there for his daughter's wedding. Simon's parents arrived. For them it was an emotional reunion with Martin and Louise. They were meeting again after twenty-five years, and yet, the years were no boundary to friendship. The connection was still there between them, and the years fell away, as they talked about memories that went so far back. After seeing the photos they felt great happiness to finally meet Martine. They were only able to stay for a very short time, but they felt excited and happy to be there for the celebration, and yet they were deeply saddened seeing Martin so ill.

Martine and Simon went to the pastor of the church, where Martine and her parents had been worshipping, and they asked about their wedding. The pastor asked a few questions and pointed out that he would not be able to marry them in the church, citing as the reason that Simon was worshipping in a synagogue as well as in a church and was not baptized. He did not even seem sympathetic when he explained that these were the regulations. He could marry them in the side room of the church community center, but a wedding venue in the garden was not meeting with his approval either. Martine had to think that even though this man was calling himself "pastor", he was not really the good shepherd, but an administrator who strictly went by the book and its paragraphs. Martine's voice was calm but determined, when she heard what he told them. "Thank you, but in this case I decline. A meaningful civil ceremony will be good enough for us. It is my belief that God's blessings are not confined to a church." With that they left, and Martine was somewhat taken aback and disillusioned. It had been a display of rules and regulations that created division rather than unity. Simon found it incredible that two ceremonies would be needed, one at the city hall and a religious ceremony. It sounded complicated and like a lot of red tape. But these were the regulation in this country. In Canada one ceremony was enough, either a religious ceremony or a civil wedding. He put their sentiments into words. "One wedding at the city hall is plenty to make it all official on paper! Let us celebrate afterwards in the garden with all friends and family here. And we will celebrate in Toronto with our friends there." Martine had another thought. All his relatives were Jewish, and she wanted to honor his tradition: "Wouldn't you want a Jewish wedding there?" It was a thought that appealed to both of them, and Simon's parents promised to make the necessary arrangements as soon as they returned back home. All the relatives in Canada could be present to celebrate.

Their wedding day was a beautiful, happy celebration in the flower-bedecked garden on a sunny day in mid-July with the family, close friends, and neighbors. Martin was radiant to be part of the celebration and see the happiness of his daughter and his new son-in-law. For the next few days they planned to take a short trip, finally being together, no longer needing to sneak away to Simon's room at the guesthouse for a few stolen hours. Simon wanted to take her to Niagara Falls for the second part of their honeymoon once they were in Canada. They explored a scenic area not far away, hilly vineyards, old castles, and the river valley. It was a dream-like time for them of being immersed in their love and passion for each other. One morning they sat at the breakfast table, happily planning the next day, when the innkeeper told them that there was a telephone call for them. Michael was on the phone. Dad Laumann had been readmitted to hospital, his condition had rapidly deteriorated and become terminal. The message left them stunned and grief stricken; it felt to them like darkness had suddenly fallen on the day despite the brightness of their love and this light-filled beautiful morning. They held on to each other and cried. Hastily they packed and travelled back, hoping to still be able to say good-bye to Martin. They hurried to the hospital, where they joined the family. Simon's parents had seen the serious condition of Michael's father before they flew back home and told Michael and his family to stay. It was a quiet vigil at the bedside of Dad Laumann but a very short one, and it was like Martin had waited for them. For a brief moment there was the old spark and a smile in his eyes, and his glance went over his family, but shortly after his eyes closed, and he looked like he had fallen asleep. He had said good-bye to all of them.

The funeral was over. They sat together in the living room. Dad Laumann's armchair was empty. They cried and they remembered. There was gratitude for his life, gratitude that he still saw his grandchildren and was still there to celebrate the wedding. But there was also deep sorrow for all of them. Martine's visa was ready, and the family had talked together and thought about the future. Louise was calm and more composed than the others. She had witnessed the long illness of her husband, but she also knew that the family would be leaving very soon, which hurt. It was Michael who started to voice his thoughts. His mother needed a break, a time to get away. "Mom, we all have been thinking a lot. You need time for yourself. You have to recover too. A wedding and a funeral within ten days is simply too much!" He paused. "I don't want to pressure you into something you do not want at all, but listen to me all the same. We believe that it would be good for you to come with us instead of being alone here." He saw her hesitant look and continued: "Come with us, see how we live, take some time, and go with an open mind. Go for a month or more, but come along. It is a wonderful country. You may like to live there. But you have to find out and see for yourself." Mom Laumann was twisting her hands in her lap. She knew her son so well. Michael saw life situations with a lot of clarity, always direct, pragmatic, and very similar to Martin. She saw Martine, who nodded affirmatively. She always wanted her mother to worry less, and it showed in her face now, that she was anxious for her to join. There was Rose, as loving and steady as always, her eyes on her, encouraging, almost pleading, and Simon's loving, reassuring glance resting on her, telling her that she had a second son in him. Louise was struggling with her inner turmoil even though she saw the glances of encouragement, love, and support for her on the faces of her children. She rose from her chair, her face showing her effort to make a decision. "I need to think; I need to go for a walk, and I have to do it alone." She turned to them, a woman who had the strength to come to terms with difficult choices. "I'll be gone for a while. Please don't worry about me; I need this time to hear myself think and figure things out."

She left and walked. She walked through the neighborhood, looking at all the houses, thinking and reminiscing. She had seen destruction and rebuilding here, and yet some older, familiar landmarks were still there. Her steps took her to the field path. She passed the overgrown garden with the apple trees. The old chicken coop was still there, now decrepit and leaning. She could look at this place seemingly from a distance. The apple orchard, which for a long time had filled her with panic and horror, was now like a faded photo in an old album. She acknowledged that it did not trigger feelings of anxiety and pain in her any more. Next she walked into the town center, crossed the market place, the church square, and passed all of those familiar places that she had known for over twenty-five years. Her steps led her to the cemetery. At the fresh grave she stood still. Her eyes filled. It was another place of remembrance. Martin was buried here. But for her his memory was in her heart and with her wherever she went, and she had the deep faith that his soul was with God. She walked back and had to reflect on what Martin would tell her. He always had the will to soldier on, whether it had been hardship or illness. Life must go on! She had to go on too, hard as it was. It would be in his sense. Suddenly she realized that it was getting later, and the evening shadows were turning longer. The evening ended with a glorious sunset. It was like a proclamation of the colorful continuity of life from sunrise to sunset with the promise of the gift of a new day. Her thoughts became clear, and her mind was made up. Her walk had been a good bye for now. She would go along with her children for a visit to experience the other country. She would know more about her future once she had stayed and experienced it. A large bookstore in town was still open. In the past she bought Michael's and Martine's schoolbooks and school supplies here. She went in, bought an English dictionary and a travel guide about Canada and started to walk back home. It was time to learn more. This time it was concerning her. Nobody was ever finished learning, and for her it was a step into something new.

All of the family members were busy helping together in the kitchen and preparing supper, when she entered. She noticed tension and a question in their eyes. With a smile she looked at them and held out the books she had purchased. There was a collective gasp of understanding of what she was telling them. Michael spoke for everybody: "Oh Mom, it will be so good for all of us that you are coming along." There were hugs and tears.

The last days of Michael's and Rose's stay were coming to a close. Martine and Simon were packing their belongings for their trip. They said good-bye to their friends and neighbors. Louise packed luggage for an extended trip. There had been so many details to look out for, paperwork to complete, so much to think of, and a whirlwind of activity. Now as they were boarding the jet, everybody just wanted to relax. Martine felt tired and leaned back in her seat. She was quieter than the rest. Simon observed her. Comfortingly he put his arm around her, gave her a pillow, asked for a glass of water and hoped that she would rest and feel better. Michael felt sorry for her. "Poor thing; problems of a first time flyer! I just remember the trip by boat, and I was sick like a dog!" His friend quietly agreed, even though he knew that motion sickness was hardly the problem. Nevertheless she as well as everybody else was looking forward to the trip, and everybody was full of happy anticipation. It was a calm journey, as the plane was gliding westbound, still at a low altitude, where the landscape in Europe looked like a toy box with the small towns and the red tile roofs spread out below. The jet was soaring into high altitude, and an endless dark blue sky stretched out. They talked about their time, the incredible events of joy, excitement, and the dark shadow of Martin's passing, and now they were anticipating the arrival in Toronto.

The plane landed at the airport, and the family was tired but elated at the same time. Simon's parents picked them up. With their warmth they welcomed Martine as a new daughter, and they went to their home. Louise felt the heartfelt and sincere welcome both, Ruth and Paul, extended to her; it was a warm and comforting feeling that touched her. It was a feeling of arriving home, even though it was a home that she needed to explore first. They talked for hours about all of the events, the weeks full of joy, and the end darkened by sorrow. The children had fallen asleep on the couch. Michael announced that his mother would come with them and stay at his home. "What about us?" Martine and Simon looked at her. She was unconcerned. "Of course I'll come and visit you too. But I have to play with Chris and get to know to little Tim. They have to get to know to their grandma too." Martine and Simon smiled at her. "You'll be very busy being somebody else's grandma next, together with Grandma and Grandpa Hoffer, which should be by March next year," Martine announced. Louise took a moment to process this news, while the room around her erupted into shouts and laughter. When she understood what Martine had told her, she laughed out loud, her first liberating, joyful laughter since Martin had passed away, and Simon's parents were ecstatic at the news.

Louise looked into the round of people she loved and felt lifted up by their happy exuberance and zest for life. New beginnings, she thought... Life was about a constant building of connections and bridges. There were bridges to a new life for Simon's family, for Michael, Rose, and now for Martine. She could not look into the future, but she knew after the news, which Martine had told the family, that her own life situation could be subject to change. But then her entire life had been about changes, and she felt more excitement than apprehension. She had witnessed so many new beginnings and bridges from the past to the present. After surviving World War I, she saw life grow again out of dust and ashes. She experienced a time of unstable recovery, which was only short-lived. Next there was the shadow of dictatorship and ultimately the most sinister time of war and destruction in Europe and elsewhere. She knew despair and struggle along with the people of this time. Even though she experienced violence of the worst kind, she and Martin recovered from this too. Martine was the new life after a destructive war and violence, and she was a blessing to both of them. The somber shadow of Martin's illness was present, but nevertheless they both saw their daughter grow up. Martin always told her that life had to go on, even when he was struggling with his chronic illness. She thought of the one evening with its sunset that was like a promise for a new and brighter day; it was the evening when she decided to travel with her children. It was so often that life meant walking through darkness, but even in the darkness of grief there was hope for light. Louise knew that her own story would not end here. Life was full of unexpected chances to build. The road went through ups and downs. She was part of the bridge that stretched across continents and connected people. The building process of life and its bridges was a wonder that was always continuing to unfold in a colorful pattern of brilliantly bright shades, darkest shadow, and every shade of color in between. She did not know and could not predict this process in its details. From the past she knew that it involved challenges, surprises, and trust. Life was about building bridges, and it filled her with a sense of wonder and deep gratitude to be part of it.